THE
OF

COMPANY
SUCCESSFUL
INVESTORS

FINANCIAL TIMES
Prentice Hall

In an increasingly competitive world, it is quality
of thinking that gives an edge – an idea that opens new
doors, a technique that solves a problem, or an insight
that simply helps make sense of it all.

We work with leading authors in the fields of
management and finance to bring cutting-edge thinking
and best learning practice to a global market.

Under a range of leading imprints, including
Financial Times Prentice Hall, we create world-class
print publications and electronic products giving
readers knowledge and understanding which can then
be applied, whether studying or at work.

To find out more about our business and professional
products, you can visit us at www.financialminds.com

For other Pearson Education publications, visit
www.pearsoned-ema.com

Pearson
Education

TERRY BOND

THE COMPANY OF SUCCESSFUL INVESTORS

PROFIT FROM THE POWER OF INVESTMENT CLUBS

FINANCIAL TIMES
Prentice Hall

An imprint of Pearson Education

London • New York • Toronto • Sydney •
Tokyo • Singapore • Hong Kong • Cape Town •
New Delhi • Madrid • Paris • Amsterdam•
Munich • Milan • Stockholm

PEARSON EDUCATION LIMITED

Head Office:
Edinburgh Gate
Harlow CM20 2JE
Tel: +44 (0)1279 623623
Fax: +44 (0)1279 431059

London Office:
128 Long Acre
London WC2E 9AN
Tel: +44 (0)20 7447 2000
Fax: +44(0)20 7240 5771

Website www.financialminds.com

First published in Great Britain 2002

ISBN 0 273 65600 7

British Library Cataloguing in Publication Data
A CIP catalogue record for this book can be obtained from the British Library

10 9 8 7 6 5 4 3 2 1

Designed by Claire Brodmann Book Designs, Lichfield, Staffs

Typeset by Pantek Arts Ltd, Maidstone, Kent
Printed and bound in Great Britain by Biddles Ltd, Guildford & King's Lynn

The publishers' policy is to use paper manufactured from sustainable forests.

I BELIEVE *THE* COMPANY OF
SUCCESSFUL *INVESTORS* COULD
BECOME A CLASSIC AS THE DEFINITIVE GUIDE
TO FORMING AND RUNNING AN
INVESTMENT CLUB

JIM SLATER

FOR HELLE, WHO STILL
LIVES WITH US

CONTENTS

ACKNOWLEDGEMENTS

Thanks to ... Helen, my wife, who
provided the room service and the TLC;
Jim Slater, a good and inspirational man;
Jeremy King, a wise and gentle man;
Graham Quick, who has endured my
sense of humour with fortitude; Kipper
Williams, who makes me smile;
ProShare, the *Independent* newspaper
and those at the late, lamented website
UK-iNvest who allowed me to raid the
writings I originally did for them; a host
of other friends who, knowingly or
unwittingly, played their part by sharing
with me their knowledge and
experiences; and most of all the
thousands of investment club members I
have met and talked with in the past 10
years. You made this book possible.

FOREWORD

I first met Terry Bond at an investment conference in the early 1990s. I liked him immediately and have since grown to admire his integrity and ability and his enthusiasm for spreading the word on the attractions of investment and investment clubs. For many years now, Terry has worked tirelessly with ProShare to develop the investment club movement and has done a wonderful job as evidenced by the 11,000 clubs that have already been formed in Britain. His contribution to the ProShare Manual and more recently to devising the Investors' Toolkit demonstrate his attention to detail and grasp of the subject. Without Terry's advice and guidance the UK investment club movement would have been a pale shadow of what it is today.

I believe that investment clubs are a wonderful way for aspiring investors to get to know more about the subject and to increase their wealth at the same time. It seems to me they offer a number of very important advantages:

1. They are an excellent source of help and inspiration for private investors who, through joining a club, can share the fun with others, obtain moral support and improve their own investment performance.

2. With a good spread of club membership (e.g. a solicitor, accountant, estate agent, shopkeeper, restaurant manager, engineer, including a mix of men and women) the club's circle of competence is increased dramatically. Every one of its members adds something to the overall knowledge and know-how of the group, helping to make their investment decisions much more valid.

3. Within every club there is always a faster gun – someone who knows more about investment than the other members and can add to the knowledge of the group.

4. It is easier in a club to stick to a discipline and to gain moral support from other members, especially when times are difficult (and sometimes they will be).

5. Last, but not least, the cost of newsletters and necessary investment services like company *REFS* can be shared to reduce the expense to a very affordable level per member.

Terry's excellent book takes you by the hand and, step by step, explains how to form an investment club. Most importantly, Terry shows how to select shares, and how an investment club should be run to maximize its chances of success. *The Company of Successful Investors* is very readable and laced with amusing anecdotes. My favourite is the one about his father-in-law, Wilfred. I bet it will be yours too.

Jim Slater

ABOUT THE AUTHOR

Terry Bond has had a busy business career. He's been a national newspaper journalist, broadcaster and author; business partner of the round-the-world sailor Sir Chay Blyth; owner of an international public relations business and a European property company; and sales and marketing director of a major plc.

Now he is a successful private investor with a substantial portfolio involved principally in British and American equities. He is chairman of a biotechnology investment company, BioProjects International, and a director of ProShare (UK) Ltd, the organization which looks after the interests of the investor in the corridors of power. He is also British director of the World Federation of Investment Clubs. At ProShare he is responsible for guiding the development of the investment club movement – it has gone from 350 clubs to over 11,000 clubs in four years – and is himself a member of three investment clubs.

PREFACE

The phenomenon of investment clubs has taken the financial world by surprise. They are proliferating at an amazing rate as private investors realize that clubbing together with friends and colleagues provides a pool of knowledge to outstrip the abilities of the best-informed City analyst. Here in the UK the movement has almost reached cult proportions. In less than four years ProShare, the organization that oversees the development of clubs, has provided the guidelines for more than 11,000 clubs to set up and the numbers increase by hundreds every month. Even the powers that be – the Inland Revenue, the Treasury, stockbrokers, quoted companies and the like – have entered into the spirit of investment clubs by adapting their rules and providing advice which allows the movement to flourish.

The club principles are simple. A group of friends each agree to contribute a small amount of their savings every month into a collective pot. The object is to create a portfolio of shares that will outperform the markets. Monthly discussions on what to buy and sell utilize all the members' experience and opinions, and decisions are completely democratic. Novice investors learn how the market works, experienced investors benefit from the knowledge other members have of particular sectors and businesses. And along the way everyone has a lot of laughs and a great deal of fun.

But beginners beware. The secret of investment club success is profit. And you will only achieve this if you organize your club properly and choose shares that go up in value.

The Company of Successful Investors tells you how to get there.

Deep breath now. Let it out slowly ... slowly. That's it. Now
push ... push ... PUSH ... Good, that's good. It's coming, I can
see it ... just one more push ... that's it. Here it is! Wonderful!
Break open the champagne! I'm delighted to tell you that
you have given birth to a magnificent and perfectly
formed baby. And that wasn't so bad, was it? I bet
you're glad now that you attended Doctor Bond's
ante-natal clinic and did all the things
he told you to.

The midwife

THE BIRTH

None of us is as smart as all of us.

Anon

A
PATHETIC PUNTER

So, you want to be comfortably rich. Don't let's exaggerate this, you are not yearning to be a fat cat dashing about the world in your executive Lear jet accompanied by a bevy of beautiful people who are dedicated to satisfying your every whim – although that would be nice, wouldn't it? No, you will be quite happy with a secure financial future. Able to take luxurious overseas holidays at least once a year, upgrade the furniture and carpets in your house whenever necessary, buy a new car when the ashtrays get full. Be honest, not only do you want to keep up with the Joneses; you would like to pass them and wave as you go by.

It's not easy though, is it? For most of us the dye of life is cast and our income is already fixed. We can do little more than pay our bills, contribute to our pensions and perhaps salt a modest amount away for the future. Usually there's some left over at the end of the month and that should be the acorn from which our big oak tree will grow. But how do we make sure that happens? Which is the repository that will receive our savings and help turn them into a valuable nest egg?

Let's look at the options. With all due respect, the banks and the building societies are worse than a waste of time. Sure, they are safe havens for your money in that there is little or no risk with their deposit accounts, but those interest rates! Pathetic. The incontrovertible fact is that their rates almost always lag behind the annual increase in the cost of living so your money is losing its value while it stays with such moneylenders. We're agreed then, this is certainly not the route to take if you want to be rich.

Top up your pension – now there's an idea. Careful though, all those problems with pensions mis-selling and seemingly rock-solid companies that are having trouble paying out what they promised. Make sure you absolutely understand what you are letting yourself in for and, more importantly, what you will be getting out at the end. I paid into a pension fund from the age of 25 and when it matured the pensions company

BE HONEST,

NOT ONLY DO YOU WANT TO

KEEP UP WITH THE JONESES;

YOU WOULD LIKE TO PASS THEM AND

WAVE AS YOU GO BY.

told me it was worth well over six figures. Hooray, said I, send me the cheque. Oh no, said the pensions people, it doesn't work like that. You can have a comparatively small lump sum and then we'll pay you a paltry amount every month until you die. That's no good, I protested. You say the pension is worth six figures and I want it all now, while I'm still young enough to enjoy it. Who wants to be a 90-year-old millionaire? Sorry, said the pensions people, them's the rules, take it or leave it. I had no choice but if I

had my time over again I would put my spare cash to much better use.

Faced with these depressing comments you will probably be tempted to try the other end of the scale, and take a gamble. Have a bet. After all, it is spare cash, you've paid all your bills and this is money you have earned so you can do whatever you like with it. Squander the lot on the National Lottery – maybe this week the finger will point at you. And then again, maybe it won't. In fact, there is more chance of Elvis Presley calling at your house this evening and inviting you to accompany him on his comeback album.

How about a day at the races? That would be fun. All the colour and excitement of the racecourse, the friendly, rosy-cheeked bookie who takes your pounds and promises to give you 10 times as much back when your horse romps home. The buzz of anticipation as the horses are loaded into the starting stalls, the roar of the punters as the field thunders past the grandstand, the cheers as the winner passes the post ... and the puzzlement on your face as you look vainly back down the course for your horse, the one whose jockey is wearing that pretty blue shirt, your favourite colour. Never mind, there's always roulette, or poker, or the football pools. Try them all if you must but in your heart of hearts you know it's all a waste of time, the odds are loaded against you.

Don't despair! There is one game in town that, provided you are sensible, can help you to grow your spare cash from a little acorn to that mighty oak and – trust me – you will have a great deal of fun along the way. The game is equity investing, buying and selling shares, and around the world people are realizing that securing their share of successful companies is a grand way to steadily build up personal wealth until they become comfortably rich.

Of course, when you think about it, it's obvious. Identify a company that is making good profits for its owners, become a part-owner yourself and share in those profits. That's what my with-it friends in the City, always keen to coin a phrase, call a 'no-brainer'. Predictably though it's not quite as easy as all that, otherwise everyone would be doing it. And, I won't kid you, many have tried and failed. But it can be done, it has been done by hundreds of thousands of folk, and you are perfectly capable of joining the winners. Why am I so certain? Because I have done it myself. I have made a personal fortune from buying and selling shares yet not so many years ago I thought the stock exchange was a place where you swap your beef-flavour gravy cubes for chicken-flavour ones ...

Immodestly I can tell you that I have become a very successful private investor but I hasten to add that I learned the hard way.

Here's how it all began. I had a few thousand pounds saved in the bank and

AT LAST!

THE WAY TO GET RICH QUICK.

BUY SHARES FOR A FEW PENNIES TODAY

AND TOMORROW, BINGO,

THEY WILL BE WORTH POUNDS.

AMONG THE WORST HIT WERE THE HOPE STOCKS, THE PENNY DREADFULS, AND AMONG THE BIGGEST CASUALTIES WERE MY FIVE. WITHIN TWO WEEKS MY £10,000 WAS WORTH £1,900 AND FALLING.

on a visit to my in-laws' house in Somerset I came across a copy of a penny-share tipsheet to which my father-in-law subscribed (the laws of libel prohibit me from telling you the title). As I read my excitement grew. At last! The way to get rich quick. Buy shares for a few pennies today and tomorrow, bingo, they will be worth pounds. I snaffled the tipsheet and couldn't wait to get back to my Sussex home and trust my nest egg to the stock exchange. I perused the penny-share publication from cover to cover and picked the five penny punts that sounded to me the most likely to shoot skywards. Having picked my winners how was I supposed to back them? I had never owned shares before and I knew only vaguely how the system worked. I rang the bank manager (you can tell how long ago this was, because banks had proper managers who you could ring up and talk to, not like today when you have to make do with a work-experience teenager if you want to discuss your financial situation).

The manager could not have been more helpful. Did I want specialist advice from one of his stockbroker colleagues? No thank you, I had already selected the shares I wanted to buy: £2,000 invested

in each of five companies, a total of £10,000. The manager invited me to call into the bank next day just to confirm my instructions. In the event this proved to be something of a problem. Overnight there was the most horrendous storm that caused havoc on the South coast. Woodland was devastated and buildings seriously damaged as the gales reached over a hundred miles an hour. Fortunately my home escaped with minor damage but the journey to the bank was slow and hazardous as I negotiated fallen trees and roof tiles. No matter, I got there in the end and signed the share purchase orders. It was an exhilarating feeling, a buzz of adrenalin as I entrusted my hard-earned savings to the five wonder stocks. Now all I had to do was to wait until they doubled in value. How long would it take, I wondered. A week? A month? It wasn't really important, I could afford to wait.

There is a clue to the outcome of this story in the previous paragraph. The terrific storm that hit Britain's coast was in mid-October, 1987. It was headline news for a couple of days until another significant event knocked it off the front pages. Black Monday. The stock market crash. Share prices collapsed. Among the worst hit were the hope stocks, the penny dreadfuls, and among the biggest casualties were my five. Within two weeks my £10,000 was worth £1,900 and falling. I couldn't stand the strain, I sold.

For a couple of days I was completely shell-shocked, hardly able to believe what had happened. Then I resorted to a technique I adopt whenever an unexpected trauma occurs, I went for a walk. I am not talking about a toddle to the village pub. I mean a long, long, solitary walk taking all day and with no particular destination in mind. No company, no mobile phones (none in those days anyway), no distractions and nothing to think about but the matter in hand.

I know I am not the sharpest knife in the drawer when it comes to brains, it takes me a while to assess any situation, but it soon became apparent that there was only one person to blame for this disaster. Me. I had committed the cardinal error that is the pitfall waiting for all suckers who think they have discovered the secret of getting rich quick. I had spent my money without having the faintest idea what I was doing. Like the mug punter who places a big wager on a knackered nag because he swears the horse winked at him from the parade ring, or the casino clown who puts her all on number seven because she had a dream about dwarfs and Snow White the night before, I was relying on Lady Luck and little else.

It was a salutary lesson. By the end of the walk I had made two decisions. First, I would not buy another share for a period of two years. Second, during those two years I would read and learn everything I could about the stock market and its workings, how to pick companies that were going to do well, timing, technique, the lot. Because the fact is that, despite my awful initial experience as a shareholder, I had caught the bug. I had tasted the excitement of owning shares, albeit the wrong ones, and next time I wanted to get it right.

Soon afterwards, fortuitously, my consultancy work took me on a two-year posting to the Costa del Sol in Spain which was a great place for holidays but a third-world country when it came to the comforts of everyday life. For example, during the whole of the two years my wife and I existed without the aid of a home telephone (I discovered from the local *telefonica* service that in Spanish *mañana*

DESPITE MY AWFUL INITIAL EXPERIENCE AS A SHAREHOLDER, I HAD CAUGHT THE BUG. I HAD TASTED THE EXCITEMENT OF OWNING SHARES, ALBEIT THE WRONG ONES, AND NEXT TIME I WANTED TO GET IT RIGHT.

does not mean tomorrow, it means sometime never). All day and every day we shared a telephone box at the end of the road with other frustrated residents and an army of giant ants. The only television channel I could understand was Gibraltar TV which started at seven in the evening and closed three hours later. Our neighbours were shadowy and silent figures who lived behind high walls and were invariably hiding from the police, the wife, the business partner or the taxman. For most ex-pats the days consisted of playing golf or bridge and drinking more than any liver could sensibly stand. I soon forsook the lotus-eating lifestyle and settled down to a rather hermit-like existence. I had taken a plentiful supply of books and from Juan at the local newsagents I bought the *Financial Times* every weekday and the *Investors' Chronicle* once a week. I was learning.

When we came back to England in the early 90s I was determined to become a private investor. I had a grasp of the theory and now I wanted practical experience. I became a member of ProShare, the organization that had recently been established to explain to individuals the advantages of sensible share investment, and I also joined an evening class at Worthing Technical College. From 7 p.m. for two hours every Wednesday a local accountant called Fred talked to our band of 10 would-be investors about all aspects of the stock market. He covered everything from straightforward equities and investment trusts to such instruments as options, derivatives and futures. It was a nine-week course and, as so often happens in

these situations, the individuals in our class became friends. On the last evening we all went to a local pub with Fred for a farewell drink and it was then that I broached an idea I had heard about from ProShare. Investment clubs. People getting together on a regular basis to pool an amount of money they could each easily afford with the aim of investing in shares and learning about the stock market. Every member would be entitled to suggest an investment and at the end of each meeting a democratic vote would be taken on which share to buy. Frankly, I knew little more about investment clubs than that. All those obvious questions, like what happens if someone wants to leave the club, or do we have to pay tax on the profits, or can a club buy shares in its own name, had not occurred to me. Thankfully these vexing queries did not cross the minds of my fellow students either and by closing time there was unanimous agreement that we would meet the following week to discuss the idea in detail. Even Fred, although he was slightly dubious that his professional integrity might be called into question, had warmed to the idea. I confess I was chuffed because I had been unsure about the kind of reception such a radical thought as pooling funds would receive. After all, we're British and the last thing a Brit wants to talk about is his or her private finances. If you don't believe me, try it. Ask a friend to detail his or her salary and then give you a list of precise figures for their mortgage, hire purchase and savings. In Britain such queries are a good way to lose a friend, whereas across the pond the Americans are only too happy to discuss such intimate matters with almost total strangers. However, I need not have worried about my Worthing friends. They were totally taken with the concept of an investment club and so began my association with a movement that has helped me to become a successful professional investor.

For the last decade I have been totally absorbed by investing and investment clubs and I am completely convinced that it is imperative for the private investor who wants to maximize his or her personal profit potential to be a member of at least one successful club. Notice that word,

'successful'. It's the key. Simply starting a new club or joining an existing one is not sufficient, you must be sure that your club is a winner, not just in terms of profit but also pleasure. In the last few years well over 10,000 clubs have been formed in Britain alone but sadly they are not all winners. Indeed, there's no hiding the fact that a significant few have been so unsuccessful that they have wound up.

In the pages that follow I will pass on to you the essential ingredients for creating a successful club. Get the formula right and you will be comfortably rich, waving to the Joneses as you go by.

I'm not a great fan of statistics, they can be made to show what you want them to show and often they hide a multitude of truths. However, if they come from a reputable source and can be used to illustrate a point I have no rooted objection to using them. So if you are tempted to doubt my contention that the stock market is the place for your savings, take a look at the facts revealed by the latest Barclays Equity Gilt Study, which is produced each year.

If you had put £100 into a bank savings account as the new century dawned at the end of 1899, a century later at the start of 2000 it would have been worth £13,601. Not bad? The same £100 invested in the stock market at the same time would, over the same period, have grown to £1,209,836.

Of course the cost of living rose inexorably over the 100 years. Adjusted to take account of that your £100 in the savings account would be worth just £257. The £100 in equities would be worth £22,817.

Taking the period of a whole century is a bit silly because it is a time span that doesn't relate to our lives. So let's look at a more realistic scenario revealed by the Barclays study. Suppose you were born just after the Second World War, and your parents were so well-heeled and far-sighted that they decided to invest £100,000 so you could enjoy your old age. You're in your mid-fifties now, thinking about retiring while you are still young enough to enjoy the third age. In a savings account since 1945 the £100,000, with all the interest reinvested, would have grown to £177,000 – very nice but not enough to retire on. In the stock market for the same period the £100,000 would be worth £4,132,000. I bet you could manage on that for a few years.

They told me to buy this stock for my old age. It worked wonderfully. Within a week I was an old man.

Eddie Cantor

CHAPTER

FOOLS

RUSHIN

Once upon a long time ago – I guess it was the best part of 40 years back – a rather scary looking lady doctor called Barbara Moore, who must have been well into her 60s, captured the attention and the imagination of the great British public by walking from Edinburgh to London. I seem to recall it took her about three weeks but it could well have been longer. She was a game old bird, thin as a lath, and as she strode along the Edgware Road on the last lap of her journey the world's press followed her. Hundreds of cameras and television crews recorded her achievement for posterity.

While I can't remember the exact year, I do know that she arrived in London on the Thursday before Christmas. How can I be so sure? Because the events of the few days that followed are for ever imprinted on my memory. It was the time when I learned that rushing in where angels fear to tread can lead to a lot of personal aggro.

My father-in-law at the time was a self-made rich man who had been aptly named Wilfred and could best be described as brash. He knew everything. He could do anything. He owned a dozen haberdashery shops and several main dealership car garages, two of which he had built with his bare hands. For pleasure he drove racing cars he constructed himself and drank whisky. I, on the other hand, could not change a light bulb, earned a pittance as a junior reporter on a Midlands Sunday newspaper, drove a Morris van and drank pints of beer. Wilfred was firmly of the opinion that I knew nothing and was practically useless. His daughter had chosen badly, we were not close and our conversations were inevitably strained affairs.

Barbara Moore arrived in the capital to the acclaim of clapping crowds and that evening, as we watched the television pictures of the event, my father-in-law was adamant. 'Wonderful woman!' he exclaimed, pouring himself a scotch and not offering me one. 'There's not another person in the world that could do what she's done.' He looked across at me, daring me to contradict him. 'I'd give anyone 500 quid if they could do it quicker than her.' I ignored him. He was just a silly old fool given to making outrageous statements when he'd had a few scotches.

But next day I couldn't get Wilfred's bold statement out of my mind. I rang him at his biggest garage to confirm the £500 offer. I explained that in my opinion it was quite a good local news story, someone offering a cash prize for the first person to beat Barbara Moore's record, and that if I wrote a report in the *Sunday Mercury* that would be good publicity for his garage. Of course, Wilfred could not back down. He knew that I knew that he'd made the offer and if he tried to backtrack he would lose face. I dispatched a photographer to snap him standing proudly on the forecourt of Willenhall Motor Services.

Next day the page 3 lead story in the *Sunday Mercury* was headed: MIDLANDS GARAGE BOSS OFFERS £500 FOR SOMEONE TO BEAT BARBARA. Hmmm, I thought as I read the piece, it must be a thin news day today. Surely the story doesn't warrant that much of a display?

How wrong can you be? Astonishingly, when I got home that evening it was the second item on *News at Ten*. There he was, a slightly confused Wilfred, confirming in his strong Black Country accent that yes, he thought Doctor Moore was a wonderful person, a fine example of mature and fit womanhood, and he was prepared to pay £500 to anyone who could beat her walking record from Edinburgh to London.

Next day was Christmas day and therefore there were no newspapers. It was a typically festive occasion, one of those atmospheric family gatherings at Wilfred's house, a montage of children's whines, whispered disagreements between adults, disappointing presents, dirty nappies and underdone turkey. For a change though, Wilfred was relatively pleasant. I think he was secretly rather pleased that he'd been on the telly and when that evening he and I went for a Christmas drink at his local he was quite a celebrity. Fuelled by the booze and the spirit of Christmas we returned to his house in mellow mood.

Of course the bonhomie couldn't last and sure enough it didn't. At 8 o'clock on Boxing Day morning the doorbell rang and a bleary-eyed Wilfred opened the door to reveal two young Germans, one youth and one girl. 'Vot izz zee starting time?' demanded the youth. 'Vare izz zee starting place in Edinburgh?'

So began countless days of chaos. Literally hundreds of people from all over Britain, and scores from Europe, made their way north to Edinburgh then turned round and started to walk south. The television pictures said it all, a never-ending snake of loonies all bent on picking up Wilfred's £500. There was no organization of any kind, no starter, no timekeeper, no checkpoints, no agreed route, nothing. Wilfred and his long-suffering wife had to move to a secret address (the local pub) because their home was besieged by people wanting to officially register for the race.

The daily papers were full of it. Those wilderness days between Christmas and the New Year are notoriously barren as far as news is concerned and this was manna from heaven for the national press. Under-age children, octogenarians, blind people and wheelchair-bound folk, all of them hungry for the money. There was a human-interest story every mile of the way. After 10 days I received a call from the *Daily Mirror*. One of the walkers, another Terry, was a few miles from London. Could I get Wilfred down to Trafalgar Square to present the cheque? I picked him up from the pub and drove south at speed. I'm not sure whether his tremble was because of my driving or the trauma of recent days.

The pictures in the papers next day showed Wilfred complete with fixed grin, obviously false teeth and glazed eyes, presenting Terry with his cheque. All the stories were the same too, referring to Terry's great achievement in beating Barbara Moore's record. All except the *Daily Telegraph* which used the same picture but started its report with the fact that a lorry driver had come forward to claim that he had given Terry a lift for several miles southwards in the Jedburgh area.

I will not go on further with this sorry tale, which continued for months and involved the *Daily Mirror* setting up a surprise confrontation between Terry and the lorry driver, except to say that we stopped Terry's cheque. Eventually, as with every news story that ever there was, this one lost its interest value. Wilfred quietly gave his £500 to an abattoir worker from Birmingham who seemed a genuine sort of bloke. About the only good thing to come out of the whole episode was that Wilfred did not speak to me for at least two years.

By this time, dear reader, I'm sure you are asking yourself what on earth this event has to do with investment clubs. Well, I mention it because it was the perfect example of fools – or, rather, this fool – rushing in where angels feared to tread. I rushed to write the news story without thinking of the havoc it could cause. As a cub reporter on a provincial newspaper I had not realized the power of publicity in the national media and I had not considered the possibility that anyone would be silly enough to take up Wilfred's daft challenge.

Another such well-meaning but ill-thought-out move involving national newspapers was responsible for the birth of the investment club movement in Britain. Around half a century ago – to be precise, it was the summer of 1951 a chap called Barry Groombridge wrote a letter to *The Thunderer*. That was the nickname of what was then the most famous and feared newspaper in the world, *The Times*. Every opinion former of the day – peers, politicians and all the others who felt they were a cut above the common herd – read *The Times* and was influenced by its editorials. If the mighty organ decreed that the government was doing a good job it usually meant the incumbent gang could look forward to another term, but if the paper sneered at our national policies those responsible could contemplate five years in the dole queue. By mutual agreement *The Times* was at the cutting edge of progress, if it sneezed the repercussions were felt around the world.

Needless to say the competition to have a letter published in *The Times* was fierce. The paper received 10 times more correspondence than it had room for. So our Barry was a lucky fellow, his letter was given an airing and again *The Thunderer*, albeit unwittingly, drew attention to a subject that has since affected hundreds of thousands of lives.

I haven't been able to secure the exact text of Mr Groombridge's letter but the gist of it was: 'Sir, On a recent visit to the United States I encountered a strange phenomenon. All over the country people with an interest in the stock market are forming themselves into clubs, pooling a regular amount of their savings and purchasing equities. The clubs meet on a regular basis – typically once a month – to discuss possible investments and then vote democratically on which ones should be bought. It occurs to me that if the shares are chosen carefully and therefore go up in value this benefits (a) the club members and (b) the American economy as a whole. If any of your readers are interested in joining me in the formation

A THOUSAND CLUBS WERE SOON FORMED AND

THE NUMBER GREW BY THE WEEK.

BUT WITHOUT DETAILED GUIDANCE,

AND FACED WITH THE INDIFFERENCE OF

THE AUTHORITIES AND COMMERCIAL NECESSITIES

SUCH AS BANKS AND STOCKBROKERS,

THE MAJORITY SOON SHUT UP SHOP.

of a club in Britain I would be pleased to hear from them.'

This innocuous note opened the floodgates. Literally thousands of people inundated Barry with requests to join his club. Poor chap, he didn't know which way to turn, just imagine the cost in stamps of replying to all those letters, never mind the fact that he had little or no idea how to actually form a club. Rules? Constitution? Tax liabilities? Age limits? Barry had some outline thoughts on how it might work but putting flesh on the skeleton was something he had not thought out carefully.

The solution to such a dilemma invariably relies on who you know rather than what you know and here Barry was a lucky bunny. He was acquainted with a successful Liverpool-based accountant called Bill Lowe. A rotund and jovial character, Bill shared Barry's vision of investment clubs and took on the mantle of organization. He formed the National

Association of Investment Clubs, sought advice and guidance from his friend Ken Janke who ran the National Association of Investors Corporation (NAIC) in America, and – hey presto! – the movement in the United Kingdom was born.

Bill produced some basic guidelines for clubs then with a small band of volunteer helpers, plus some spare hands in his Liverpool accountancy office, spent evenings and weekends sending out information to all the enquirers. As he addressed the last envelope and posted it he breathed a sigh of relief. A job well done, now he could relax. Little did he realize that the job was only just beginning. Queries began to pour in to his home and office. Banks were uncertain what sort of account an investment club should open. Brokers were refusing to have clubs as customers because they didn't know how to deal with them. The Inland Revenue branches were unable to give guidance on how tax should be handled.

Could husbands and wives be in the same club? Did the clubs need to include a qualified adviser in their list of members? Could shares be registered in the name of a club? Could a new club advertise for members? Could there be proxy votes? If one member did all the research could he be paid a commission? Despite his valiant efforts to answer everything and satisfy everyone Bill was fighting a losing battle. He had a business to run, a family to support, and he did not have the staff or the funding to cope with a movement which, like Topsy, just growed and growed.

A thousand clubs were soon formed and the number grew by the week. But without detailed guidance, and faced with the indifference of the authorities and commercial necessities such as banks and stockbrokers, the majority soon shut up shop. In the four decades that followed Barry Groombridge's letter to *The Times* the investment club movement briefly flared in popularity to 1,500 clubs then for lack of nourishment had dwindled to about 350 clubs, loosely part of an association but muddling along without any real guidance because running a national organization takes time and money.

Enter ProShare. It was originally set up by the London Stock Exchange and industry in the early 1990s to sing the praises of sensible share ownership to the great British public. And the people responsible for setting the agenda quickly realized that there was one sure-fire way to introduce people to the attractions of share ownership while at the same time making sure that they learned enough to avoid losing their savings. Investment clubs.

Bill Lowe, the pioneer, was enthusiastic. He worked closely with the ProShare people who were able to introduce funding and marketing expertise into the equation. Sadly, before he was able to properly appreciate the extent of the rebirth of the movement, Bill Lowe died suddenly. It was a great pity, he was a jolly chap who had put tremendous enthusiasm, money and time into forming the embryo of the movement and he would have been thrilled to see the result of his efforts today. Thousands of clubs in Britain, tens of thousands around the world.

THE DEVIL IS IN THE DETAIL
AND BY NO MEANS ARE ALL CLUBS SUCCESSFUL.
AN UNACCEPTABLE PROPORTION OF THEM FAIL
BECAUSE EITHER THEY DON'T MAKE PROFITS
OR THE PROCEEDINGS ARE SO DIRGE-LIKE
THAT MEMBERS GET BORED.

So why are clubs so popular? Who gets them going? How do they get off the ground? Who joins them? What makes them tick? How do they become successful?

We will consider each of these questions separately but first let's define exactly what an investment club is because, believe me, there is nothing complicated about it. An investment club is a group of people who agree to pool some of their spare cash on a regular basis and use the collective funds to buy shares on the stock market. Club members meet, usually once a month, to discuss which new shares to buy and whether they want to sell any of the shares they have bought previously. To help them decide which lucky companies are going to benefit from their largesse the club members carry out research on the various suggestions and listen to the input of other members who may have a specialist knowledge of particular companies and industries. All members are encouraged to express an opinion and all decisions are arrived at by democratic vote.

Easy isn't it? However, I have to tell you that the devil is in the detail and by no means are all clubs successful. An unacceptable proportion of them fail because either they don't make profits or the proceedings are so dirge-like that members get bored, attendance dwindles and the whole thing collapses. But fear not, dear reader, it will not happen to your club because you are going to read the pearls of wisdom contained in these pages, apply the techniques to your club and thereby ensure its success.

First though, we will deal with some of the basic queries I listed a few paragraphs back.

Popularity

Investment club members come in all shapes and sizes. Male and female, fat and thin, youngsters, pensioners and lots in between. But they all have one thing in common. They want to make their spare cash work for them. They dream of being rich and they are prepared to do something about it. And that makes them different.

Once upon a time I was the business partner, confidant and friend of a chap called Chay Blyth. When I met him he had just left the 3rd Regiment of the Parachute Brigade in the British Army with the rank of sergeant and a certain notoriety because he had rowed across the Atlantic with an army officer. Scottish through and through, Chay had a burning ambition. He wanted to be the first person to sail single-handedly around the world, the wrong way – westwards, against all the prevailing winds and tides. Now you must admit that's quite an ambition, particularly when you have no boat, no money, almost no sailing experience, a huge mortgage and a wife and baby. But Chay was not the sort of fellow to let these minor distractions bother him. He asked me to help and, although I was secretly convinced he was barmy, I agreed.

I won't take up valuable pages telling you how we did it, but the fact is that we did. The British Steel Corporation were wooed by us and agreed to put up the money – well over £100,000 – to build a 60-foot yacht which was royally christened *British Steel*. We begged and borrowed equipment, food supplies, waterproof

THAT DECISION TO ACT
RATHER THAN JUST DREAM ABOUT THINGS
IS WHAT SINGLES OUT INVESTMENT CLUB MEMBERS
FROM THE CROWD. THEY WANT TO MAKE THEIR MONEY
WORK FOR THEM AND THEY ARE PREPARED
TO PUT A BIT OF EFFORT
INTO ACHIEVING IT FOR THEMSELVES.

clothing, and goodness knows what else. The *Sunday Mirror* bought the newspaper rights, ITN and Southern Television put mini-cameras on board, Hodder & Stoughton bought the book rights, and one bright September day Chay set sail from The Hamble. Ten months later he returned, having completed one of the epic solo voyages of the twentieth century. There was a huge flotilla of craft in the Hamble estuary to greet him plus a bevy of royalty and other dignitaries waiting on the pontoon to shake his hand.

At the press conference in the Royal Southern Yacht Club 10 minutes after he set foot on shore he was asked whether he considered himself different from other sailors. 'Certainly,' he replied with typical Chay modesty. 'Most sailors dream about sailing around the world. I dreamed about it too, but I'm different because I stopped dreaming and went ahead and did it.'

That decision to act rather than just dream about things is what singles out investment club members from the crowd. They want to make their money work for them and, rather than watch others drive along the road to financial success, they are prepared to put a bit of effort into achieving it for themselves. Luckily, it is a darned sight easier than rowing the Atlantic or sailing round the world so there are far more of us who can and do act to turn our dreams into reality.

Who gets the club going?

The answer to that is straightforward: *you* – or, at the very least, you are going to provide the initial motivation. And before

you slam the book shut and say, 'Well, that lets me out. If he's trying to persuade me to start a club he's got another think coming,' do me a favour and read on for a while. And, in the interests of reader participation, put a tick next to one or more of the following reasons why it shouldn't be you:

1. I haven't got time to organize a club. ☐
2. I don't know enough people who might want to join. ☐
3. I don't know much about the stock market or investing. ☐
4. I'm a dunce when it comes to sums. ☐
5. I've never run a meeting in my life. ☐
6. The thought of being the focus of attention fills me with horror. ☐

If you ticked 1 you are squealing like a pig before its been stuck, you haven't the faintest idea how much time is involved and you will be pleasantly surprised how few of your precious leisure hours it will take up.

If you ticked 2 you are almost certainly wrong, you only need a couple of people who you think might like the idea. Sit them down, chat the concept through with them and I can virtually guarantee they will be enthusiastic. Ask them each to invite two of their friends to your next meeting and without any great effort you have the nucleus of a club.

If you ticked 3 then you are missing the point of investment clubs. It is precisely because members realize that they are not investment experts that they join. The knowledge of all the members is combined to provide a formidable whole and, don't worry, in every club there are always better-informed and dimmer members than you.

If you ticked 4 you are worried about keeping records and making returns to the taxman. You are almost certainly numerically challenged – meaning, you can't do sums. So in your list of founder

members make sure there is someone who will undertake the treasurer's job, there are plenty of them about. Equally, you should try to identify someone who will be happy to keep minutes of the meetings.

If you ticked 5 pause for a moment. Are you sure you wouldn't be good at it if you tried? If you are absolutely certain then look at the next sentence.

If you ticked 6 then the answer is simple: choose someone else as leader

of the pack. Notice I said you should at least be the motivator of the club. That doesn't necessarily mean the chairperson. You should identify one of your friends or contacts you know would be happy in the role and ask them to be the front man or woman.

So, you have run out of excuses. But do I get the feeling you are still wriggling, not prepared to take on the responsibility yet? Thinking, perhaps, that you can avoid all the hard work by joining an existing club? Then let me give you two reasons why that is not a good idea.

First, you will have a hard job finding a club that wants you. It's nothing personal, just that we are British and as a race we do not like discussing such emotive subjects as money and investing with strangers. We are only prepared to consider these sort of intimate matters with those we know and trust. As I mentioned earlier our American cousins are much more outgoing, any bus ride or train journey will prove that. You might all be strangers when the trip starts but after half an hour you are all best buddies, knowing what every one of your fellow passengers does to earn a crust, where they live, how many times they've been divorced, how much they earn and so on. Brits are slightly different. The bus or train could be stuck in a snowdrift for a week and when the passengers are finally rescued they won't even have exchanged Christian names.

Second, we have an aversion to saying no. A couple of years ago I had the bright idea of producing a directory of investment clubs. It would give the name of the club together with a contact name, address and phone number for the chairman or secretary. This would be of use to clubs generally, enabling local clubs to get together for social meetings or perhaps to arrange joint visits to local quoted companies or have special speakers on investment topics. Good idea? Not on your nelly. My letter to clubs asking for the requisite information was met with nil response and when I asked why, I was told in no uncertain terms by over 80 per cent of the clubs that they did not want to be included in the directory. Why? Because they were worried about being approached by strangers who wanted to join their ranks and they did not want the embarrassment of saying no, neither did they wish to be pestered by a shower of unsolicited direct mail leaflets from financial services providers.

There's another very pertinent reason why you can't join an existing club. The investment club concept is such a brilliant idea that as soon as one starts the word gets round and before you know it there's a waiting list of friends, and friends of friends, who all want to join. If the club is successful this situation will never change and indeed many clubs decide to start offshoot clubs to cope with the demand from people they know.

Of course there are a few clubs that are looking for members, they have their names published in *Dividend*, a regular magazine ProShare mails to investment club members. But they're few and far between and knowing your luck there won't be any in your neck of the woods. Anyway, do you really want to join a club

THE INVESTMENT CLUB CONCEPT IS

SUCH A **BRILLIANT IDEA** THAT AS SOON

AS ONE STARTS THE WORD GETS ROUND

AND BEFORE YOU KNOW IT THERE'S

A WAITING LIST OF FRIENDS,

AND FRIENDS OF FRIENDS,

WHO ALL WANT TO JOIN.

of strangers? Remember, they got together in the first place because they knew each other. You will be the new bug, the outsider. And if they are short of friends to join them and have to resort to inviting people they don't know to join, it might be because they are a group of no-hopers or anoraks. That's not the sort of club you want to be in, is it?

No, there's only one thing for it. You have got to start a club of your own. At least that way you will be able to create the kind of club that suits you and has members that you choose. Right? Good, glad I've convinced you.

Now let me tell you how easy it is.

First, get on the phone to ProShare (the number is 020 7220 1750) and ask them to send you half a dozen copies of their free leaflet 'A Way to Learn, A Way to Earn'. It explains in just a few paragraphs what investment clubs are and how they can play an important part in your financial future as well as adding a fun dimension to your social life.

Now identify a few people who you think might be interested in the new

club. They could be friends, neighbours, work colleagues, or even members of your own family. (Before you decide who to approach make sure you read and digest the next chapter of this book, it will save you from making mistakes that could influence the success or failure of your venture.) Give each of the chosen few a copy of the 'Way to Earn' leaflet and suggest they have a look at it before you even discuss the idea of a club. Don't worry about their response, I promise you it will be positive. Naturally there will be a few who say thanks but no thanks, however, the vast majority will contact you within 24 hours so enthused that they can't wait to get started.

Invite the enthusiasts to an informal chat at a mutually convenient place, your home or perhaps a pub. If it is the latter make sure you pick an early lunchtime or early evening so you can nab a quiet corner, you don't want your conversation to be overheard by all and sundry because the subject is so interesting you will soon attract a crowd of earwiggers.

Don't have a set agenda. Just chat. Talk about the concept first, the idea of pooling a few bob and the expectation of building up your meagre funds into something meaningful. Be honest between yourselves, if you don't know anything about stocks and shares, if you always ignore the business pages of the newspaper, say so. No point in kidding anybody in this situation, you can be encouraged by the fact that 60 per cent of people who join investment clubs have never bought a share in their lives and the vast majority of them wouldn't know how to go about it. And be encouraged by another statistic, of that 60 per cent know-nothings, at least half of them will be running their own personal share portfolio within two years.

It might be that at this first meeting one of your merry band is already an investor and has a knowledge of how the shares business works. If so, fine, he or she can fill in the others on how comparatively easy it is. If not, agree that as soon as your club is formed you will contact a stockbroker to come and explain the basics of investing. As a starting point contact a few of the brokers listed later in this book, the ones that are keen for investment club business. If they are worth their salt they will come to your meeting and there will be no question of them charging, the stockbroking world is extremely competitive and they are after not just your club business but the personal portfolios of all your members.

However, I'm running ahead of myself. We are still at the chatting stage and you will find that as the discussion progresses the form of your club begins to take shape, even though the membership is as yet largely faceless. The talk will revolve around when and where to hold your club meetings, what sort of people you would like to see join, and there'll be a few laughs as you think of names for the club. (Incidentally, try to be original, there are already over 50 Midas Clubs, at least 20 Millenniums, and a dozen Viagras).

As you all prattle on, perhaps talking about local companies in which the club might buy a few shares, each person will be asking him- or herself three questions: Is this for me? Can I afford it? Who else would I like to see as members?

The 'Is this for me?' question basically means 'Am I going to enjoy it?' and that is a very personal thing. So let me outline what you are letting yourself in for. Make no mistake, this is an additional commitment but it need not be onerous, this is not going to dominate your life. It will be a pleasant and sometimes exciting leisure activity, taking up one evening a month for the meetings and however much extra time you are prepared to devote to it. I estimate the average club member gives no more than two hours a month extra to club activities, usually researching the facts about a particular share or keeping an eye on the price of the share he or she has been asked to watch (more about this later).

Can you afford it? Again, very personal and only you know the answer. I will be discussing subscriptions later but suffice to say now that the money you put into the club must be money you can afford to lose. I don't want to give the wrong impression but it is quite likely that in the early days while your club is finding its feet the members might make some unwise investment decisions. The chosen shares might go down and there is a possibility that you will lose money. Should this happen it must be an aggravation and not a disaster. So my advice is only to put in money you can afford to lose and if the worst occurs and you do pick some dogs to start with you can smile, put it down to experience and vow to do better next time.

And the final universal question everyone at your informal chat meeting is silently asking him- or herself: Who would I like to see in this club and who don't we want at any price? Although you probably don't realize it yet, that is the most important question of the three.

....

Money can't buy you friends but it can get you

a better class of enemy.

Spike Milligan

CHAPTER

YOU'RE
ONLY AS
GOOD AS YOUR
MEMBERS

Cedric is a chemist. Not the kind who prepares the potions that the doctor prescribes or sells you something for the weekend. No, Cedric works in the laboratories of one of the world's largest pharmaceutical companies doing clever things with proteins and cultures. It's an environment he enjoys because he is involved in groundbreaking experiments that could make a difference to mankind and he has the stimulation of working alongside a score or so of equally motivated chemists.

As a breed, chemists are a thoughtful lot so it's small wonder therefore that during lunchbreaks in the company's restaurant – a much more pleasant word than canteen – the conversation often revolves around what will happen in the future, not just in biotechnological terms but also in their personal lives. Spending their days poring over pipettes is all very well but there comes a time when even vocational chemists have to consider what is going to happen to them and their loved ones when they can no longer light the Bunsen burner. So, when Cedric, munching on his chicken-tikka-masala-with-mayo-on-brown sarnie one lunchtime, mentioned the idea of an investment club, several pairs of chemists' ears pricked up.

To his credit Cedric was reasonably well versed in the subject, he had read about such clubs in one of the Sunday newspapers, and by coincidence had obtained a leaflet which outlined the rudiments of how a club operates. The discussion became enthusiastic, even animated, inevitably there were more questions than answers, but by the time the chemists trooped back to their laboratory benches a significant number of them were sold on the concept.

Cedric is by nature a doer rather than a talker, the ideal sort of chap to start an investment club. Within a week he had obtained a copy of ProShare's manual which is the bible most clubs use to guide their ongoing activities. It contains all those things you need to set up your club – draft rules, club constitution, Inland Revenue tax forms and so on. He ordered the manual from ProShare and it came with a free supply of those 'Way to Earn/ Way to Learn' leaflets I mentioned earlier. He distributed leaflets to his colleagues, and talked to the landlord of a nearby pub about using a private room for an exploratory meeting. The landlord, himself a far-sighted sort of fellow, could see the wisdom of providing the room free because it stood empty most weekday evenings and if the chemists were going to meet on a regular basis for a pie and a pint it would serve to boost his takings.

The inaugural meeting was arranged and gratifyingly a dozen chemists turned up. They had already chatted the whole thing through during several lunchtimes so the proposals relating to the club's basic structure were agreed with the minimum of discussion and absolutely no dissension. The chairman was to be Cedric, after all, it was his idea in the first place, and anyway he was the only one who had read the manual. The secretary was to be Jean because she had reasonably legible writing (remember, they were all chemists). Andy – nickname Anorak because he wore one and was one – agreed to be treasurer because he understood spreadsheets.

The matter of the subscription had been the subject of endless lunchtime discussions so by the time the inaugural meeting came round it had been fully aired and there was general agreement. Everyone would put in £250 to start with, then the monthly subscription would be £50.

After considering various names, some rude, some not even funny, they settled on the Chemikazi club. A bank account was authorized, brokers chosen, and Cedric circulated a questionnaire to everyone present.

Because this questionnaire is the point of my story it is reproduced here.

Name:

Address:

Home telephone:

Work extension:

E-mail:

Brief curriculum vitae:

Interests and hobbies (note everything, no matter how seemingly mundane):

Stock market sectors I would be happy to keep an eye on:

The members were asked to take the form home, fill it in and return it to Cedric. Over the next few days, as he received the questionnaires back through the post, he realized with a growing sense of dismay that there was a danger of the club getting off on entirely the wrong foot. It was that last section of the questionnaire that flagged up the warning. All 11 forms said, 'Pharmaceuticals'. The club's area of expertise in that sector was undoubtedly deep, certainly strong, and at the club meetings they would be able to talk with authority on the discovery, development, manufacture and marketing of prescription and non-prescription medicines until the cows came home but there the Chemikazi circle of competence would begin and end.

The essence of any investment club is the variety of experience and opinion that the members bring to it, so you and the few friends you invite to chat around the idea in the first place must approach this matter very carefully. Indeed, I venture to suggest that you will be setting the path for the success or failure of your club.

Here is the single word you should be able to apply to your membership list – VARIETY. Ideally you need a balance of:

- age
- talent
- experience
- sex.

THE ESSENCE OF ANY INVESTMENT CLUB IS THE **VARIETY OF EXPERIENCE** AND OPINION THAT THE MEMBERS BRING TO IT, SO YOU AND THE FEW FRIENDS YOU INVITE TO CHAT AROUND THE IDEA IN THE FIRST PLACE MUST APPROACH THIS MATTER **VERY CAREFULLY.**

Age

Let me tell you about Little Sue, a former colleague of mine. In the City office where we worked she was known as Little Sue, not just because she was a tad under five feet high, but because we had another lady of the same name who stood six feet tall in her stockings. You've guessed it. She was Big Sue. To confuse you further there were those in the office who felt it was politically incorrect to refer to Little Sue's lack of stature so they preferred to make fun of her Cockney accent by calling her London Sue.

Anyway, for the purposes of this tale she will be Little Sue. She worked in the accounts department, a quiet soul who, if a goose had waddled into the office, would not have said boo to it. When someone suggested the idea of an office investment club she was hesitant about joining but agreed to attend the exploratory meeting. She sipped her glass of Chardonnay, listened, and didn't say a word.

It was the same at each of the first three monthly sessions of our new club which, with a predictable lack of imagination, we called Moneypenny. Sue turned up at the meetings, listened some more, paid her subscription but made no verbal contributions to the proceedings. At the fourth meeting, a rather grey evening in February, the chairman opened the session with no sign of Sue and I'm sorry to relate she was not even noticeable by her absence. It wasn't until she came into the room, flustered, loaded with designer shopping bags and full of apologies, that we registered she was late.

'So sorry,' she said, plonking herself down and pouring a glass of wine from the communal bottle. 'I've had a hell of a day. Lunchtime, I went down Next. It's a bun fight in there. Not a stitch left on the rails. Then, teatime, I had to stay late at the office.' The City suits who were her fellow Moneypenny members nodded politely but disinterestedly. Half of them hadn't understood a word she'd said. They hurried on with their learned deliberations while Sue silently and contentedly slurped her Chardonnay.

Came the time when the chairman went round the room to elicit any investment suggestions from the members. When it came to Sue's turn she piped up without hesitation: 'Next.' It took a while for the older farts among us to realize that she was referring to a shop. You could almost hear the penny dropping as it dawned on them Next was a clothes store for teens and 20-somethings. A fashion house. Sue went on to explain: 'The Spring range came in today and it's knockout,' she enthused. 'The colours, the styles, they're just brill. I'm telling you, there'll be fighting in the streets for this gear.'

The more with-it members of Moneypenny busily translated Little Sue's announcement for their elders and soon everyone understood that Next's spring range, just arrived in the store, had caused a sensation among its target audience. But then Little Sue produced her real surprise, her masterstroke. 'I've looked up the financial facts and noted them down,' she said. 'It's a bit of a scribble I'm afraid but I think I've covered all the points you talked about at the first three meetings. There are photocopies for everyone.' Sue handed round her sheets of A4 paper and we studied them. Everything was there – five-year history of profits and earnings, analysis of the price movements, even a crudely drawn graph. Apart from a couple of minor blips it was the classic growth stock. Steady increase in turnover and profits, good earnings for shareholders, and a price that indicated the City was not particularly impressed.

The miracle of Little Sue's suggestion hit most of us at the same time. We were in a position that most private investors and clubs only dream about. We were privy to the purest piece of insider information. Ours was probably the first investment club in the country to realize that Next had a winning range, so appealing that the customers were fighting over it. And we knew before those City analysts who wouldn't get the news until takings from stores scattered around Britain filtered through to the corporate bottom line. As far as Moneypenny was concerned no more research was necessary, we filled our boots with Next shares using all the cash we had available. Clever us, the price went up and up.

OURS WAS PROBABLY THE
FIRST INVESTMENT CLUB
IN THE COUNTRY TO REALIZE THAT NEXT
HAD A WINNING RANGE,
SO APPEALING THAT THE CUSTOMERS WERE
FIGHTING OVER IT.

That's not the end of the story. Nine months later, as we basked euphorically in a 70 per cent increase on our investment, Little Sue – by now the toast of the club – came with the news that the winter range at Next was 'pants'. For those who do not follow these colloquial developments the expression 'pants' means that Sue and her mates were not too impressed with the store's seasonal garments. We could not believe our luck. Again, we were insiders. It was going to be a cold winter for the Next sales tills. No hesitation, we sold and in the following months watched smugly as the Next price dwindled.

I quote this true story about Little Sue to illustrate these facts:

- A variety of ages is a real asset to an investment club.

- The 'insider' information gave us an advantage over all the statistics merchants in the City.

- Sue's knowledge provided us with expertise in an area that is alien to most of us (for instance, if I walked into a Next store a silence would fall on the place and the security guard would probably take me on one side for a discreet word).

- The views of younger people can bring a fresh perspective to your club's investing technique.

Footnote: Within two years Little Sue was voted in as chairperson of Moneypenny. Unfortunately, after six months in office she left to have a baby. We miss her still.

Talent

The tale of Little Sue illustrates equally the need to have talent in your club. Not only was she of an age that most of us had sadly long forgotten, but it was obvious that she had style. Small she may have been but she was always dressed in a way that made admiring heads turn and the glances were from women as well as men.

Often a talent such as Sue's is God-given and cannot be learned. You've either got it or you haven't and if it's not there, no matter how hard you try, it will be beyond you. Be aware of this and choose your members to fill gaps where you know you are weak. Let me give you a personal example of what I mean.

I'm no good at sums, I haven't got the talent for it. Luckily, my friend Melvyn is a chartered accountant and finds figures orgasmic. He can do gigantic sums in his head.

Here's another personal shortcoming. Man management is not my forte. I do not have the authority to stop boring people from talking without offending them, or to cajole idle folk into pulling their weight. When I was in a position of power in a corporate organization I would agonize for days about reprimanding anyone and the thought of having to sack a useless member of a team gave me nightmares. Fortunately, my friend David has the charisma and experience to get the best out of people.

When I write I tend to babble on – you may have noticed – rather than simply putting down the facts. A good job then that my friend Peter is succinct and to the point when it comes to preparing a written report.

Melvyn, David and Peter were my priorities a couple of years ago when I drew up the list of potential members for a new club I decided to form, the Pall Mall Investment Club. It comprises people I have met and worked with over four decades in various parts of the world, most of them never knew each other before the formation of the club so I was the only common link. Normally if you put a group of strangers into a room it creates an uncomfortable atmosphere, but I knew my friends. From that first exploratory meeting, which we held at The Reform Club in Pall Mall, it was obvious the rapport I felt with each of them was infectious. We formed the club that evening and I'm delighted to say it is still alive and well and has David as chairman, Melvyn as treasurer and Peter as secretary. They are excellent officers and I take the credit for identifying their talents at the outset.

So when you compile your list of potential members bear in mind the official positions in the club that must be filled. But don't make the mistake of telling the people the main reason you are asking them to join you. If I had said to Melvyn, 'I want you to become a member of the Pall Mall club because you are a good bookkeeper,' he would rightly have been quite offended. In real life he is a top London accountant charging several hundred pounds an hour for his services, so to suggest his role in the club would be to keep a set of simple books would

be offensive. And if I had asked Peter if he would mind noting down what was said at the meetings and then circulating the minutes he would have reminded me that as a super-rich Mayfair-based property developer he has a bevy of assistants to do that sort of work for him. So be subtle, make them feel wanted for their wisdom and deep thoughts – then make sure that at the inaugural meeting they are honoured by being chosen for the official jobs. You will see my talent is as a scheming bullshitter.

Experience

It's the commodity you can't buy, and is the advantage the investment club has over the individual investor and the City suits. Each of us brings a unique bundle of experience to the club meetings. We have all trodden different paths in life and had a variety of ups and downs. In education we have reached various levels and achieved a variety of qualifications. In work we have utilized our own particular skills and concentrated on our chosen aspects of business – finance, management, marketing, manufacturing and so on. Outside work few of us share exactly the same enthusiasms. Some people enjoy watching or taking part in sport during their leisure hours while others cannot bear the thought of physical exercise, preferring to spend spare time going out for a meal or to the pub, or indulging in a spot of do-it-yourself. Thank goodness, we are all different and therein lies the secret of a successful investment club. Put this miraculous cornucopia of wisdom and enthusiasm in the same room and you can make investment decisions that are based on real live knowledge. You have a circle of competence that is superior to any analyst.

··

Sex

Don't get excited. I'm not suggesting that this is part of the extra-curricular activities in your club. What I do believe is that you should consider having both male and female members.

I can already hear the strident voices rising, particularly among the all-women clubs, which have proved their abilities statistically by achieving consistently better returns from their portfolios than all-men clubs. (By the way that's an American statistic that has been handed down in folklore. However, a recent survey carried out by ProShare tended to confirm it. Personally, I find it difficult to believe – but, then, I am a man.) On the whole I find mixed clubs are more able to make a balanced judgement about investments. I realize this is a generalization and is based primarily on my personal experiences, but there's a logical feel to it. In my opinion – and, after all, this *is* my book – women are more sensible than men and less subject to knee-jerk reaction. We males on the other hand are more decisive and less emotional. Between us we make a good combination when it comes to well-thought-out and timely investment decisions.

To sum up: Choose your members carefully and try to achieve a balance in

IN MY OPINION WOMEN ARE
MORE SENSIBLE THAN MEN
AND LESS SUBJECT TO KNEE-JERK REACTION.
WE MALES ON THE OTHER HAND ARE
MORE DECISIVE AND LESS
EMOTIONAL. BETWEEN US WE MAKE A
GOOD COMBINATION WHEN IT COMES TO
WELL-THOUGHT-OUT AND TIMELY
INVESTMENT DECISIONS.

your club. There is an additional consideration you should have in the back of your mind but this is one I cannot give you definitive guidance on. The very best clubs are those that reach their decisions by co-operation rather than confrontation. Therefore your members must gel together, enjoy each other's company and respect each other's opinions. Too often clubs fail not because they are suffering financial losses but because of temperamental conflicts within the club.

It's impossible to be specific about people who can cause disruption so let me describe a few of the types I have encountered on my tours around the clubs of Britain.

- **Arfur Dailey (or his wife, Erindoors Dailey)**. Arfur is a real character, life and soul of the party, always there with a merry quip and an optimistic comment. His whole demeanour is of a man well connected, friends in high places, contacts that can provide insider information to put the club on the road to riches. His enthusiasm is infectious and he is excellent company.

  One evening Arfur will turn up at the club meeting positively beaming. 'Boys and girls, is this your lucky night!' he will announce. 'Break open the bottles of bubbly, we can celebrate in advance. Have I got a winner for you!' This is not a question, it is a statement of fact. Arfur is sure. It is our lucky night, there is nothing more certain than the winner he has for us. Arthur then reveals the name

of this miracle share, and it is equally certain that you will never have heard of it. Someone might even have the temerity to voice that the share's name is unfamiliar. Does Arfur sneer? Not at all. 'Well spotted,' he smiles. 'That's the beauty of this one. A brand new opportunity, we're the first to be offered it. My best contact – owes me a favour, no names, no pack drill, walls have ears – is letting us in on the ground floor. But we've got to get in quick before word gets round.'

What does the company do? Such a question seems superfluous and Arfur shrugs it aside. 'Can't be precise about that, squire,' he says with a nod-nod, wink-wink. 'That's technology. Not my line. But trust me, the share price is pennies today and it will be pounds tomorrow.'

Carried away by Arfur's silver tongue and elated by the sheer excitement at being in at the start of something big, the club buys the share. To avoid giving the wrong impression I should emphasize that Arfur is a genuine bloke who honestly believes that his contact has given him a winner. And it is just possible – miracle of miracles – that on this occasion he is right and the share does show a profit. Outsiders have been known to win races. It is just conceivable that it might happen a second time and Arfur will become the club Messiah. But I guarantee that it will not happen a third time and if you continue to listen to him and follow his hot tips Arfur will unwittingly and unintentionally lead the club down the road to disaster.

- **Mr Wotif.** Hail, rain or shine Mr Wotif wears a pullover. In the winter it is dark grey and has long sleeves, in the summer it has no sleeves and a Fair Isle pattern. When he goes to work he wears a brown jacket over his pullover and there is a neat row of biros in the inside pocket. But in the evening, because this is leisure time and therefore casual dress is called for, he leaves the jacket off. He always, but always, wears the same tie, knitted for him by Mrs Wotif.

Mr Wotif invariably prepares a question for the monthly club meeting. Strictly speaking it should come under 'Any other business' at the end of the meeting but Mr Wotif can't wait that long because there may not be enough time for his question to be discussed fully. So he raises it immediately after the chairman's remarks and always starts by saying: 'On a point of order, Mr Chairman ...' This ensures he gets a full hearing because no one can be absolutely sure that his question doesn't relate to something the chairman has said.

The subjects of Mr Wotif's questions are far-ranging and complicated but they have one thing in common. They bear absolutely no relevance to the main purpose of the evening, which is to select shares that will go up in value. 'What if there's a storm this evening and the roof of the pub collapses? Is this club properly insured?' 'What if you and the treasurer decide to go on holiday together and your plane crashes, Mr Chairman? Who will sign the cheques and be authorized to instruct the club stockbroker? How is our money protected?' 'What if our broker has a fire in his premises and all our records are lost? Because we are in a nominee account what proof have we got that we own the shares? And will we be able to buy and sell while the broker sorts things out?' 'What if I decide one evening that I have a slight head cold coming on and feel it would be inadvisable for me to attend the meeting? Could I send Mrs Wotif along as my proxy and could she vote on my behalf? And could she voice a personal opinion on each recommendation or should we postpone the decisions until she has had a chance to appraise me of the discussion which has taken place?'

The problem is that Mr Wotif has always thought his questions up carefully so that, while they are usually about obscure and irrelevant matters, they have just sufficient interest to warrant an answer and provoke a discussion. Before you know where you are the club is taking up valuable time talking about the daftest of subjects. Mr Wotif is happy. When he gets home he undresses quietly and in the dark because Mrs Wotif is asleep. Then he puts his pullover back on and slips between the sheets, quietly satisfied because his question has dominated the proceedings.

Timewasters like Mr Wotif must be avoided at all costs. It is vital that you remember the whole basis of your club is to discuss and select shares. Several clubs I know have a strict rule that business unrelated to specific shares must take up no more than 20 minutes per meeting and I am aware of three clubs that use alarm clocks to signal when time is up.

- **Emma Toobusy**. At first sight Emma is the perfect member for your club. She has a rich husband, two children at boarding school, and a wide circle of influential friends. And she is so enthusiastic about the idea of the investment club that she can't wait for you to get it started. 'Dwarling, it's too, too marvellous,' she trills. 'Our little group pooling money to invest on the stock exchange – how thrilling! Of course I don't know anything about shares and that sort of thing so I'll leave all that side of it to you. Now I can't attend the first meeting because we're going to the country but please, count me in. I don't care what the subscription is, I'll sign a blank banker's order and you can fill it in.'

You gently explain to Emma that one of the main reasons for joining an investment club is to learn about buying and selling shares. She nods politely but is really not too interested, she leaves that sort of thing to rich hubby. And the thought of becoming involved with research

into potential investments horrifies her. She's much too busy. Nevertheless Emma is a lovely lady and she's perfectly happy to pay her monthly subscriptions and attend the social functions. The temptation is to take her money and make decisions without her. My advice: don't. You would be silly to have her as a member. The strength of an investment club is the expertise and opinions that its members bring to a meeting, plus their willingness to help with research and learn about investing. The subscriptions are a minor (albeit essential) part of the process.

- **Abbi Superior**. As she will tell you at the drop of a hat, Abbi is a private investor in her own right. Been at it for years, and the profits she made in millennium year were the talk of Goldman Sachs. She knows Jim Slater intimately, writes to John Templeton regularly and rumour has it Warren Buffett sometimes gives her a ring when he needs a woman's opinion.

Whenever another member suggests a potential investment Abbi is usually ready to comment. 'Sounds fine as far as it goes,' she says condescendingly. 'But have you considered the ROCE? And did you deduct the intangibles from the NAV before you calculated the PTBV? I looked up the chart and the neckline on the double bottom was very low.' Abbi never deigns to explain what the initials stand for, or the significance of a neckline on a double bottom, unless she is asked to do so. Then she explains slowly and painstakingly with many sighs, making the questioner feel uncomfortable and inadequate. Nobody enjoys that sort of putdown so at the next meeting the questioner remains silent or, worse still, just doesn't turn up.

Abbi doesn't set out to be a clever clogs, she simply doesn't have time for beginners because they do not speak her language. She belongs in a club of professional investors where she can share her opinion and thoughts with other bores.

No doubt I have exaggerated Arfur, Emma *et al* but I'll bet those of you who are already in an investment club can identify at least one of your members who bears a passing resemblance to someone in this gang. Your members are the lifeblood of your organization so choose them with care.

....

Man stand for long time with mouth open

before roast duck fly in.

ancient Chinese proverb

CHAPTER

ABOUT TO

BE BORN

Because I can't know your personal status – are you thinking of starting a club? already a member of one? contemplating joining an existing outfit? just interested in knowing how they work? – I do not intend to dwell on the nitty-gritty of how to set up a club. Such details as draft rules, constitution, tax forms and so on are included in ProShare's manual. I find that in practice most clubs have the manual at every meeting; it's treated rather like a bible when a point of order comes up.

However, I do want to devote some space to the inaugural meeting, the first official gathering of a new club, because it is very much a scene-setter for the future. And for those old salts who are experienced clubbers and think they know it all, take a few minutes to read this chapter. It might ring a few bells and identify some gaps you wish you had filled at the beginning.

For our purposes, I have made the assumption that you, dear reader, are the driving force behind a new club.

So, the club is about to be born. The pregnancy has gone well, you've had the private chats and the informal get-togethers in small groups or maybe even collectively, you have identified the potential club officers, your friends have recruited their friends, everyone's read the little leaflet 'A Way to Learn, A Way to Earn' and it's time for you to give birth. You are going to convene the Very Important Inaugural Meeting, destined to be what is perhaps the most significant session your club will ever have. I do not exaggerate, it is the first and a major milestone in your club's history because this is the occasion that will (a) create the environment and atmosphere in which your future meetings will be held and (b) establish the pattern for your investment strategy.

AT THE END OF THE EVENING (OR MORNING, LUNCHTIME, WHATEVER) EVERYONE THERE MUST KNOW EXACTLY WHAT THEY HAVE LET THEMSELVES IN FOR, BE HAPPY WITH THE COMMITMENT IN TERMS OF MONEY AND TIME, AND BE FIRED WITH ENTHUSIASM FOR THE JOB.

At the end of the evening (or morning, lunchtime, whatever) everyone there must know exactly what they have let themselves in for, be happy with the commitment in terms of money and time, and be fired with enthusiasm for the job. The secret is to prepare the whole event carefully. It's difficult to be precise with my guidance because situations vary between clubs, but what is imperative is that things should run like clockwork.

Well beforehand

Write to everyone concerned at least two weeks before the meeting with a chatty covering letter giving details of the venue, date and time of the inaugural meeting. I emphasize chatty because at this stage at least some of the prospective members are still not committed and there's a fair chance that their partners at home have greeted the news of the proposed club with a sigh and a comment like: 'But you don't know anything about shares.' This first 'official' communication should paint a relaxed but nevertheless enthusiastic picture of a fun evening out, an event to look forward to with pleasurable anticipation.

I suggest your letter should read something like this:

Dear Jack [or Jill]

Good news! I've been able to book the back room at the Black Horse for our club's inaugural meeting on Wednesday, 29 February. We have a lot to talk about so I would like to make a start promptly at 7 p.m.

Enclosed with this letter are the agenda and drafts of the proposed rules and constitution for the club. They are the ones suggested by ProShare but there may be a few changes to suit our particular purposes so I would be grateful if you would read them and be ready to make your comments at the meeting. Also enclosed is a brief questionnaire which I hope you will fill in and post to me in advance or hand in on the night. It will enable us compile a membership list and also give us an idea of the stock market sectors in which we have experience.

As you will see one of the items for discussion is the format future meetings should follow and we can consider such vital matters as refreshments then. However, on this occasion, I have taken the liberty of making an executive decision and arranged for the pub to serve us fish and chips at 8.30 p.m. The break at that time will enable us to replenish our glasses from the bar. The pub is charging us a very reasonable fiver a head for the food and we pay for our drinks as we go along. Incidentally, Sid the landlord is kindly letting us have the room free – he hopes to make enough from us at the bar!

There should be a dozen of us at the meeting and I know we're all looking forward to starting a successful club where we will learn a lot, laugh a lot, and hopefully make some money too!

See you on the 29th.

Yours sincerely

Terry

PS If you don't fancy fish and chips give me a ring a couple of days beforehand and I will cancel your portion and ask if they have an alternative.

The venue

Whether it is a pub or a club, the village hall or your own front room, it must be big enough. People want to feel comfortable, some might even be strangers to one another so they won't like being crammed in like sardines. And for goodness sake make sure there are enough chairs. If someone comes late he or she doesn't expect to be made to feel like a pariah from the word go, standing out like a sore thumb – always remember, we are talking about people's leisure time and if they feel the slightest bit unwelcome you won't see them again.

If you are meeting in a pub or club make sure the way to the private room is well signposted. There's nothing more embarrassing than trying to catch the eye of a busy landlord when you are not going to buy a drink but merely ask where the meeting is or, worse still, asking one of the customers who will almost certainly not know what the hell you are talking about.

You must get there first and make sure the room is laid out as you want it. Ideally there should be a large table or set of tables around which everyone can sit – most people will want to make notes and therefore want something to lean on. They will also want somewhere to park their fish and chips and drinks.

On the assumption that you are the prime mover in this new venture, you must initially take charge. No point in being a wilting flower, you must start as you mean to go on so just five minutes after the appointed time bang on your bit of the table and welcome everyone to the meeting.

TIP Splash out yourself and buy a dozen small notebooks and pencils, enough for everyone at the meeting to have something to write on and with. The club will have an administration kitty so you will be able to recoup your expenditure, and it's a nice touch.

I suggest that you begin the proceedings before the meeting proper with a few well-chosen words of your own. You will know what to say because you will be acquainted with most of the people there and the background to the formation of the club. You are looking to establish an all-friends-together atmosphere, at the same time explaining that investing is a serious business because personal money is involved. Don't read your little homily verbatim from a script, but it's OK to have a crib sheet with single-word reminders of what you want to say. *Practise in the mirror at home, time yourself beforehand, and on no account make these opening remarks more than five minutes long. No matter how important you think your messages are do not exceed that time otherwise you will lose your audience. They are not there to listen to speeches, especially from you.*

You will know how committed and informed your prospective members are; nevertheless I would make the point at the end of your remarks that although this is the inaugural meeting and that by their very presence everyone there has indicated their intention of being a

YOU ARE LOOKING TO ESTABLISH AN ALL-FRIENDS-TOGETHER ATMOSPHERE, AT THE SAME TIME EXPLAINING THAT INVESTING IS A SERIOUS BUSINESS BECAUSE PERSONAL MONEY IS INVOLVED.

member, there will still be the opportunity to opt out. You are going to discuss such vital matters as the level of monthly subscriptions and whether there should be a lump sum payment to get the club off the ground. The final decisions on such delicate matters may not suit some people who would, however, not like to admit in public that they simply can't afford to join the club. In these cases I believe you should leave the door open for anyone who is not happy after the meeting to make a discreet phone call to you next day and simply not be registered as a founder member.

At the end of your welcoming comments, formally declare the meeting open and follow the items on the agenda.

1. **Apologies for absence.** In any gathering of 10 or more there are bound to be people who, for perfectly legitimate reasons, cannot attend. That's fine, they can be sent minutes of the meeting and accepted as founder members.

2. **Election of a chairperson.** Let's face it, unless you've made other arrangements this is likely to be you, and quite right too because the club is your baby. On the other hand if you definitely don't want the job, make sure you have set someone up well beforehand and that he or she is willing to accept. You make the proposal – making it clear that you are happy with the idea – and be certain you have a seconder already in place. A vote is taken on a show of hands, then the official chairperson takes over the proceedings. If there is any doubt about who should do this job then you can appoint a caretaker chairperson for this meeting only, but this isn't very satisfactory because it's a wishy-washy start to your club's life.

3. **Election of honorary treasurer.** Hopefully, you will have identified who this is going to be well before the actual meeting and, of course, obtained his or her agreement to do the job. You will have made plain that, even if the treasurer is a pen pusher and not yet in touch with the real world of cyberspace, the job will not take more than an hour a month.

Much better though that the treasurer has a basic knowledge of computing and a PC at home because the software program which is available from ProShare enables the whole process to be updated at the push of a button. Election for the position of treasurer should be a formality but follow the rules and have a show of hands.

4. **Election of honorary secretary.** Here again, you should decide who it is going to be well in advance of the meeting. Indeed, the chosen person should have been taking notes from the outset of the inaugural session with a view to recording the happenings and producing the minutes for circulation. If there is only one nominee for secretary a show of hands will suffice.

5. **Discussion on and adoption of the constitution and rules of the club.** This might well test the mettle of the chairperson. Because you have circulated the drafts beforehand – quite rightly, because these are important matters and should be considered carefully – there are likely to be those who feel bound to comment. There may also be those who are happy to spend the time discussing obscure points (remember Mr Wotif?). The chairperson's task is to let everyone have an input but to speed things along by pointing out the dangers of becoming bogged down. It should also be explained that while minor changes can be made to the drafts any major alterations might affect the legality of the document and would need the advice of a solicitor. Obtaining such advice would be a cost to the club because it is not available from ProShare. This item on the agenda is probably the first occasion on which the chairperson's ability will be tested. You, or the person you have persuaded to do the job, needs to let everyone have their say but you must terminate waffle because time and boredom are your enemies. Be firm yet gentle, and if there's a radical difference of opinion on any point, call for a vote.

6. **Discussion and decision on the level of the monthly subscription and a lump sum initial payment (if any).** This will have been talked through at your get-togethers and hopefully a consensus opinion will have been reached. Nevertheless, it must be discussed and formally agreed because each person is making a long-term financial commitment. If you have club members of various ages and financial standing it is perfectly acceptable to have a variety of monthly contributions, providing that you democratically stick to one-member-one-vote on all resolutions – there must be no second-class citizens. The important thing is that the subscription should be set at an amount everyone can comfortably afford. Most clubs decide to have a one-off initial lump sum payment so

they can start investing in the real world as soon as possible. Fantasy portfolios are all very well but there's nothing like the real thing. As a guide I suggest a lump sum around £250 and monthly subs anywhere between £25 and £100 (the latter for the fat cats). I know clubs where the members pay £1,000 a month but in my opinion that's too much, and I suspect that when a part of the portfolio falls out of bed the smiles are replaced by furrowed brows.

7. **Appointment of bankers.** This is going to be easy or not-quite-so-easy. Hopefully, even in this day and age when general banking enquiries seem to be dealt with by a disembodied voice and a confusing series of numbers to press, or at best by someone just out of school, you have a contact at your bank who will understand when you want to open an account for your investment club. Ideally the bank you approach will know what you are talking about when you say investment clubs but if not tell them that what you want is a Clubs and Societies account or a Treasurer's account. Nowadays some of the bigger stockbrokers offer banking facilities to their customers (indeed, some insist on it) but if you decide to go down this route make sure you get an account with a cheque book rather than just a credit card. It will often be necessary to pay out funds for items other than shares and the treasurer will want to be able to carry out these transactions easily.

8. **Appointment of a stockbroker.** Shop around (see the chapter on stockbrokers). Most of the big stockbrokers, and in particular the execution-only brokers, are keen to act for investment clubs and have tempting offers to get your club's custom. The appeal for the broker is: (a) you have new money to invest every month so they are going to earn regular commissions; (b) inevitably you will be active customers, buying as well as selling, so yet more commissions; and (c) if the brokers are efficient your members may open personal accounts with them.

9. **Appointment of club trustees (optional).** The investment business is fast moving towards a paperless society. Shares are held on behalf of individuals and clubs in the nominee accounts of stockbrokers and this results in minimum administrative work and speed of settlement for everyone concerned. However, there are still investors and clubs that prefer to have the security of a share certificate. If your club insists on it you should appoint trustees, who must sign a Declaration of Trust, to act on behalf of the club in share transfer transactions and to have their names on the share registers of companies (companies will not issue shares in the name of individual clubs). Be aware of three possible snags if you opt for the trustee route: (a) several of the execution-only

brokers will not want your business because they will only deal through their nominee accounts; (b) a trustee must always be readily available to sign transfer documents and this can present problems with holidays etc.; (c) if a trustee dies or resigns the club will often have to pay to have the shares re-registered in the name of the new trustee. You will probably guess that I favour the nominee account method, particularly because most share certificates can easily be forged so I do not see how they offer any degree of security.

10. **Treasurer to advise on payment of subscriptions.** There is only one way to receive members' subscriptions, and that is by banker's order paid in by every member on the same day each month. That way the club knows its exact financial position and can invest accordingly. Please don't fall for the plea from the chap or lass who want to pay by cash because they are in a business where they handle readies. It might work well for a few months but, trust me, it will all end in tears.

11. **Membership.** As soon as word of your new club gets around you will inevitably receive enquiries from friends or acquaintances who want to join. So at this stage it is worth discussing how big you want the club to be. Remember, you can't have more than 20 because you are regarded in law as a partnership and

that's the legal limit (there are some exceptions to this rule but an investment club is not one of them). My advice: don't rush into anything or recruit new members ad lib just because you want to boost your numbers. Carefully choose people who can contribute, and I don't mean just their monthly subscription.

12. **Initial discussion on investment policy.** It's a fair bet that by now everyone is feeling a bit jaded. You have covered a lot of ground and you are full of fish and chips. The last thing members want to do is discuss investment policy but it should be on the agenda just to show you mean business. I suggest you simply distribute my four tablets of stone – see Chapter 5 – which you have photocopied beforehand (you have my complete permission to reproduce them without fee). Agree that an investment philosophy and system will be the main item on the agenda for the next meeting. This will give everyone a chance to get their thoughts together.

13. **Any other business.** Doubtful, but some hardy soul might want to raise something.

14. **Date, time and place of the next meeting.** Does this evening of the week suit everyone? Was this pub OK? Fish and chips good? Wine and beer palatable? Fine. If not, ring the changes.

The morning after the night before

It's not over yet. When you wake up and you're staring at the ceiling thinking through the events of a few hours before, try to remember the little points. Did everyone join in or was there anyone who didn't say a word? Were there any items of discussion where someone's view was not accepted, and did he or she take it gracefully? Was there a prospective member who, by his or her comments and force of personality, demonstrated the possibility that they might be a disruptive influence? Did anyone show hesitancy when the vote on the subscription level was taken?

The temptation is to let things ride and see what happens but my advice to whoever has been appointed chairperson is to take the bull by the horns and make a few discreet phone calls. You are constructing a club that you want to grow strong and successful and this will only happen if your members are content with their contributions and look forward to your meetings. If you have any doubts or you think there's a possibility that any of those at the meeting might be having second thoughts you should take the initiative and ring them.

TIP Make sure the club secretary distributes the minutes by e-mail or snail mail *within 48 hours of the meeting*. This kind of efficiency will provide a continuity to your club's activities and members will be able to diary the date of the next meeting well in advance. And make sure those who apologized are on the mailing list.

YOU ARE CONSTRUCTING A CLUB THAT YOU WANT TO GROW
STRONG AND SUCCESSFUL
AND THIS WILL ONLY HAPPEN IF YOUR MEMBERS ARE
CONTENT WITH THEIR CONTRIBUTIONS AND LOOK
FORWARD TO YOUR MEETINGS.

THE CIRCLE OF COMPETENCE QUESTIONNAIRE

Whether yours is a new club or already well established this is an essential requirement if you are to realize your full potential. You have a unique pool of knowledge and experience. Collectively the members possess remarkable in-depth strength when it comes to considering which shares the club should invest its money in. But this strength, this circle of competence, can only be truly effective if it is properly identified and harnessed. The best way to do this is to survey your members and build up a complete picture of where their expertise and enthusiasms lie.

This is not a 'let's spend 10 minutes chatting about it at the end of the meeting' task. It needs mature reflection by each member so I suggest a sensible method is to send a questionnaire to everyone's home. It is a good idea for the chairperson to write the covering letter because it adds gravitas and emphasizes the importance of the exercise. The covering note should ask the members to spend some time considering their answers.

In Chapter 3 I gave you my idea for a questionnaire. You can of course customize it to suit your club. From the replies you will be able to draw up a complete picture of your club's circle of competence. The areas of expertise will be identified and the chairperson should produce a resumé for discussion in conjunction with the decisions to be made regarding the club's investment strategy.

A by-product of this questionnaire is that you will have volunteers to keep tabs on particular sectors. Explain that this is not an exacting job, just a matter of keeping in touch with the news and giving a brief one-minute update at each club meeting. This ensures that as many members as possible feel involved and participate in the success of the club.

....

People may bet on the hourly wiggles in the market,

but it's the earnings that waggle the wiggles

in the long term.

Peter Lynch

THE TABLETS OF STONE

W e come now to what is perhaps the most important part of this book. We are going to establish the principles on which your investment strategy will be based. This will be your philosophy, your approach, the wisdom which will guide all your deliberations. And you will follow it, not just because it works, but because unless you do there is a very real danger your club will become part of a sad but significant statistic. Let me quote from a book published by our good friends at the National Association of Investors Corporation in America:

'We've found that one quarter of all investment clubs go out of business within the first 24 months because of conflict between those who believe in long-term investing and those advocating speculative trading. Be sure your members agree on a long-term philosophy before you get started.'

You don't want to be a loser and, worse still, you would not want to be responsible for guiding you friends along the losers' route. So put aside those stupid notions of getting rich overnight by trading shares two and three times a day, wheeling and dealing, ducking and diving. Just remember that silly fellow in the *Sunday Times* who gave up a perfectly good job to become a day trader. Last time I looked he was about £30,000 down and still falling. I meet a lot of people in the City and I can promise, hand on heart, I do not know one

successful day trader but I am well acquainted with a score of failures.

Be a winner. It's important that you take a sensible and reasoned approach to you investing activities and I'm delighted to tell you there is a proven method for you to follow. All over the world, and especially in the UK and the USA, there are investment clubs that started by putting peanuts into the pot and are now very rich and powerful because they accepted four simple guidelines.

Here are the tablets of stone:

TABLET ONE
Invest regularly, no matter what the market is doing.

TABLET TWO
Reinvest all earnings.

TABLET THREE
Choose undervalued growth companies.

TABLET FOUR
Diversify your portfolio.

Read, learn and inwardly digest. Stick with these principles and you will build a winning club. Now let me clarify each principle.

Invest reguarly, no matter what the market is doing

Even Mystic Meg, who is daft enough to believe she can predict who is going to win the lottery, would not dream of trying to second-guess Mr Market. Why? Because he's a loony, that's why. Completely unpredictable, making decisions on a whim, sometimes totally logical and other times moving prices in a contrarian and stupid direction. You can't reason with a mercurial madman and if you try to do so you will end up frustrated, furious and poor.

Yet we all say: What's the market done today? Up? Down? We should have bought, we should have sold, we missed the boat. We are obsessed with timing but we forget one simple and incontrovertible fact: for decades the market's overall trend has been upwards. Despite wars, strikes, recessions, booms, depressions and what have you, over time the graph line goes skywards and if you have the right ingredients in your portfolio your line will outstrip the rest.

Get it into your head that when you are buying a share you are becoming part-owner of a business. You have chosen that business because you believe that it is successful and will continue to be so. Of course you watch the market movements, and in particular the price of the share, because if it goes down for no apparent reason that may well be a signal to buy even more of the same. It is called pound cost averaging and that is the essence of investing. You buy more shares for your pounds when the price is lower, fewer when it is high. This way you even out the caprices of the market. Later in the book I will explain how to decide when the price of your company is high, low or about right. Suffice to say at this point that your decision should always be driven by the continued success or otherwise of your company's business and not by the movement of such an ephemeral thing as the FTSE 100.

By all means watch the market movements. Get to know the patterns, spot the opportunities, but do not make a decision based solely on the charts. Buy companies, not markets, because companies are real and tangible and can produce things and make money for themselves and you. Markets can't do any of that because they are nothing.

REMEMBER,
A GOOD COMPANY TODAY
WILL MOST LIKELY BE
A GOOD COMPANY TOMORROW;
A SOW'S EAR TODAY IS UNLIKELY
TO BE SILK PURSE TOMORROW.

And choose your companies carefully, basing your decision on the facts. Remember, a good company today will most likely be a good company tomorrow; a sow's ear today is unlikely to be silk purse tomorrow.

Reinvest all earnings

For this purpose, the earnings we are talking about are dividends. These are the cheques that drop through your letterbox once or twice a year and you are invariably unimpressed with their size. You have thousands invested in a company yet all they send is a few measly quid, just a tiny percentage of the total you have invested. If you get anything between 4 and 6 per cent it is as much as you can expect. But add that to your capital growth – the increase in the value of the share price in a year – and suddenly you are talking a major contribution.

Let's take an easy example. You buy a share for £1 and in a year, according to the price quoted in the paper, it has gone up just 10 per cent. Add in a 5 per cent dividend and you have a total of 15 per cent profit for the year. *Keep up that modest increase every year, reinvest all the dividends you receive and every five years you will double the value of your investments.*

Believe me, an average compound increase of 15 per cent (that's the rise in share price and the dividend added together) should not be too difficult. Here's an example of what it means and, because I am not a mathematician and tend to get distracted by fractions, I'll stick to round figures.

Let's be ultra-conservative and say you have a club of 15 members and each of them pays in just £20 per month. From scratch, in five years your club will have a portfolio worth well in excess of £22,000.

Now suppose all the members are in their 20s and pay into the club until they retire. In 40 years at an average rate of return as low as 10 per cent their club portfolio would be worth nigh on £2 million. That's a nice nest egg isn't it? I know it's easy for me to quote future statistics like these but when I paint the pictures I err on the side of caution because I don't want to exaggerate what is achievable. In reality your club increases will probably be much better than those I have quoted because it is a proven fact that as your club gets older and more experienced it will become much better at this investment game. Doubling the figures I have just quoted is perfectly possible as long as you follow this approach to the letter.

So reinvest those little dividends, it makes an amazing difference over time.

Choose undervalued growth companies

Companies are like babies and the investors are their parents. Companies are living, moving, people things that need feeding and taking care of so that they can grow. When they are small they need particular attention because these are the vulnerable years and they do not

THE TABLETS OF STONE **61**

have the experience to avoid pitfalls and make sensible decisions. Sometimes they are naughty and have to be taught right from wrong, that's the job of nannies (the directors). When they go out into the big wide world they must have their hands held tightly by nanny because that's where the nasty men are, people who don't like children, feel threatened by them and think nothing of trampling the young ones underfoot.

If the companies survive these formative years – and, sadly, many don't – they can grow into fine young adults, the apples of their parents' eyes, and hopefully bright enough to arrange mergers of their own, have babies, and at the same time keep their proud parents in luxurious old age.

We will consider the whole question of growth and where to find it when we examine the Investors' Toolkit in Chapter 6. In the context of investing it means regular and steady increases in a company's turnover, profits and share price. To be of any use at all these rises will have occurred over a number of recent years, establishing a pattern that, barring accidents, will continue for the foreseeable future. How many years? In my view four is a minimum, five is better and six is ideal.

The growth may be started in any number of ways. Maybe it's a new product, a new idea, a new service, a new market or even a new industry. But the growth will be nurtured and strengthened by an experienced, dedicated, vigorous, forward-thinking management. There is the key. That is the common denominator of all

growth companies. That is what you are looking for. This information comes from the heart because I spend much of my life looking at companies and trying to assess their potential and I know that the quality of the management is the ingredient without which there will be no significant growth. I like to see a well-established and settled management but unfortunately nothing is for ever and it is the nature of things that people leave, retire or die. So what you must hope for is that the bright boys and girls who are responsible for the past growth have established a culture within the company that is sustainable despite their departure.

Diversify to reduce risk

When we look at the balance of a portfolio, these things matter:

- How many?
- How big?
- Where from?

The question most often asked at investment club seminars is, 'How many shares should we have in our portfolio?' In my opinion this is not half as important as deciding on the quality of the stocks. Nevertheless, it should be agreed at the outset of your club's life. You should restrict the number of shares to a list that you can manage comfortably and this should be dictated by the number of active members you have in the club (and, please note, I emphasize the word 'active'). A conservative and rough rule of thumb is: 12 willing members in the club, a maximum of 12 shares in the portfolio; eight members, at the most eight shares; 20 members, no more than 20 shares and so on. Because choosing shares is only half the job – you can't make profits until you sell – each member should have responsibility for monitoring a share. These are general guidelines and can be adapted according to the nature of your membership. It is perfectly acceptable for members to watch two shares or even more, provided the club is confident that it will be done efficiently. For instance, you may have an experienced investor who is at home most of the day and actively involved in managing his or her own portfolio. It would be quite reasonable for that individual to watch up to three shares. Equally, there may be a member who genuinely does not have access to share prices and therefore can't keep tabs on a particular stock on a regular basis. Suffice to say that the club should hold the number of shares that it can comfortably monitor on a minimum twice-daily basis.

Let me emphasize that when you have reached the maximum number, you don't sit back and relax. Keep searching for new, exciting and undervalued opportunities. Until you are certain of a new potential investment buy more of the same – put more money into your existing holdings – but at the same time create a waiting list of shares that you like. And when you have a gem that you just can't wait to buy, and you know everything about it and are totally convinced of its pedigree, then examine your existing shares and pick the one that you would be least upset to lose. Then make the change.

Of equal importance is the size of the companies in the portfolio. You want a balance of big, small and medium-sized companies. Let me explain why. Large companies (and I class these as ones with a market capitalization of more than £2 billion) are likely to have a more predictable rate of growth and, when the bad times come and markets turn down, they are in a better position to absorb the pain and cope with the downturn. They are also easy to deal in – no problems about a shortage of stock or anything like that – and comparatively

YOU SHOULD RESTRICT THE NUMBER OF SHARES TO A LIST THAT YOU CAN MANAGE COMFORTABLY AND THIS SHOULD BE DICTATED BY THE NUMBER OF ACTIVE MEMBERS YOU HAVE IN THE CLUB.

NEW CLUBS SHOULD BUY

THE BIG COMPANIES FIRST BECAUSE

THAT WILL GIVE A **RELATIVELY SAFE BASE**

FOR YOUR ACTIVITIES AND

YOU WILL BE **BETTER ABLE** TO

WITHSTAND A FEW KNOCKS.

inexpensive, the spread is less because the market maker is prepared to take lower profits from a safe and busy share.

Medium-sized companies – those with a market capitalization between £300 million and £2 billion – are in the area where the undiscovered gems are. This is the section you should trawl to find the real winners, outfits with a proven product that have the experience and ability to attack their markets, push the boundaries and challenge the big boys at their own game.

And no portfolio is complete without its share of tiddlers (comparatively small fellows with a market cap of less than £300 million). These are the blue sky boys who promise much and in buoyant markets they may double, treble, quadruple in price. But beware, when bubbles burst theirs is the first to go pop and there is a danger you will be left with nothing more than crushed hopes and shattered dreams. Don't be tempted to bet more than you can afford to lose on these babies.

Here's my idea of the perfect portfolio balance in terms of pounds invested:

Large companies	**25%**
Small companies	**25%**
Medium-sized companies	**50%**

New clubs should buy the big companies first because that will give a relatively safe base for your activities and you will be better able to withstand a few knocks. And here's a tip: try to choose your smaller stocks from companies whose headquarters are in your locality. That way you will be able to monitor them more easily because news about them – new appointments, fresh orders, expansion plans and so on – will most likely be featured in your local paper and in addition you may be able to make some contacts on the inside.

A note here about analysts. Brokers' analysts tend to ignore smaller companies as not worth their while, so it is difficult for the individual or club to source an unbiased assessment. You may be able to obtain what is called an Analyst's Report on a small company but please check its provenance because it will probably have been produced by a company which charges the company for writing it. I find it difficult to believe that in these circumstances the analyzing company will be keen to criticize the hand that feeds it.

Finally on this diversification theme you must obviously exploit your circle of competence. At the outset you will have identified the club's strengths in terms of areas of expertise, knowledge and talent. Pick shares from sectors which reflect these abilities and allocate the shares to be monitored by those most qualified and interested in them.

Whether yours is a new club or one that is already formed it is vital that you adopt the foregoing four principles. So vital that I would like you to read from the start of this chapter again so that you completely understand what the tablets of stone are and why they are there. Then, at the very next meeting of your club, read them out loud. It is very, very important that each member of your club accepts the principles and the reasons for them being in place. Disharmony is the hidden disease that is waiting to strike any club, so you must all be singing with gusto from the same hymn sheet.

Stop crying, dear, you mustn't be frightened. School's a nice place. You'll meet lots of other little ones and there's plenty of playtime as well as lessons. And the headmaster, Mr Bond, is a lovely man, such a good teacher and ever so patient. You see, he was little once and he remembers how scared he was on his first day at school because he was worried he wouldn't be as clever as the others in the class. Then he found all the other youngsters felt the same so he promised himself when he grew up and became a teacher he wouldn't use big words and try to show off.

Proud Parent

PART

2

SCHOOL

....

Select stocks the way porcupines make love.

Very carefully.

Bob Dinda

THE INVESTORS' TOOLKIT

Now we are going to learn how to become competent and successful investors. It's not particularly difficult – all you have to do is to pick shares that go up in value. That is not a trite phrase just to give you a smile, it's a statement of fact.

When I decided to join the investment game in the late 80s I honestly knew nothing about it and I had absolutely no contacts in the business. Since leaving school I had worked hard for a living, first as a journalist, then as a public relations adviser, and finally running a series of businesses of my own. The companies I created covered everything from advertising and marketing to yachting holidays and world-wide property sales. Most of them were sold to bigger fish at a profit so I knew how to start and sell small businesses but when it came to publicly quoted companies and the stockmarket I was green as a stick insect. Nevertheless, I decided to rush in where angels would be frightened to walk and, as I admitted at the beginning of this book, I made mistakes. This happened not because I was thick but because I was an ignoramus. And I was daunted by the sheer complexity of it all. I knew there must be shortcuts to success – in every field of endeavour this is the case – but I soon realized that I wouldn't be able to identify these paths to glory until I had at least a grounding in the basics. The problem was that in most of the books and journals I studied the basics were hidden in a jungle of jargon.

I hacked through the jungle and now I am going to pass on to you what I learned. And as you read remember the aim of the exercise: we want to understand the company in which we are planning to invest our savings so that we can assess for ourselves whether it has a bright future and the shares are available now at the right price.

We are going to look at the sort of information we need and the sources for discovering the information, then we are going to decide how best to interpret it. But first of all we are going to get organized.

Go back to square one. Why are you in an investment club? Quite obviously you are there for enjoyment, the company of friends and the opportunity to make a few bob along the way. But there are two other objectives that must not be forgotten: (a) you want to learn how to become a successful investor in your own right; and (b) you intend to create a portfolio of your own that will keep you and yours in the manner to which you *could* become accustomed. This latter aim will only become a reality if you play a full part in the club's activities, understand exactly what is going on and gain the experience that involvement will give you.

You must not let the chosen and willing few in the club do all the research work. For true success everyone should play a part in finding out all the facts about potential investments.

Carrying out research on a share can be a lonely old business. Basically it is detective work and some people prefer to do it by themselves because they can concentrate better, others are motivated if they can do it in pairs or threes. Your club will have its own set of circumstances and they will dictate what is best for you: if members live relatively close to each other groups for research are a good idea, if the membership is scattered individual enquiries might be the only option, although e-mail and the telephone break down distance barriers. Put the matter on the agenda for discussion at your next club meeting. Talk it through and get a feel for what members want. Don't be deflected by the suggestion that it might be wise to appoint an investment sub-committee of members who would be prepared to do all the fact finding and then come to the monthly meeting having decided which shares to invest in. That's passing the buck to a few willing horses and in the long run it can lead to the ruination of the club. The horses will become less willing when they realize: (a) they are doing all the hard work; and (b) they have to carry the can when prices drop. Those who aren't involved in the share selection will feel surplus to requirements and stop attending the meetings.

In the long run investment sub-committees are a recipe for apathy among the majority of the membership.

So get the agreement of everyone to be involved in research. Then the most important thing to decide is exactly what information you are looking for and how to find it. That should be the subject of an entire meeting early on in the club's history. You will have followed my advice and agreed on the tablets of stone and the balance for your portfolio. What we are going to concentrate on first is the tablet which refers to your stock picking: *invest in growth companies*. When you and your club understand how to do this then you will be well on your way down the yellow brick road.

Let's refresh our memories and define a growth company again. It's a business whose sales and earnings are moving ahead faster than inflation and have been

CARRYING OUT RESEARCH ON A SHARE CAN BE A LONELY OLD BUSINESS.

BASICALLY IT IS DETECTIVE WORK AND

SOME PEOPLE PREFER TO DO IT

BY THEMSELVES BECAUSE THEY CAN

CONCENTRATE BETTER, OTHERS ARE

MOTIVATED IF THEY CAN DO IT IN PAIRS OR THREES.

doing so for some time, and whose records suggest the company will be far more valuable five years in the future. (Incidentally, this is my definition rather than an official one. I like it because it is easy to understand.)

When we have identified a stock like this we need to check whether the present management is running the business at its maximum potential and whether today's share price represents good value for money as far as new shareholders are concerned.

Enter the Investors' Toolkit.

Immodestly, I claim the Toolkit as my baby although I hasten to pay tribute to my friends Graham Quick of Hemscott and Jeremy King late of ProShare who acted as midwives at the very difficult birth.

The Toolkit was conceived on a trip I made to Detroit in 1998. I was there for ProShare with my colleague Tony Hobman and we were studying the methods of the NAIC, the National Association of Investors Corporation, which has played the major role in developing the investment club movement in the United States. With around 60,000 clubs to its credit the NAIC was way ahead of ProShare in terms of maturity so it was appropriate that we learned from their experience.

The chief executive, Kenneth S. Janke Snr, and his staff could not have been more helpful. Ken is a leading figure on the world investment stage and it is his mission to spread the word about the value of clubs. His main message to us was, 'Too many clubs close because they don't approach stock selection properly.

Help them to learn how to identify the right shares, but keep it simple.' The Americans do it with a sophisticated collection of investor aids to educate their members and, by far the most popular, used by the vast majority of successful clubs in the US, is their Stock Selection Guide. This was the document I decided to adapt for the British investor and the result is the Investors' Toolkit.

In essence it is a do-it-yourself system for investigating a share you fancy to decide whether it falls in the undervalued growth share category. Graham Quick and I developed the system, based on his knowledge of investment techniques and figures (he's a chartered accountant), and my vision of the criteria that had to be satisfied before we could identify an undervalued growth stock. When we had completed the first draft of the Toolkit I sent a sample to a random dozen clubs and asked for their comments. My request to them was: if a single member of your club is not able to check a share out satisfactorily within an hour of opening the Toolkit, let me know. They did. Their comments were constructive and to the point. 'It wasn't just a single member who couldn't do it, none of us understood it,' 'Full of jargon,' 'Thank you, but no thank you. We'll stick to a pin and the *Financial Times*,' 'We gave up.' Chastened, Graham and I went back to the drawing board again. And again. And again. After many months of beta testing we got to the product that is used today by thousands of clubs as the starting point when they want to check out a share for that part of their portfolio which houses undervalued growth stocks. I must point out here that the system is not suitable for researching such sectors as banks or insurance because their systems of doing business are not appropriate for Toolkit analysis, but for companies which produce or sell products I believe the Toolkit is an invaluable starting point for your researches.

So, what's in the Toolkit and how does it work? First, the contents. Open up the intriguing ProShare purple box and you will find:

- A CD-ROM of *REFS (Really Essential Financial Statistics)*. This is supplied by HS Financial, now part of the Charterhouse Group of Companies, and contains up-to-date financial facts on every company quoted on the London Stock Exchange. As far as I am concerned (and the *REFS* people don't pay me a penny for saying this) it is the single most important piece of kit the serious private investor can acquire. For us its invention can be considered in the same breath as the wheel and sliced bread. I explain how to make the best use of *REFS* in Chapter 7.

- Fifty identical copies of the four-page Share Appraisal Form (SAF). You complete a form for each of the companies you want to investigate. The information is available from various sources and much of it is contained on the *REFS* CD-ROM.

- A manual containing a step-by-step explanation of how to complete the form and how to interpret the results. You might have guessed I'm a stickler

for plain English and I have long ago ceased to become embarrassed when I have to admit that I don't understand a word, a phrase or an acronym. The City is full of smart alecs who burble on about nil-paids, leverage, bulldogs and bullets. Ask them for a clear definition and they go all coy.

These are the three main ingredients in the Toolkit. Various other bits and pieces are also included but it would be invidious to list them because they are subject to change and in any case they are not essential to the working of the system.

I believe the best way to demonstrate how the Toolkit works is to take an actual example of a company and fill in the SAF. While this is much better than making up a company name and twisting the facts to get the results that would suit me best, it is dangerous for me because there is a time lag between me writing this (mid-2001) and you reading it. Sod's Law says the price of the company will fall out of bed because I have chosen it but, what the hell, let's live dangerously.

The company I have chosen to put under the Toolkit microscope is Tesco. There's no particular reason for this, except that I'm sure as I can be that, even if you pick up this book in 10 years from now, good old Tesco will still be around. Mind you, in this world nothing is certain.

Before we begin, let's go back to basics again, just to remind ourselves where we are trying to get to. We want to look at Tesco dispassionately and in depth to decide:

TESCO

PRICE (p)

5p Ords vs FTSE All-Share vs norm eps

	97	98	99	00	01	02	03
HIGH	177	202	197	286	276		
LOW	111	157	157	156	236		
AVE PER	17.4x	20.2x	19.1x	21.5x	22.9x		

RELATIVE	%
1M	-4.5
3M	-10.3
6M	-6.9
1Y	+20.4
Beta rel	-0.09

SEDOL: 884709
EPIC: TSCO **BLMBG:** TSCO

ACTIVITIES ANALYSIS (01AR)			
		T/O	Pr
Food retailing	%	100	100
Property development	%	0	
UK	%	88	94
Rest of Europe	%	8	6
Asia	%	4	0

PRICE (HMS 200)
25-MAY-01 **241p**

market cap	£16,707m
position	17th
index	FTSE 100
norm eps (pr)	13.0p
turnover (01AR)	£20,988m
pretax (01AR)	£1,054m

			m	s
DY (pr)	%	2.35	⊙	⊙
PER (pr)	x	18.5	⊙	⊙
PEG (pr)	f	1.59	○	○
GR (pr)	%	11.6	○	○
ROCE	%	14.4	⊙	○
MARGIN	%	5.59	⊙	●
GEAR	%	57.1	○	○
PBV	x	3.12	⊙	○
PTBV	x	3.21	⊙	○
PCF	x	10.9	⊙	○
PSR	x	0.78	⊙	○
PRR	x	na	⊕	⊕

nav ps (01AR)	77.3p
net cash ps (01AR)	na

SECTOR: Food & drug retailers. **ACTIVITIES:** Operation of retail superstores and associated activities.

DIRS: J A Gardiner (ch)*, T P Leahy (ce), D E Reid (dch), A T Higginson (fd), T J R Mason (mktg), R S Ager (cs), J Gildersleeve, P A Clarke, D T Potts, G F Pimlott*, J W Melbourn CBE*, C L Allen*, Dr H Einsmann*, Veronique Morali*. **HEAD & REG OFF:** Tesco House, Delamare Road, Cheshunt, Hertfordshire, EN8 9SL. Tel: (01992) 632222. Tlx: 24138. Fax: (01992) 630794. **REGISTRAR:** Lloyds TSB Registrars, Worthing. Tel: (0870) 600 0158

SHARE CAPITAL, HOLDINGS, DEALINGS			
(1) 6932m 5p Ords (Dirs 0.11% [d]); (2) ADR.			
T P Leahy (ce)	m	1.62	2+
A T Higginson (fd)	k	194	2+
J A Gardiner* (ch)	k	607	1+
D E Reid (dch)	m	1.74	2+
T J R Mason (mktg)	k	677	2+
R S Ager (cs)	m	1.20	2+
J Gildersleeve	m	1.10	2+
P A Clarke	k	112	2+
D T Potts	k	145	2+
G F Pimlott*	k	27.3	

BROKERS: Deutsche Bank AG London; Morgan Stanley & Co International Ltd. **AUDITORS:** PricewaterhouseCoopers.

OUTLOOK: (9-Apr-01) AR: ce - "We are establishing an international business with real capability and growth prospects that will make a substantial difference to the Tesco group over the next 10 years".

NEWSFLOW: (19-Jul-00) Ann: The company and iVillage Inc, operator of the leading women's network online, announce the creation of an international joint venture, iVillage UK. The venture is to serve the womens online market in the UK and the Rupiblic of Ireland. (13-Dec-00) Ann: The company has adopted Kewill Systems PLC's Internet-based supply chain trading solution, Kewill.Trade, to manage its supply chain. (13-Dec-00) Ann: The company has entered a contract with ID Data PLC for 18 months worth £1.80m. ID Data will cover the provision and personalisation of all loyalty club card requirements. (15-Dec-00) Ann: Tesco is to form a joint venture company to develop hypermarkets in Malaysia. Tesco Stores (Malaysia) Sdn Bhd will be 70.0% owned by Tesco and 30.0% owned by Sime Darby Berhad. It is expected that £215m will be invested to open around 15 hypermarkets.

year ended 22 Feb		1997	1998	1999	2000	2001	2002E	2003E
turnover	£m	13887	16452	17158	18796	20988		
depreciation	£m	317	358	401	428	468		
int paid (net)	£m	24.0	65.0	82.0	91.0	107		
FRS3 pretax	£m	750	760	842	933	1054		
norm pretax	£m	750	832	881	955	1070	1193	1336
turnover ps	£	2.14	2.51	2.59	2.81	3.09		
op margin	%	5.57	5.54	5.62	5.55	5.59		
ROCE	%	16.8	17.3	15.6	15.5	14.4		
ROE	%	13.3	15.2	14.5	14.5	14.6		
FRS3 eps	p	7.83	7.93	8.93	9.89	11.1		
norm eps	p	7.83	8.86	9.37	10.2	11.3	12.6	14.1
norm eps growth	%	+7.41	+13.2	+5.76	+8.96	+10.7	+11.5	+12.0
tax rate	%	31	30	28	28	27	27	27
norm per	x					21.3	19.1	17.1
peg	f					2.00	1.66	1.42
cash flow ps	p	14.6	12.6	14.4	17.5	22.1		
capex ps	p	3.47	3.95	5.79	5.44	6.30		
dividend ps	p	3.45	3.87	4.12	4.48	4.98	5.48	6.12
dps growth	%	+7.81	+12.2	+6.46	+8.74	+11.2	+10.0	+11.7
dividend yield	%					2.07	2.27	2.54
dividend cover	x	2.27	2.29	2.27	2.28	2.27	2.30	2.31
shrholders funds	£m	3890	3903	4382	4769	5356		
net borrowings	£m	829	1387	1921	2318	3059		
net curr assets	£m	-1328	-1771	-1929	-2145	-2695		
ntav ps	p	59.6	59.1	63.1	67.9	75.0		

	2002 ESTIMATES				2003 ESTIMATES			
Brokers (5 not shown)	Date	Rec	Pretax £m	Eps p	Dps p	Pretax £m	Eps p	Dps p
Peel Hunt PLC	23-Feb-01	HOLD	1180 +	12.4 +	5.40			
Merrill Lynch	27-Mar-01	ACCU +	1205	13.1	5.70			
SG Securities	30-Mar-01	BUY	1202	13.1	5.60	1435 +	15.6 +	6.40
Tilney I/M	30-Mar-01	OUTP	1034	11.2	4.97	1140	12.0	5.34
HSBC Securities	11-Apr-01	RED	1195 +	12.5 +	5.30	1355 +	14.1 +	6.00
Lloyds TSB Private Banking	11-Apr-01	BUY +	1190 +	12.6 +	5.50 +	1300	13.8	6.10
UBS Warburg	11-Apr-01	BUY		12.8 +	5.55		14.6 –	6.40
Credit Lyonnais Securities	12-Apr-01	ADD –	1200 +	12.6 –	5.60 +	1345 +	13.9 –	6.20 +
Seymour Pierce Ltd	17-Apr-01	CORE	1200	12.4 –	5.58 –	1500	16.0	7.44
Gilbert Eliott	26-Apr-01	HOLD –	1190 +	12.7 +	5.50 –	1330	14.2	6.10
Williams de Broe	1-May-01	BUY	1200	12.6	5.50	1350 –	14.1	6.00
BNP Paribas	4-May-01	NEUT	1194	12.5	5.50 +	1352	13.9	6.07 +
ABN AMRO	7-May-01	SELL –	1201 +	12.6 –	5.67 –	1381	14.5	6.49
Lehman Brothers	14-May-01	BUY	1039	11.6	5.28	1152	12.9	5.87
Teather & Greenwood	15-May-01	HOLD	1200	12.6	5.55 +	1360	14.3	6.05 +
ING Barings Charterhouse	21-May-01	BUY	1190	13.0 +		1314 –	14.0 –	
Consensus			**1193**	**12.6**	**5.48**	**1336**	**14.1**	**6.12**
1M change			+1.09	+0.01	-0.00	-5.48	+0.03	+0.04
3M change			+13.5	-0.04	+0.04	+29.9	+0.06	+0.12

GEARING, COVER (01AR)			
		Incl	Excl
intangibles		nil	
net gearing	%	57.1	58.8
cash	%	5.21	5.36
gross gearing	%	62.3	64.2
under 5 yrs	%	35.9	36.9
under 1 yr	%	26.4	27.2
quick ratio	r		0.20
current ratio	r		0.39
interest cover	x		5.86

KEY DATES	
next AR year end	22-Feb-02
int xd (1.34p)	27-Sep-99
fin xd (3.14p)	17-Apr-00
int results	19-Sep-00
int xd (1.48p)	25-Sep-00
year end	24-Feb-01
annual report	9-Apr-01
prelim results	10-Apr-01
fin xd (3.50p)	18-Apr-01
agm	15-Jun-01

Fig 6.1 The *REFS* page containing Tesco's financial facts

- Is it a market leader?
- Has it proved itself to be a financial success?
- Is it being run efficiently?
- Will it continue to be successful?
- Is today's share price attractive to us?
- Do we believe the price will rise?

Let's suppose that one of your members – call her Helen, because it is a lovely name and it will earn me brownie points at home – has recently visited the new Tesco store in your area. She did her weekly shopping there and returned home so impressed that she wants the club to consider an investment and has tabled Tesco for a discussion at your next meeting.

Helen knows it's a club rule that every proposition must be accompanied by as much information as possible so she contacted the company's registrars (Lloyds TSB in Worthing) and obtained the latest annual report. Now she has decided to have a go at filling in the Investors' Toolkit SAF herself. It is her first attempt at completing the form so we are going to follow her progress. I should add that Helen's club has a quarterly subscription to *REFS*, which will provide her with many of the facts she will need. For those of you who are not conversant with it I explain the secrets of *REFS* in Chapter 7 (no, don't look now, you'll lose the thread of Helen's Tesco investigation). And don't worry too much if you don't have a *REFS* book easily available, the information needed to complete the SAF can be found in several other sources

including the Tesco annual report and the company's website.

The form has four pages (see Figure 6.2) but this shouldn't take long.

Share Appraisal Form

Section one

Easy. Name of the company, the date Helen is filling in the form, a club reference number and Helen's name. This will enable the form to be filed in the club archives and referred to in the future.

There's a space for the **market capitalization** of the company, which is calculated by multiplying that day's share price by the number of shares issued by the company. The mid-price on this particular day is 241p, there are 6,932 million 5p ordinary Tesco shares owned by shareholders or available in the market place, which means the market cap is £16,707 million. Make no mistake, we are looking at a big boy here. This company is one of Britain's Top 20.

Gearing. What does that mean? Helen's not too sure so she consults the manual, which is part of the Toolkit. All is revealed. Gearing means borrowings and is calculated by taking the total amount borrowed by the company then subtracting such items as cash at the bank and other easily realizable assets. The borrowings are then expressed as a percentage of shareholders' funds. Helen views this sort of talk with dismay. Identify the borrowings? How different is an easily realizable asset from one that's difficult to realize? It's all beyond her and

---

SECTION 1

Company: *Tesco*

Date: *30-6-2001* | Reference number and your name: *Helen 001*

Market Capilization £ *16,707 m* | Gearing *57* %

Latest Financial Year to *24/02/01*

What does the company do and why do I like it? *In a world where brand leadership counts,*

Tesco holds the title. Quality, price, range, service — they compete with honour on all fronts. And in a world where so much is uncertain one thing will never change — we have to eat. Demand will always be insatiable. News at the annual meetings in June all seemed very positive and the chief executive said sales for the group in the first quarter of the year had increased by 14 per cent.

It is a difficult time for investors at the moment, and I believe that at such times we should put our faith in strong, forward looking companies that are well managed.

That is a perfect description of Tesco.

If we decide to buy Tesco we must view it as a long-term hold because in this sector elephants don't gallop. As you will note from the graph they plod steadily uphill. As a good base for our portfolio that's exactly what we want.

Wealth warning:
Please be aware that the value of investments and the income from them can go
down as well as up and you may not get back the amount of your original investment

---

Fig 6.2 ProShare Investors' Toolkit – Share Appraisal Form

SECTION 2 – HAVE THE COMPANY'S BUSINESS AND PROFITS GROWN?

		Sales		Profits for Company		Profits for shareholders	
1. Most recent year to	2001	£m 20988	£m	1070		11.3	p
2. Next most recent year to	2000	£m 18796	£m	855		10.2	p
3. Three years ago to	1999	£m 17158	£m	881		9.37	p
4. Four years ago to	1998	£m 16452	£m	832		8.86	p
5. Five years ago to	1997	£m 13887	£m	750		7.83	p
6. Increase (1–5)		£m 7101	£m	320		3.47	p
7. Percentage increase (6/5)*100		51	%	43	%	0.44	%
8. Average Annual % Increase		10	%	85	%	0.09	%

SECTION3 – ARE THE PEOPLE IN CHARGE DOING A GOOD JOB?

Year	1997	1998	1999	2000	2001	Average of 5 years
Company profits (1)	750	832	881	855	1070	898
Sales (2)	13887	16452	17158	18796	20988	17456
Operating margin % (1/2)×100	5.4	5.05	5.13	5.08	5.1	5.14

Year	1997	1998	1999	2000	2001	Average of 5 years
Company profits (3)						
Capital employed (4)						
Return on capital (ROCE) % (1/2)×100	16.8	17.3	15.6	15.5	14.4	

* There is an adjustment in REFS for interest, so this figure may not be exact.

** On the REFS report the ROCE value is given, but not the component figures to calculate it – these can be found in the companies Report and Accounts if necessary.

Fig 6.2 *Continued*

SECTION 4 – IS THE SHARE GOOD VALUE FOR MONEY TODAY?

		High Each Year A	Low Each Year B	Earnings Per share C	PER at High D = A/|C	PER at Low E = B/C	Average PER F = (D + E)/2
Most recent year to	2001	276	236	11.3	24.4	20.9	22.65
Next most recent year to	2000	286	15.6	10.2	28	18.3	21.65
Three years ago to	1999	197	15.7	9.37	20.5	16.25	18.62
Four years ago to	1998	202	15.7	8.86	22.8	17.2	20
Five years ago to	1997	177	111	7.83	22.6	14.2	18.4
Total		1138	817		118.3	84.35	
Average		227.6	163		23.7	16.9	20.3

Today's share price is   241   p

How does it compare with the share price five years ago?   HIGHER/lower

It has increased over the five year period by?   67 %

In how many years has the share price been as high as the current price?   2 years

Today's PER is   18.5   (Latest Share Price/Latest Ernings Per Share)

In relation to past PERs this is   HIGHER/lower

SECTION 5 – EARNINGS PER SHARE GRAPH

Fig 6.2 *Continued*

SECTION 6 – REASONS FOR PAST GROWTH

Reason	Details	Still expected to be effective over next five years – YES/NO
Introduction of new products and services	Yes. Constantly introducing new lines	Yes
Development of existing products	Yes. 'Own brand' has emphasis on quality	Yes
Achieving a larger market share	Now the largest and seems to be unassailable	Yes
Technological changes in production		—
Management skills	Appear to be consistently good	
Enhanced marketing and promotion	The best	Yes
Fasion trends	Don't seem to be pioneers	Not Known
Acquisition of new companies	Seem to prefer joint ventures overseas	—
Recovery of cynical business	N/A	N/A
Other reasons		

SECTION 7 – IT'S MAKE-YOUR-MIND-UP TIME...

Put an affirmative tick or a negative cross after each of the following statements:

- I understand this company and what it does.   ✔
- I am completely confident that the company has a sound five-year financial record.   ✔
- I believe the management of this company has developed the product and profits in a cost-effective and profitable manner.   ✔
- The information I have discovered leads me to believe that this company will continue to produce increasing dividends for its shareholders.   ✔
- My knowledge and common sense tells me that the share price today indicates that the company is undervalued in the marketplace.   ✘
- I like this company so much I would like to own the whole business.   ✔

If you have 4 ticks then this company is worthy of serious further consideration.
If you have a single cross then forget this company. There are plenty of others out there.
Be completely honest with yourself.
In share dealing it is always better to be safe than sorry.

Fig 6.2 *Continued*

she is about to pack up and forget the whole thing when she reads in the Toolkit manual: 'Don't worry. We direct you to sources where the calculation is done for you. You just note down the figure.' Phew! Thank goodness for that.

But why do we want to know about the borrowings anyway? What do they tell us? Well, a high gearing percentage is significant because it indicates how vulnerable a company is. If a hurricane hits world markets and banks call in overdrafts, the highly geared companies are the first to suffer. A high gearing also indicates that a company could be particularly sensitive to changes in interest rates. A very rough rule of thumb is that gearing of more than 50 per cent is a possible cause for worry. Helen has also been told it is worth comparing a company's borrowings with others in the sector to make sure it isn't out of line. In *REFS* she looks up Safeway (60 per cent gearing), Sainsburys (27 per cent), Morrison Supermarkets (–3.67 per cent, which means they have money in the bank) and Somerfield (13.2 per cent).

Tesco's borrowings are comparatively high. It's worth making a note.

There's a space on the form to fill in the date of the latest financial-year-end figures. That's because you are relying on information that is factual and it is provided in detail just once a year. In this case Tesco's year-end was 24 February. Bear in mind any time lag when you are comparing figures.

What does the company do and why do I like it? Helen's a sensible lass, she knows the answer is not just 'It's a supermarket which sells a lot of things I want.' She reads the Toolkit's instruction manual:

There is a saying among successful professional investors – 'Know what you own and own what you know.' It means simply that you should be quite clear in your own mind about what the company you are examining does to make its profits.

Consider the products or services the company provides then ask yourself: 'Do I *understand* them? And if I don't, do I

A HIGH GEARING INDICATES THAT A COMPANY COULD BE PARTICULARLY SENSITIVE TO CHANGES IN INTEREST RATES. A VERY ROUGH RULE OF THUMB IS THAT GEARING OF MORE THAN 50 PER CENT IS A POSSIBLE CAUSE FOR WORRY.

know someone who does? Or, failing that, will it be quite easy for me to find out and understand?'

If the answer is 'No', forget this particular company and start to research another one because unless you or one of your friends or a member of your investment club understands the business and what it does you cannot expect to make an objective assessment of its potential.

If the answer is 'Yes', do you believe that the product or service has got a bright future? Is it as good or better than its competitors and do you think people will continue to want to buy it?

This is research at its most basic but it is vital if you are to get a complete picture. Talk to people who know about the kind of business you are looking at. Get their thoughts about the company. Is it going places? Has it got a good reputation? Do its customers think they are getting quality and value for money? At the same time you should comb the financial pages of the newspapers and other publications for news, check on the Internet, visit the reference library and send for the annual report.

Happy that you understand the company and what it does? Good. Now, in a few short but honest sentences, note down what attracted you to the share in the first place. Whatever the reasons – a tip from a knowledgeable friend, something you read in the paper, a discussion with people whose opinions you respect – write them down.

At the end of your research you will be able to check whether the facts confirm your instincts.

Helen has a PC and can access the Internet. She calls up the company's website and studies each section. It is comprehensive and easy to read. A main reason for the borrowings must be the supermarket's expansion plans – new stores cost money. Next she checks on news sites such as hemscott and ft.com. She searches the archives for stories and gets a clearer picture of the Tesco present-day operations.

Now for a really sensible move. Helen returns to her local Tesco on Saturday morning, not to buy this time but to observe. Her eyes are those of a potential part-owner of the store. How quickly are shelves replenished? Does the fresh food section look perky and bright? Are the staff smiling? How many checkouts are there and are the queues unacceptably long? She carries out a personal test, approaches an assistant who is obviously busy counting tins of beans. 'Could you take me to the Tabasco?' asks Helen. 'Certainly, madam,' says the assistant without the sign of a sigh. 'Follow me.' Helen has to buy the Tabasco but it was worth it, Tesco's staff training impresses her. No matter how irksome the request, the customer is king.

Back home Helen makes a précis of her notes and fills in the front page of the SAF.

Section two

Helen's got the *REFS* Tesco page so this part of the form is child's play. Sales means the total of everything Tesco sold in all its stores during the relevant year. Profits are what was left after all the suppliers, staff, overheads and so on had been paid. Profits for the shareholders are the dividend, the amount paid from the profits to the shareholders and it is expressed as an amount per single share. Helen follows the manual instructions, copies the figures down and does the simple sums.

In answer to the question **Have the business and profits grown?** She can see that they have and the good news is that the annual increases have been steady. That's comforting, because sudden spurts bring problems of their own. It also eliminates the 'busy fool' possibility because the profit margin, while not stupendous, is reasonable and shows that all the Tesco effort has been worthwhile.

Section three

Helen's looking at management now. The supermarket business is a game of fierce competition and narrow profit margins. The management must consistently run a very tight ship. Helen follows the instructions in the manual, notes down the profits and the sales figures for the last five years and does a simple sum. It reveals the operating margin is low – in this business that is expected – but reasonably consistent.

For the bottom half of this section Helen cheats. The company profits have to be compared with the capital employed in the company so that we can assess whether the profit is a reasonable rate of return for the funds we shareholders and others have provided. The profit figure is easy to identify. The capital employed figure is not. To give you a full and relatively jargon free definition: *Capital employed is the sum of the ordinary and preference share capital plus reserves, debentures, loan stocks, all borrowings including obligations under finance leases, bank overdraft, minority interests and provisions. Deductions include investments in associated companies.*

Fortunately for Helen and the rest of the investing world, people like expert analysts do this horrific calculation for us so there is a life-saving line in *REFS* which gives the return on capital employed (ROCE). Helen notes down the ROCE history and it seems OK and reasonably consistent, but there was a drift in the 2001 figures of over one percentage point. That needs watching.

Section four

In your search for good growth companies it is relatively easy to find one that has a

record of steadily increasing sales and earnings for at least five years. If it is in a sector of business that you consider is expanding, and your company is a market leader, you begin to get really excited. But if its value has already been recognized by the stock market as a whole – and more often than not that is the case – you should not consider buying the shares. To put it crudely, you have missed the boat. What you must do is put it on your club's watch list and keep an eye on the price in the hope that it will drop to a level where it represents a bargain.

This section of the SAF aims to indicate whether today's share price represents the true value of the stock. It is not infallible, indeed some will say it is too simplistic, but I like it and in my experience it works.

As she fills in the form Helen is looking at the share price movements over recent years and comparing them with the earnings of the company.

The share price and earnings-per-share (EPS) figures are copied from earlier in the form. Now we're looking for the price-to-earnings ratio (PER). This is a vitally important statistic and in Chapter 7 I go into the detail of how it is calculated and its real significance. At this stage though it is worth including the definition from the Toolkit manual:

The 'P' part of the PER is simply the share price. It's the one that you see quoted in the newspapers or on the Teletext pages every day. It represents the midway amount between what buyers are prepared to pay for a share and sellers are prepared to accept.

The 'E' part refers to the earnings, that amount you worked out a few minutes ago, the EPS or earnings-per-share.

Divide the 'P' (price) by the 'E' (earnings) and you have the P/E ratio. The figure represents the number of years it would take for the company to pay you back for your investment, assuming that the price and the profits stayed the same. It's a good guide to what other investors think the company is worth, so if you compare today's PER with that average over the last few years you can easily work out whether you might be looking at a bargain or a hyped-up share.

Helen does a quick calculation of today's PER for Tesco, based on the price of 241p on the *REFS* page she is using. It is 18.5, which is lower than the average for the last five years. That's a good sign.

Section five

You can't beat a bit of visual analysis. This is the easiest way to demonstrate to numerically challenged club members what the trend has been for the past five years and, equally important, what the analysts think will happen in the future. Make no mistake, these analysts are clever chappies and chapesses, paid big bucks to predict the future for their clients. Inaccuracy can cost them their jobs so they spend their working time studying the companies in their charge in minute detail, talking to the management and the opposition, examining the sector as a whole, factoring in national and international market movements. Their crystal ball gazing has a

method to it and when the analysts' consensus opinion is published is it usually reasonably accurate.

Helen creates her own scale on the left-hand side of the graph and is able to demonstrate Tesco's steady rise in earnings together with the cautiously optimistic forecast of the experts.

Section six

During her researches our Helen has learned a lot about Tesco. She has revealed a steadily growing company that has chased and overtaken all the opposition. It is fighting in a very competitive ring – the French, the Germans and the Americans are over here in force trying to capture a slice of the action – so it is important to try to identify just why Tesco is so successful. What makes it a brand leader?

Helen does her best to put her finger on the main reasons. The suggested list doesn't really fit the bill so she saves her main comment for the 'Other reasons' section.

Section seven

Based on everything she has discovered about Tesco Helen is able to put five ticks out of a possible six in the **Make-Your-Mind-Up-Time** boxes. The only one she's not too sure of is the question about whether the share is undervalued today. The PER is slightly lower than the historical average but it is about the same as other supermarket groups in the sector. Perhaps it is a reflection of the

WHAT THE TOOLKIT DOES IS
ENABLE INVESTORS AND CLUBS TO DO THEIR OWN RESEARCH
AND GET A FEEL FOR THE COMPANY
IN WHICH THEY ARE INVESTING MONEY,
SO THEY ARE NOT BLINDLY
FOLLOWING TIPS OR HUNCHES, OR GAMBLING
WITHOUT KNOWING THE FACTS.

stock market as a whole? This is a question for the whole club to discuss, but Helen still likes the share sufficiently to table it as a recommendation at the next meeting.

The Investors' Toolkit is not an end in itself when it comes to share selection. There are many other matters to be taken into consideration before a final decision is made. Directors' dealings, for example, and the whole question of increasing competition from foreign-owned companies which will undercut prices to achieve market share.

What the Toolkit does is enable investors and clubs to do their own research and get a feel for the company in which they are investing money, so they are not blindly following tips or hunches, or gambling without knowing the facts. And because they do the research work themselves they are understanding the processes that go towards uncovering a gem. Believe me, when it happens there is no buzz like it.

Final checks

Because I wrote it I have no compunction in stealing the part of the Toolkit which advises what to do when you have completed the SAF.

Before you pick up the phone or hit the 'BUY' button on your computer spend a little more time making absolutely sure that this is the share for you.

Read the last annual report again. You know enough about the company now to have a pretty good idea about its position in the market place and its future potential. Look at the chairperson's statement. Do you consider it a fair reflection of your opinion about the company? Do his or her points of emphasis coincide with your thoughts on the company's strengths and have he/she or the other senior management personnel covered all the areas you believe are important?

Now look at the company's website. Most companies that have passed through your Share Appraisal Form with flying colours will have a site on the Internet because they have a history going back several years. Does the site impress you? Is it up to date? Can you set up a communications link direct with the company, by telephone, fax or e-mail, so you can contact them with queries? It might even be worth trying their Internet home delivery service – at the very least it will save you pushing one of those trolleys with the wonky wheels.

Finally, ask yourself two questions:

- **Will this share fit comfortably in my portfolio?** You must make sure that you have a balanced portfolio of shares. You must spread your wealth over a variety of sectors and sizes of company. In this way you will dilute the risk and minimize the impact of market fluctuations.

- **Do I like this share so much that I would like to own the whole company?** Think of your most treasured material possession – your house or car for instance. Are you so sure of this share that you would be prepared to mortgage your greatest treasure to buy it? If the answer is 'Yes', then go ahead – BUY!

WHAT HAPPENS NOW?

You must learn the meaning of a very important word. PATIENCE.

Unless you are extremely lucky, your new baby, the share you have just bought, will initially disappoint you. Like most babies it will probably just lie there doing nothing for the first few months. You expected it to be a lively little soul, growing bigger by the day, but such is the unpredictability of this world that the baby may even take a turn for the worse during the start of its life with you.

Don't worry. Be patient. If the reasons that you chose the share are valid then it should begin to perform as you predicted but you must be patient.

And you must watch the share like a hawk.

In the early stages keep in daily touch with the share price, note any dramatic variations – good or bad – and find out why. It may be a piece of news about the company or one of its competitors, or simply market sentiment. Whatever the reason you need to know and understand it because this share is part of your portfolio family and you need to keep a constant check on its health.

As time passes and hopefully the share gains in size and strength you will become familiar with its movements and carry out a routine health check once a week or even less. But be ever vigilant for any deviations and ready to take action if necessary.

SO WHEN SHOULD I SELL?

Remember, when you made the decision to buy shares in this company it was on the basis that you would be happy to own it for at least five years. You bought because you decided this was a good company with a proven track record, you liked the product or service it produced and you believed its future was bright. *While this picture remains clear and unaltered you should not sell the share.* You bought for the long term and to share in the company's prosperity. So be aware of the daily influences that affect the share price but, unless the picture fundamentally alters, keep faith with your decision.

Don't sell . . .

- just because the price has not risen. You must be patient.

- just because you have made a paper profit or loss. Never forget you bought a great company that, given time, should produce great rewards.

- just because you haven't done any buying or selling for a while, and feel you should be an active trader. That's the worst reason in the world.

Consider selling . . .

- if the reasons you originally chose the share are no longer valid. Despite your most diligent research, unforeseen circumstances can alter the overall picture and the fundamental facts.

- if the balance of your total share portfolio changes. Price rises and new acquisitions can create an unacceptable weighting in size or sector. In this case the share should be compared against the others in your portfolio.

- if, as you update the Share Appraisal Form (we recommend you do this whenever the company issues a new set of figures), the overall picture loses clarity. Study it carefully and ask yourself 'Would I still buy today?'

IF IN DOUBT, BE A COWARD

When you have considered all the facts, if you are still undecided whether to sell a stock – why not sell part of your holding? You will be hedging your decision and creating an opportunity to further diversify your portfolio.

BUT

If sales and earnings gains continue to meet or exceed your minimum requirements, and the profit margin keeps rising, and the PER does not exceed the historical PER by more than one-and-a-half times . . .

KEEP THE FAITH!

It is important not to ignore forecasts that are uncongenial.

Jib Fowles

HELP IS
AT HAND

You've heard the expression 'two minds with but a single thought'. Well, as far as I can ascertain, that's how *REFS – Really Essential Financial Statistics* – was born. Talk to different people, including the two protagonists, and you will get different stories but this one rings truest.

In 1992 Jim Slater wrote a book called *The Zulu Principle*, sub-titled *Making Extraordinary Profits from Ordinary Shares*. In it he praised the up-to-date information contained within regular publications produced in America by Value Line, Standard & Poors and Moody's. He also bemoaned the fact that there were no such services for British investors.

An accountant and keen private investor, Peter Scott, read the book and wrote to Jim saying he had developed a system for compiling the data but wanted guidance on exactly how it should be presented to the British investor. I work with Jim now and I know how, when he is presented with a proposition that excites him, he becomes single-minded in his determination to drive it to success. Peter Scott and Jim worked day and night to produce their amazing publication. It took 18 months of hard slog but, my goodness, it was so worthwhile.

At the risk of repeating myself, *REFS* is the finest aid ever produced for the investor. Despite its price, there are thousands of subscribers, ranging from professionals (I have noticed that all the biggest institutional analysts have several copies in their offices) to enthusiastic amateurs. Most seasoned investment clubs have access to *REFS* either because they subscribe directly or one of their members does. There are also a fortunate few clubs who have persuaded their local libraries to order copies.

The main *REFS* volume has a whole page devoted to each of the companies quoted in the main listings of the London Stock Exchange and in a supporting volume there is half a page devoted to the 500-plus stocks on AIM (the Alternative Investment Market). In addition the smaller book contains dozens of pages of analysis and market information on such items as index changes, new issues, highest growth rates, highest and lowest PERs and PEGs, highest return on capital, highest dividend yields, directors' dealings and so on and so on.

REFS appears as a huge 1,800 page two-volume tome every month, or it is available on CD-ROM, or you can download pages on the companies you want to research from the *REFS* Internet site where the information is as up to date as yesterday's closing prices. With the CD-ROM or online version you can customize searches by putting sieves in place to sort out shares which meet your chosen criteria each month.

Of course there are subscription costs involved. They vary depending on how often you want to have the information. Look on the website www.companyrefs.com or ring 020 7278 7769 if you want details of the printed or CD-ROM versions. For the online information look on www.hemscott.net or ring 020 7847 0076.

I contend that investors and investment clubs cannot do their job speedily and efficiently without *REFS*. However, I have one gripe about it and I have battled in vain with the publishers for some time, urging them to produce an idiot's explanation of how the private investor should interpret each section of a *REFS* page. Only in this way will he or she be able to understand the heartbeat of the company under scrutiny. So, fed up with waiting for the publishers to heed my wise advice, I am going to dissect a page and explain each section in language you will understand.

For no particular reason other than I quite like the share, I have chosen to look at Pearson (*REFS* page follows as Figure 7.1), who incidentally have had the good sense to publish the book you are reading now. That should do wonders for their profits.

At first sight a *REFS* page is a mass of figures and small print, rather off-putting for those visiting the tome for the first time. Like a new pair of shoes, it takes some getting used to. But with practice you will agree it is a treasure trove and your eyes will laser in on the information you seek. Many *REFS* subscribers – and I am one of them – flick through the publication page by page when it arrives at the beginning of the month. With 1,700 companies to look at it takes quite a time but not as long as you might imagine because at a glance we can assess whether a share is of interest to us. The key is in the top corners of the page – on the left-hand side is a chart and on the right a shaded rectangle. Graphs on the

one side, moons on the other. Steady rises on the left and black moons on the right, and we are interested.

To enable you to share the secrets of *REFS* I'm going to give you a detailed explanation of these two sections of the page because they contain an analysis of the financial facts, then a brief overview of the information on the rest of the page.

....

The chart

What a wealth of information there is in this little gem. The top line gives you a clue. **25p Ords vs FTSE All-Share vs norm eps**. That's just jargon which says that the graph compares the price of Pearson's shares (25p Ords) over recent years with the performance of the market as a whole (FTSE All-Share) and Pearson's profits (norm eps).

Now to the chart itself. There are the three graph lines contained on the chart and keys on the left-hand side and along the top. Check each of the bullet points below against the page to make sure you can locate them.

- Above the graph is a list of recent and future years and on the left-hand side a price range.

- The graph line that runs across the top of the shaded area plots the price movement of the share.

- The graph line that is unbroken but punctuated with small circles is the normalized EPS progress over the years (don't panic! I will explain EPS when I deal with the moons in a moment). The small circles indicate the company's financial year-end.

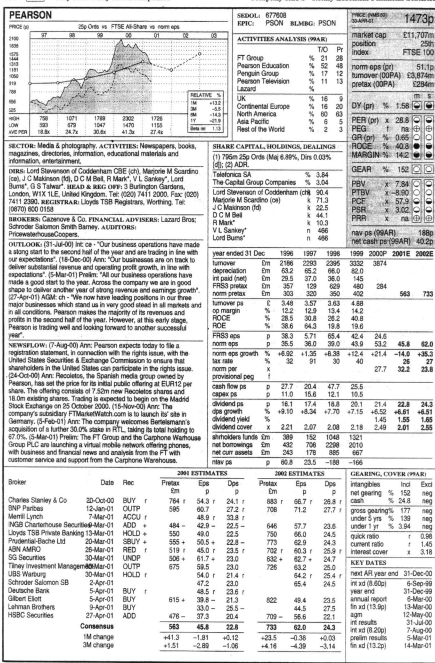

Fig 7.1 Pearson *REFS* page

Where this graph line becomes broken and moves out of the shaded area is where the brokers' consensus forecast of what is going to happen to the EPS in the future kicks in.

- The dotted graph line indicates the share price movements relative to changes in the FTSE Actuaries All-Share Index over the period. This is known as 'relative strength'. It enables you to see how this share has performed compared with the market as a whole. If the graph line moves up, the share price has exceeded the growth of the All-Share Index, conversely if it moves down the share has underperformed the index.

- Below the graph is a list of annual high and low points in the share price and the average PER for each year (again, explained in detail further on in the chapter).

In the right-hand corner of the chart is a small panel headed **RELATIVE %**. This relates to the performance of the share compared with the market as a whole over four periods – a month, a quarter, six months and a year. The other figure in that panel, the **Beta relative**, indicates how volatile the share-price movement has been compared with the market. The calculation is made by taking the average price of the index and the average price of the share every month over the past two years. This gives the market a Beta of 1. Therefore a Beta of more than 1 means the share was more volatile than the market, below 1 it was less volatile and therefore less risky.

The moons

At the top right hand of the *REFS* page there is a shaded elongated rectangle. It contains statistics that appear on other parts of the page and the publishers have decided to highlight them because they are of particular interest and significance to investors. The information in the rectangle provides a financial snapshot of the company. It is split into eight sections and, in the middle part of the rectangle, the quoted statistics have two circles to the right of them. The circles are called moons and compare each statistic of our target company with others in the market as a whole and with its peers in the same sector. A rule of thumb is that black is beautiful as far as investors are concerned, in other words the fuller the moon, the better we like it.

Let's consider all the elements of this shaded panel in order.

- **Price.** The price shown, 1473p, is the mid-market price on the date stated, 30 April 2001. The NMS 50 in brackets indicates the normal market size and is in thousands, so the average trade is between 33,000 and 60,000 shares. This tells me that the big boys, the institutions and investment trusts, deal in Pearson shares. A normal purchase for them is, say, 50,000 shares, which means they will lay out around £725,000. Who cares? I hear you ask. That's funny money. But it is interesting to us because it indicates that for our tiddler deals, perhaps a few thousand pounds at the most, there will be plenty of shares available and our purchase will not rock the overall share price.

- **Market cap.** Stands for market capitalization. It's arrived at by multiplying the number of ordinary shares issued by the market price (1473p) and shows the size of the company. At £11.5 billion Pearson is a big one.

- **Position** and **Index.** The 25th largest company of all those quoted on the London Stock Exchange and a stalwart of the FTSE 100. FTSE stands for *Financial Times* – Stock Exchange and the FTSE 100 is an index of the 100 leading shares, measured by market capitalization. But it is important because collective investment vehicles like tracker funds, investment trusts, unit trusts and many of the major institutions slavishly follow the FTSE 100, buying when a company grows big enough to gain promotion to the index and selling when a price declines to the point where it is booted downstairs to the FTSE 250. These huge share transactions have a knock-on effect, which essentially has little or nothing to do with the commercial performance of the company.

- **Norm eps (pr).** Here's a prime example of what I mean when I contend that so much of the information in the investment world is camouflaged in gobbledegook. Hand on heart, do you know what 'norm eps (pr)' stands for? I'll tell you:

normalized earnings per share (prospective). Any wiser? Of course not. Earnings per share are the profits the company makes for the shareholders after it has paid its tax. To get to the figure you divide the after-tax profits by the number of shares in issue. The (pr) is the interesting bit because this shows that the calculation has also taken into account the brokers' consensus forecasts for future earnings, so it's a view of the company's future prospects. That's much more interesting to the investor than what has happened in the past. I'll deal with that word 'normalized' later.

Infuriatingly, companies can choose any old date for the end of their financial year. What *REFS* does is attempt to level the playing field by calculating the earnings on a rolling 12-month forward basis, so you are always looking at comparable expectations of future earnings. Don't worry about how they do the sums, just be happy that they do.

- **Turnover (ooPA).** This shows the total sales of the company for the year to 31 December 2000, not including VAT. PA indicates it is a preliminary announcement rather than AR, which stands for annual report. However, because the preliminary announcement comes from the company we know it is accurate. The figure gives an immediate impression of the size and therefore the status of the company.

- **Pretax (ooPA).** The company's profits, before tax has been paid on them, as detailed in the preliminary announcement that precedes the publication of the annual report.

In this and the following three sections you will see 'm' and an 's' over the moons. These have nothing to do with a certain currently depressed department store; they stand for 'market' and 'sector'. The blacker the moon, the more impressive that particular statistic when compared with the market as a whole and its peers in particular.

- **DY (pr).** The dividend yield. Dividends are the payouts shareholders get, usually twice a year, direct from the company they have invested in. The yield expresses the annual dividend total as a percentage of the share price. The (pr) means the figure shown is a consensus forecast of what brokers estimate the dividend will be for the 12 months immediately ahead. I always pay particular attention to this figure because there's evidence to show that shares with a high yield outperform the market.

- **PER (pr).** Price-to-earnings ratio. I'm going to take a bit of space to cover this item because it's my way of getting an instant fix on how the market values a company. Plus it is the figure quoted in the right-hand column of the share-price listings in the quality daily newspapers so you can make an instant comparison with competitors in the sector and the market as a whole. But that's meaningless unless you understand what you are comparing.

Let's take it a step at a time.

Price is easy. That's the first figure we looked at, the up-to-date quoted price. If you are buying the share you will have to pay a fraction more for it than the quoted price, if you are selling you will receive a fraction less. The difference between the buying and selling price is called the spread and the price you see is the mid-price. But forget the spread, forget whether you are buying or selling, the price at the top of the *REFS* page is a good indicator of what investors think the share is worth today.

Now, *earnings*. Not so easy. It might help if I tell you that, until I mention PER again, when I refer to figures I am talking about amounts of money.

At the end of its accounting year a publicly quoted company has to produce an annual report for its shareholders showing how much money it has received from its customers. That's the turnover. The figures must also show how much the company has paid out to its suppliers, the total amount of remuneration allocated to employees, and all the other payouts for costs such as rent, depreciation of equipment, borrowing funds and so on – they all nibble away at the turnover. What's left is the pretax profit.

At the front of the queue for profits payouts is the taxman, he must have his cut first. Subtract his slice and we finish up with the earnings. It is the net amount left for the ordinary shareholders. Divide these earnings by the number of shares issued by the company and you come up with the earnings-per-share figure. (Incidentally, these historical EPS figures are used by analysts to calculate their forecasts.)

If you divide today's share price by the earnings-per-share figure you come up with the PER, the price-to-earnings ratio. It is a comparison between two important amounts of money, the price of the share today and the profits the company has earned for its shareholders.

So, now you know how to calculate a PER. But what use is it? Well, basically it is a measure. The PER measures time, value, investor confidence and reasonableness (if there is such a word).

Forget Pearson for a moment. Let's take a simpler example. If your PER is 10 it means that, if the annual earnings of the company and today's quoted price stay the same for the next 10 years, at the end of that time the money earned for the shareholders will have covered the price they paid for their shares in the first place. Therefore all the profits (not to be confused with dividends) after the 10th year will be cost-free bonuses.

So, the PER figure you see quoted for Pearson tells you the value all the shareholders – the private investors, the pension funds, the investment and unit trusts, and the directors who have a personal stake – put on the company. In this case the figure is relatively high and demonstrates how confident shareholders are that earnings will be good in the future.

The snags come when you start to look down the PER columns. You will see that they vary from sector to sector and some are totally astronomic. This reflects investor sentiment. The sector variation illustrates investment fashion and a sky-high PER is often telling you that buyers are working on the 'Greater Fool' theory: 'I may be a fool to pay this sort of price but I'll find a

A SKY-HIGH PER IS OFTEN TELLING YOU THAT BUYERS ARE WORKING ON THE 'GREATER FOOL' THEORY: 'I MAY BE A FOOL TO PAY THIS SORT OF PRICE BUT I'LL FIND A GREATER FOOL TO TAKE IT OFF MY HANDS AT A HIGHER PRICE.'

greater fool to take it off my hands at a higher price.'

How do you check whether the PER of a particular company is reasonable? I suggest two ways. First, add up all the PERs in the sector and divide by the number of companies which have a quoted PER (for various reasons some PERs are missing). That way you will obtain the sector average and be able to compare your company with its peers. If you want to be really lazy – and I do – just look in the smaller *REFS* volume because they have done the sums for you and the sector averages are listed there. Now check back over the individual company's average PER for the past five years. How does today's PER compare? It's a good way to measure reasonableness.

Because of sector and fashion variations it is difficult to have rules of thumb for PERs. But if I am doing research into a company and I see a PER over 20 I want to know why. And if it is over 35 I will definitely leave it to the birds. Too often I have been tempted by tales of turning losses into profits and rumours of phantom takeovers that send prices and PERs soaring.

- **PEG.** Price-to-earnings growth. I don't want to spend too much time on this because it gets complicated. But it is important because it is a better indicator for a growth company than the PER when it comes to assessing whether a share is good or bad value. You get to the PEG of a company by dividing the prospective PER by the

estimated future growth in earnings per share. So if the PER and the EPS growth rate were the same the PEG would be 1. (Yes, I know it's boring and difficult to understand, but try to get your head round it. Once the penny drops you will have a quick and easy way to check whether a share is worth buying). If a PEG is less than 1 there's a fair chance it is at present undervalued by the market. Over 1 and you should check carefully because the signs are it is overvalued.

There are drawbacks to the PEG system. It is designed to measure growth stocks and is not a suitable indicator for asset situations, cyclical stocks or recovery shares. A word of warning here, and I know this to my personal cost: a low PEG is not by itself a reason to buy a share. It must be used only as an indicator and all the other tests *must* be applied before it can become a contender for your portfolio.

Note. You will see that Pearson does not have a PEG figure. This is because *REFS* classifies a growth stock as one that has at least four years of consecutive share growth and the brokers' consensus forecast for normalized EPS growth for 2001 is, as you will see, a negative figure.

- **GR (pr).** Growth rate, and again the (pr) shows the forecasts for the future are being taken into account. Incidentally, I really like that ingredient because it is the future I am thinking of buying into and I know these brokers' best guesses are usually based on good information. Taking into account the current and future years the GR shows how quickly the company plans to expand. Caution: remember the 'busy fool' theory. At the end of the day it's profit that counts.

- **ROCE.** Return on capital employed. Big black beautiful moons for Pearson here. And rightly too. The ROCE is the operating profit the company makes as a percentage of the capital employed in the company. The operating profit is the profit before deduction of such items as tax, interest, dividends and other exceptional items. Capital employed is the total value of ordinary shares (those that we buy), preference shares, reserves, debentures, loan stocks and all borrowings. Pearson's ROCE figure is exceptional, no wonder the moon is black.

- **MARGIN.** Again, black moons. That's because, when you relate the trading profit (before tax, interest and so on) to the turnover, the company has made a return of over 14 per cent and that's good. Very good, compared to the market as a whole and to the sector, which in Pearson's case is Media and Photography.

    When I look at margins I have several caveats in mind:

    - High margins mean the company is there to be shot at, the business is so good it will attract competitors. In Pearson's case that is not too much of a

consideration, the nature of the business means it has attained a unique position that is almost unassailable.

- Low margins are difficult to quantify. A small fall in sales can be disastrous, but a small rise can give a real profit boost.

- It is always worth looking at what has happened in the past as far as margins are concerned. Look for a steadily improving situation rather that a rocket boost. If there have been significant blips find out why.

- **GEARING.** Gearing means borrowings after deductions of easily realized money items such as cash the company has in the bank, treasury bills and certificates of deposit. These borrowings are compared with the money invested in the company by the shareholders and shown as a percentage. Here you will see that Pearson is heavily borrowed – 152 per cent of its capitalization. That's big bucks. My yardstick is 50 per cent – anything over that should be investigated because borrowing money is expensive so there have to be good reasons for it.

- **PBV.** Price to book value. Nothing to do with the pittance you paid for this invaluable volume. It relates the share price to the value of the company's assets. You divide the former by the latter. So what does that tell us – and in my unsophisticated opinion the answer is 'not a lot'. We are entering muddy waters here, but the problem

is: it all depends how a company interprets the word 'value'. As far as I can see there are no hard-and-fast rules. For instance, how do you value a brand name? Marmite and Magnum must be worth a fortune to Unilever but how do you put a price on the names? Then again, how do you work out how much a patent or a piece of machinery is worth? Or a footballer – should he appear as an asset on the books and at what value? The value of the PBV figure depends on the nature of the company you are looking at.

- **PTBV.** Price to tangible book value. Same as above except that you take the net asset value of the company (after having taken out the intangible factors

such as the brand names as mentioned above) and compare it with the share price. On the face of it this is a more accurate method of assessment because it takes into consideration only those assets which can easily be quantified. But be careful, in some companies those intangibles, particularly if they are related to goodwill, could be among their greatest assets. You need to dig deep and consult the annual report in detail if you are to use this statistic as a guide.

- **PCF.** Price to cash flow. This is an interesting figure. It shows how much of the company's lifeblood, the annual cash flow, you are buying when you acquire a share. You calculate the PCF by dividing the company's share price by its cash flow. A generalization is that a high PCF indicates a price which may be overvalued and a low PCF is attractive. If the PCF is much higher than the PER find out why.

- **PSR.** Price-to-sales ratio. Calculated by dividing the company's share price by its sales per share, ignoring VAT. It's a good indicator, particularly if you are looking for a recovery situation. If a company is making losses, often there is no PER or dividend yield quoted. In these instances PSR can give an indication of the value when the company comes back into profit. Generally a low PSR – below 1 – is attractive. But beware of companies with a low PSR and heavy debts – they will probably be heading for a rights issue, thus diluting the value of the existing shares.

- **PRR.** Price-to-research-and-development ratio. Only of interest if the company is heavily involved in research and development – obvious examples would be pharmaceutical or biotech companies or outfits involved in evolving computer software. Divide the share price of the company by the R&D expenditure to get the PRR. An example would be a company with a market cap of £300 million spending £12 million on R&D, the PRR would be 25. So what use is it? I would use it only as a way of checking the trend of such expenditure – are they spending more or less this year? – and as a comparison against the company's peers.

- **Nav ps (99AR).** Net asset value per share. This is the total value of the company's assets, minus all short- and long-term liabilities, provisions and charges as shown in the last annual report divided by the number of shares issued. It includes all intangible assets.

- **Net cash ps (99AR).** Net cash per share. This is money left in the bank after payment of short-term borrowings. If it was divided among shareholders in proportion to the shares owned the amount shown would be how much each share would generate.

That's it. My attempt at explaining the chart and the moons that are features of every *REFS* page.

Let me now give you a much more abbreviated explanation of the other sections in this remarkable source of information.

What happened yesterday and what *might* happen tomorrow

Immediately below the shaded rectangle are detailed statistics about the company for each of the last five years, together with consensus forecasts for the next two years. This is what the various phrases mean:

- **Turnover.** The annual sales, excluding sales taxes, government levies, excise duty and VAT.

- **Depreciation.** The amount set aside each year to cover the depreciation of tangible fixed assets. There are accepted accounting principles the company must adhere to.

- **Interest paid (net)**. The net cost of the company's borrowings during the year. This includes finance charges; interest payable on loans, overdrafts and finance leases, less any interest received by the company.

- **FRS3 pretax.** How do they expect mere mortals to understand this jargon? FRS3 stands for Financial Reporting Standard 3. This shows your actual unadjusted pretax profit and therefore reflects all items of profit or loss including those which might be regarded as non-trading or exceptional and which might be considered to distort the view of the underlying performance.

- **Norm pretax.** Take the overall profit, exclude anything that is exceptional, abnormal or non-recurring, together with any non-trading profits and losses and what you're left with is the normalized pretax profit. This reflects underlying performance.

- **Turnover ps.** You've guessed, the ps means per share. (Incidentally, we are talking just ordinary shares here, nothing fancy.) You get the figure by dividing the number of shares by the turnover and it is a very good trend tester, particularly when looking at a company which may have expanded by acquisition. In such a case the straightforward turnover could be misleading.

- I explained **operating margin** and **ROCE** when I was telling you about the moons.

- **ROE.** Let's get one thing straight, the words 'shares' and 'equities' mean the same thing in the financial world. The ROE is the return on equity capital, the amount of money invested by shareholders in the business. As an indicator it might give a distorted picture because it doesn't take into account borrowings, so always check the company's gearing figure. To my mind the previous figure, ROCE, is a much more accurate yardstick. And presumably, if the return on capital employed is higher than the return on equity, it implies the company's borrowings are being put to good use.

- **FRS3 eps** and **norm eps.** Here we go again. Jargon. Financial Reporting Standard 3. It takes into account all items of profit or loss including non-recurring or exceptional items. The normalized EPS ignores one-off happenings which might give an incorrect impression. My advice: favour the normalized results, that's what the professional analysts do (with the exception of the taxman – see below) and it is the one on which they base their forecasts. But it is always worth doing a comparison between the two sets of figures because a big discrepancy might indicate a bit of creative accounting – sorry, that's jargon, I mean it might show there's a fiddle going on.

- **Norm eps growth.** Shows what it says, how the earnings are growing in percentage terms. If you are seeking a growth company, rising EPS values are a requirement. A history of steady increase in earnings is as important as a rising turnover trend.

- **Tax rate.** One person who does do his sums based on the FRS3 pretax profit figures is the taxman. A company is subject to several forms of tax – corporation, deferred, overseas and so on. The rate shown here is the percentage of the profit paid out to cover all these taxes. In normal circumstances corporation tax will be the major slice – as I write it is 31 per cent but you can never tell when the chancellor will change his mind – so if the tax figure is lower than that the company is probably using up tax losses from the previous year. If it is much higher than the norm it may be because the company does a lot of business overseas in countries where the tax rates are heavier. Deviations either way should be looked at carefully because they could affect the company's earnings picture.

- **Norm per** and **provisional peg.** I explained these in the moons part. The provisional PEG is a bit of educated guesswork based on what brokers' research analysts expect the company to do in the future. It is used when there are just three years of earnings growth rather than the four required for a full PEG.

- **Cash flow ps.** VIS. Very Important Statistic. Cash flow is the amount of cash produced by the trading operations of the business. It's the lifeblood of the company because it has to fund all the costs and produce the profits. Here it is expressed as an amount for each ordinary share. Jim Slater says: 'Cash flow is one of the most important features in the historical performance figures. I like to compare it year by year with the normalized EPS figures to make sure the cash flow per share exceeds the earnings per share ... a persistent shortfall is very worrying *and* would put me off buying the shares.'

- **Capex ps.** More jargon. Short for 'capital expenditure'. Shows the amount of money per share invested in the operation of the company during each financial period. To enable you to sleep at night it should be much less than the cash flow per share.

- **Dividend ps.** Add up all the dividends you receive for the company's trading year, divide the total by the number of

CASH FLOW IS THE AMOUNT OF CASH PRODUCED BY THE TRADING OPERATIONS OF THE BUSINESS. IT'S THE LIFEBLOOD OF THE COMPANY BECAUSE IT HAS TO FUND ALL THE COSTS *AND* PRODUCE THE PROFITS.

shares you own, and that's your dividend per share figure. It's comforting if the amount rises each year. With larger companies *REFS* includes brokers' estimates for the two years to come.

- **Dps growth.** This compares the dividend growth with that of previous years in percentage terms. It saves you working it out for yourself. Again, an increasing percentage gives you a warm glow.

- **Dividend yield.** The dividend per share for the latest set of figures expressed as a percentage of the current share price. The estimates for the next two years are then compared with the current price so you can see if you are going to do better in the future, presuming of course that the brokers get their guesses right.

- **Dividend cover.** Shows how much profit is available to pay the ordinary dividend. When considering it, make sure the ratio is fairly constant over the years. This indicates that the dividends are at least moving in line with the growth in the company's earnings.

The last two sections of the *REFS* statistics block give bottom-line information from the company's balance sheets.

- **Shareholders' funds.** Self-explanatory. Add up all the capital from ordinary shares, plus the various kinds of preference shares and any reserves the company has, and there you have it.

- **Net borrowings.** Again, it means what it says. A total of all the money borrowed from whatever source, less any cash in the bank or funds that can easily and quickly be turned into cash. If there's a minus sign in front of the figure it means the company has more cash or near-cash than it has borrowed.

- **Net current assets.** Current assets are all the things that the company has that can be realized for money now or in the fairly immediate future. They don't necessarily have to be touchy-feely things like products in the warehouse. They can be debtors (money owed to them), short-term investments or just plain cash. Current liabilities are the opposite, things that are going to be a drain on resources. Short-term borrowings, creditors (money they owe), tax, dividends not yet paid and so on. Subtract the latter from the former and hopefully you finish up with net current assets.

- **Ntav ps.** I will refrain from mentioning the word 'jargon' again. Net tangible assets are the shareholders' funds less those intangibles defined above. If there aren't any intangibles the figure will be the same as the nav ps, analyzed in the moons section. The net amount is then divided by the number of ordinary shares. It's good to see a strong and improving amount over the years.

What the experts think

Stockbrokers come in all shapes and sizes, as you'll see in Chapter 12, which I have devoted to these strange animals.

They all perform the same basic function, they buy and sell equities on our behalf, and we like them if they do the job speedily and efficiently and hate them if they don't. But there's a vast difference in the frills that surround their activities and the charges they make for performing.

Most investment clubs use the no frills service, execution-only brokerages that appeared on the British scene in the 1990s and revolutionized the stockbroking business. When I started investing I would pay anything up to 2.5 per cent of the value of a deal for a broker to carry out a transaction. On a £10,000 purchase that's £250. Today I would grumble if the broker took more than £20. But such dramatic reductions come at a price. If I want a cheapy-cheapy service I must use an execution-only broker and he (or she) is nothing more than an order taker.

If I ring up I will speak to someone, probably called Wayne or Sharon, who knows how to look at screens and read current prices, and they're automatons when it comes to pressing a button to buy or sell shares, but beyond that they know nothing. I would do better to ask my dog Sophie for advice than Wayne or Sharon, but even if I did ask they are forbidden by law from giving it.

That's the vital ingredient missing from the execution-only service. Advice. If you want guidance on investing from an advisory broker you must pay for it. They employ extremely well-paid analysts who specialize in particular market sectors and are expected to be able to give an informed opinion on the merits of every constituent company. This analyst opinion is available

to clients of the broker and is passed on by way of individual conversations or bulletins sent via post or e-mail to registered clients of the broker. But, it'll cost you. As my old dad was fond of saying, you don't get owt for nowt in this world.

Obviously, because the essence of an investment club is that the members choose the investments, the most cost-effective way to deal is via a no frills broker. Luckily however there is a way to tap into the opinions of the experts. Most of the best brokers in the land – there are some inexplicable exceptions – have agreed to allow *REFS* to include their latest recommendation on individual companies. The brokers' consensus forecasts section of the *REFS* page (bottom left) therefore contains an analysis and recommendation from people who should really know what they are talking about. (Incidentally and sadly, you will only find comprehensive analysis – more than a couple of brokers' opinions – on medium and large companies. The big-name brokers who do this research have big spenders for clients. They are simply not interested in tiddlers, either in terms of clients or shares to buy.)

At first glance the section is self-explanatory but there are a few wrinkles that will help you get the most out of it. I will run across the headings, left to right.

- **Date.** I always read this column from the bottom up. It shows the date the brokerage house made its latest recommendation and is presented in ascending order – the most recent pronouncement is at the bottom.

- **Recommendation.** More than 50 brokers contribute forecasts to *REFS* and at my last count there were 82 different abbreviations used to interpret their analysts' thinking. That's daft. I realize that a straightforward buy, sell or hold is perhaps oversimplifying it, but 82? Anyway, to enable you to cut through the jargon I have reproduced the abbreviations used and given you an explanation of what they mean. A plus or minus next to a recommendation means it has been upgraded or downgraded from an earlier forecast by the broker, and this applies to pluses and minuses next to any of the forecast figures in the section.

    If there's an 'r' next to the recommendation it means that particular recommendation has been rendered obsolete by a results announcement. If there is a 'w' then beware. The forecast has been rendered obsolete by the company announcing a profit warning. The head honcho at the company usually makes a statement that is couched in weasel-speak, something like 'the results are not expected to achieve market expectations' but what he or she really means is 'we got it wrong lads, and so did you. The results are going to be rubbish.'

    If this happens, unless you are very lucky, you can forget your stop-loss policy. The share price usually falls out of bed before you can reach for the phone. And, like buses, profit warnings often come one after the other and with catastrophic effects.

- **Lists of figures.** These are the estimates for the next two years of pretax profits, earnings per share, and dividends per share. At the bottom of each column is a consensus or average of the opinion and the last two lines show how the consensus figures have moved in the last month and three months.

Jim Slater relies heavily on these brokers' forecasts because they are the essential ingredient of his favoured PEG calculation. He points out the more brokers covering the company, the better. More than five is ideal, and the smaller the deviations, the more comfortable he feels. But look out for the lemming effect – if a prestigious and top-notch broker makes a forecast it is tempting for a lesser firm to follow the leader. If there is only one broker's forecast there is clearly a risk with following the recommendation. Remember to watch directors' dealing and relative strength in these cases.

Contrary to the popular view Jim is not particularly sceptical about the opinion of the company's own broker, especially if the broker in question has a good reputation. This broker should be better informed and will be avoiding the risk of causing embarrassment to the client company by making over-optimistic forecasts. Jim also tells me he pays strict attention to the monthly and quarterly consensus changes. They indicate whether news about the company is positive, negative or neutral.

Jim Slater is a wily old bird, he has more experience of businesses – good

THE MORE BROKERS COVERING THE COMPANY, THE BETTER. BUT LOOK OUT FOR THE LEMMING EFFECT – IF A PRESTIGIOUS AND TOP-NOTCH BROKER MAKES A FORECAST IT IS TEMPTING FOR A LESSER FIRM TO FOLLOW THE LEADER.

and bad – than the rest of us put together. He looks at the same figures we do, but interprets them differently and more astutely. We can learn a lot from him.

But who are they? and what do they actually *do*?

Good questions. We're going to take a break from the figures for a while and look at the sections of the *REFS* page which deal with people and places. We won't spend a lot of time on them because they are easy to understand, but they do contain a range of good information and it all helps to complete the jigsaw puzzle.

Under the visual price graph there's a section which starts with the word **SECTOR**. That's the heading under which you will find the company name in the

Financial Times; in the case of Pearson it is Media and Photography. Most other papers, if they cover the stock on a daily basis, will have the same or a similar heading on the prices page. Knowing where to look will enable you to: (a) check on the share price; and (b) compare it against those of the company's competitors. Though a comparison of actual prices is fairly meaningless, I find a glance down the final column, the price-to-earnings ratios, is a rough barometer of what's going on.

Then follows a list of directors and the vital statistics of the head office, the registered office, and the company's registrars (the people who maintain the register of shareholders).

The next panel lists the names of the firms, brokers, financial advisers and auditors who provide specialist services to the company.

- **OUTLOOK.** In this section the score or so of analysts who comb the annual and interim reports on a daily basis are looking for any information which refers to the company's trading prospects. Each statement is preceded by who said it and when – '(27-Apr-01) AGM:ch' means the chairman said it at the AGM. These announcements are shown in chronological order, with the latest information last.

- **NEWSFLOW.** Facts about orders, takeovers, mergers, sales, rights issues, joint ventures and so on. Gives you a feel for how the company is doing.

Top middle column

- **SEDOL** is the Stock Exchange Identification Number, **EPIC** is the Stock Exchange Reference Code and **BLMBG** is the Bloomberg Code. Bet you didn't know that. The main reasons you need them are: SEDOL to check on your purchase certificate that the broker bought the right share for you and EPIC or BLMBG to access, on a website, price information about particular company.

- **ACTIVITIES ANALYSIS.** I always find this a fascinating part of the page. Many companies, and Pearson is a good example, put their efforts into a variety of activities. Builders, for example, may do a combination of residential and commercial development. Hotel groups might own some hotels and manage others. Pearson is involved in a wide variety of media activities, everything from newspapers and books to television. The figures under **T/O** (turnover) show the percentage of the whole sales of the group attributed to each activity. There is no need for an even balance here, we don't really care how much of the whole effort is put into a particular part of the business, but it is interesting to look at the second row of figures (**Pr**). Here the profit percentages are allocated. Compare the two and you can identify whether the effort appears to be properly distributed.

  The second part of this panel lists the same percentages for the areas in the world in which it operates. So in the big picture you can gauge how much world events, overseas economies and currency fluctuations are likely to affect your stake in the company. (Interesting, isn't it, to note that the majority of Pearson's efforts and profits come from the United States? Not many people know that either.)

- **SHARE CAPITAL, HOLDINGS, DEALINGS.** A mine of information here. Immediately under the heading come details of the shares. Taking the Pearson example, this shows that of the 795 million ordinary shares issued a total of 6.89 per cent are held by major shareholders and 0.03 per cent by directors. The letters **ADR** after **(2)** mean American Depository Receipt and tells you that the shares can be traded on the New York Stock Exchange as well as in London.

  Next are the names of the two companies that make up the major shareholding. If you want to know details about them, what sort of companies they are, you will have to look up the information elsewhere. As a start it is worth searching via the Internet or typing in www.companyname.com on the address line.

Lastly there is a list of the directors, their positions in the company, and their shareholdings. An asterisk after a name indicates that the director is non-executive, he or she is not an employee who comes into the company's offices every day to earn a crust. If a director holds more than 1 per cent of the equity it is expressed as a percentage. More than a million and there's a figure with an 'm' after it. More than 1,000 and it's a figure followed by a 'k'. Under 1,000 and it is just a figure, followed by 'n' for number.

I like every director to have a big chunk of equity. These people are my representatives at the board meetings and I want them to have just the same selfish motivation as me. If a director is on the board for any length of time and does not have a substantial holding – I'm not talking about options here, I refer to actual cash invested in the business – I will try to find out why. And if I can't immediately discover a reasonable explanation I will have no hesitation in selling the shares. If the people driving the bus don't think it is mechanically perfect I want to get off and wait for another bus.

I have rattled on about *REFS*, haven't I? Sorry about that, but it seemed a sensible way to explain some of the technical terms and jargon that surround this business. So often books just list these explanations in alphabetical order and you have to look them up in isolation or, more likely, ignore them and pass on to something you do understand.

You will have guessed that I am an enthusiast for the *REFS* publication but,

I LIKE EVERY DIRECTOR TO HAVE A BIG CHUNK OF EQUITY. THESE PEOPLE ARE MY REPRESENTATIVES AT THE BOARD MEETINGS AND I WANT THEM TO HAVE JUST THE SAME SELFISH MOTIVATION AS ME.

more importantly, so are the vast majority of serious investors, both private and professional. I doubt there is a City office that doesn't have several copies lying around and after the first few days of the month they will all be well thumbed.

I won't kid you, it is an expensive publication to subscribe to. Prices and offers do change so I can't be specific, but it is currently something like £675 per annum for the monthly updated publication. The good news is though that ProShare-registered investment clubs qualify for a substantial discount which currently brings the price down to £540 for the 12 issues. The same discount applies if you subscribe quarterly. The £295 for four issues is down to £236 for ProShare clubs. You can choose to have the two-volume paper version or the CD (but not both, unless you want to pay twice as much).

The online version of *REFS* currently cost £62 per month. The attraction of this is that you can download from the Internet information about companies you want to research and the details are as up to date as last night's closing prices.

If most of your members have computers I suggest you take the CD version or the online service. To my mind it is vastly superior because as I mentioned earlier you can load in sieves for sorting the wheat from the chaff (more about this later). Have one member holding the CD who can send the relevant page to other members on request. Should talk of such futuristic ideas as computers cause you to have a senior moment then buy the paper version, but go into strict training and have the heart and the blood pressure checked regularly because lugging it between houses or to the monthly meetings needs strength.

Whichever method of subscription you choose I believe *REFS*, like the wheels on your car, is essential if you are going to get from A (fledgling investors with little more than enthusiasm and high hopes) to B (bloated plutocrats). And this is where your investment club really comes into its own because if you have 12 members and the club takes the quarterly *REFS* it will cost about 50p per member per week. The all singing, all dancing, at-your-fingertips online service will be about £1.25 per member per week. That's comparative peanuts.

If there's anyone listening to whom I owe money,

I'm prepared to forget it if you are.

Errol Flynn in a radio broadcast

CHAPTER **8**

DON'T GIVE ME THE CHALK

For three glorious years in my late teens and early twenties I was a feature writer with a newspaper in the Midlands, the *Sunday Mercury*. Looking back now, it was the most dissolute, lazy, enjoyable interlude of my career. I was an impressionable lad, easily led, so the temptations of the good life were too much for me. I didn't even bother to put up a struggle. In the company of Mick Rhind (news and features editor and good journalist), Harry Pugh (mischievous little fellow who later became a top reporter with the *Sunday Express*) and Ivor Punnett (oddest of them all, seemingly idle but in fact a prodigious writer of detective novels) I learned three questionable skills. I'll tell you about them in a moment but first let me outline our working week. Those of you who sweat over a hot desk from dawn to dusk can read and drool.

We had to be in the office by 10 a.m. on the first day of our working week, Tuesday. It was expenses day, perhaps the most creative work of the week for most of us. The task was to remember all the bus journeys, calls from phone boxes, and casual pints bought for contacts while keeping the total around £10, which we knew would be accepted without question. This rather pleasant task took until midday. The rest of Tuesday was our own.

Wednesday morning was conference time. Led by Mick Rhind there would be a conference about which topical features should be prepared that week. It was horses for courses, Harry seemed to be forever seeking – and somehow finding – vicars who had run off with vergers' wives. Punnett (for some reason no one ever called him Ivor) got the jobs that were complicated and involved combing company reports. I was given the people stories, interviewing dying women whose last wish was to kiss Frankie Vaughan, or going to see hippy communes deep in Shropshire's Clee Hills because of their belief that coveting each other's wives was OK. After the morning conference the rest of the day was ours.

Thursday, we didn't go into the office. Harry would go chasing his vicars, Punnett would read his reports and I would spend a lazy day in Shropshire with the hippies.

Friday, we wrote our features.

Saturday we worked. From 10 a.m. to 10 p.m. we became proper newspaper reporters. On the phone or the typewriter for 12 hours solid, reporting the news of the day.

Sunday and Monday were days off. It was a tough old life.

The three skills I learned and in which, through much practice, I became reasonably competent, were:

1. Drinking beer. Ansells mild, to this day I can close my eyes and remember the taste of the dark nectar.

2. Playing cards. Brag and draw poker. Both are games of bluff and counter bluff. Sitting down day in, day out, with the same school of players you learn to read a person's character, his foibles and – most importantly – his risk limit. Everyone has such a limit, it's in built and I don't believe there is

anything you can do to change it. It can seriously affect your life as an investor and your approach should be governed by you ability to tolerate risk. That's why I recommend you read Richard Koch's book *Selecting Shares that Perform*. It includes a simple test which will enable you to assess your own risk level. Essentially it is a private test and the questions can't be answered as a group, so I suggest every member does the test by him- or herself, then you take a consensus of the results.

3. Playing darts. There was a dartboard in the social club of the *Birmingham Post and Mail* (the *Sunday Mercury* was part of that group of papers). When we tired of cards we got out the arrows. I became reasonably good, even played for the social club on a couple of occasions, *but they never let me have the chalk*.

For those of you who have never played the game let me give you a one-sentence explanation. Each player takes turns throwing three darts at the board and the total is progressively subtracted from a starting figure – usually 301 – until zero is reached. I realize it is slightly more complicated than that, but this is a book about investing, not darts. The point is that they never let me do the sums. Adding up the three-dart scores, subtracting them from the previous scores and chalking the results on the blackboard was just not my forte. I'm not an eejut, I can do it given time, but it takes me for ever and darts players won't wait.

I record this flaw in my abilities because I confess that when I contemplated the idea of becoming a professional investor my inadequacies with the chalk worried me. The only sure way to judge a company is on its record and, when all the talking has stopped, it is the figures that count. My eyes glaze when confronted with columns of figures and the thought of having trying to plough through them for hours on end was a real off-putter. Furthermore, I had been told by the pundits that being able to read company accounts was imperative and, ominously, you had to look under all the stones because of 'creative accountancy'. What that meant, I presume, is that the people who prepare the accounts are devious and are trying to hide the truth.

When things get complicated, worrying and confusing like this, and you are tempted to put the whole subject in the 'too difficult' tray, I have a tip for you. Ignore the experts. Clear your mind of all your prejudices and the gypsies' warnings you have heard. Tell yourself that you have a brain that works and is still prepared to learn something new. And teach yourself the basics of whatever subject you want to know about.

In this case we are going to learn how to read a company's annual report and accounts. *You should never buy shares without having seen and studied a copy of a company's latest annual report*. So, when a share is tabled for consideration at your club meeting, unless you have got a copy of the annual report and at least one member has studied it and can give a

WHEN THINGS GET COMPLICATED, WORRYING AND CONFUSING LIKE THIS,

AND YOU ARE TEMPTED TO PUT THE WHOLE

SUBJECT IN THE 'TOO DIFFICULT' TRAY,

I HAVE A TIP FOR YOU.

IGNORE THE EXPERTS.

brief précis of the plusses and minuses, postpone a purchase decision. I realize this advice goes against the grain, there is an eagerness to buy and a thought that you mustn't miss the boat, but sensible and successful investors insist on seeing the complete picture before they buy.

The annual report is a document which by law the company concerned has to publish. It is produced as soon as possible after the end of the company's financial year and contains detailed accounts plus, usually, comment on such vital matters as current trading conditions and future prospects. It's the way a company can explain its business to its shareholders and to the world in general. The facts it contains have to be accurate – there are strict laws governing what has to be included and there are checks made by independent bodies – so it enables its readers to judge whether the company is being run well or badly.

There is probably someone in your club who already knows the rudiments of reading an annual report. If you haven't

got such a member, contact a local accountancy firm and explain that you would like someone to come along and explain to your club in layman's language how to read the accounts that are published in an annual report. If it's a go-ahead accountancy practice, on the ball and always looking for new contacts, they will send someone with pleasure. If they demur, next time you are looking for an accountancy practice to do business with, you will know the one not to use, won't you? Keep trying, you will find a speaker somewhere.

The second club I ever belonged to, the South Downs Investment Club in West Sussex, grew out of an evening investment course I went on at a college in Worthing. The course was run by an irascible old accountant called Fred – I forget his surname – who taught us that reading accounts was not too difficult. His problem was that he became irritated if some of us did not immediately grasp a point he was making so that people like me, who were never trusted with the chalk, tended to quell our questions and so only learned half of what we should have done. Don't let that happen at your club. Tell the speaker at the outset that you want a Janet-and-John explanation and encourage him or her to use actual examples.

I find the books or articles that use 'XYZ Company' or 'Feelgood plc' to illustrate their writings are extremely irritating. Why not use actual examples? It's much easier for us to relate to a company we have heard of. With that in mind I decided that when I came to this point in the book I would select the next annual report and accounts that was delivered and tell you how I read it and what I am looking for. Hey presto! This morning the annual report and accounts for The Shell Transport and Trading Company arrived through the letterbox. 'Ho, ho,' I hear you chortle. 'Serves him right for being so cocky. Let's see him explain Shell in Janet-and-John language. It's one of the biggest and most complicated companies in the world.' Well, sucks-boo to you, because Shell does the job for me.

Before we get on to the contents of the annual report, let me explain why it has come to me. The answer, obviously, is that I am a shareholder or rather my wife, Helen, is. More than that, it is by far the largest holding in her portfolio. She has held it for longer than any other share because we believe, to use their phrase, We Can be Sure of Shell. We regard it as money in the bank.

Shell has been a world-wide financial tower of strength for decades. It generates mountains of cash. Time has proved that it is well managed despite being sprawled around the globe and it works with a culture of co-operation rather than confrontation. We like that. Long-term alliances have been formed with a complex variety of governments. It is socially aware and in a volatile business it is a steady performer and a brand leader. This is a group with a total of more than a million shareholders. The shares of their two major companies are listed and traded on stock exchanges in eight European countries and in the USA. They operate in 135 countries around the world. And yet the Financial Highlights for the year are contained in 11 simple graphs and even the detailed Financial Statements cover just three pages. Both are reproduced here on pages 116–119 . . . (the whole report is 68 pages long).

Let us look at the Financial Highlights first. Whether you have Shell shares in £££s on the London Stock Exchange or $$$s in the USA you can see that the millennium year was excellent as far as earnings were concerned. No surprise really, the price of oil escalated and stayed on a high. A look at the previous year's report would show you that the company had calculated its conservative projections on the basis of a selling price of $14 a barrel and the reality was almost double that.

Our dividend is up again. Helen cares about that because our holding is significant enough for the annual payout to provide her with a clothing allowance for the year. I have tried to explain to her the power of compounding, reinvesting all dividends, but when it's a choice between that and Jaeger there is no contest. I wonder why the American

Royal Dutch Petroleum Company

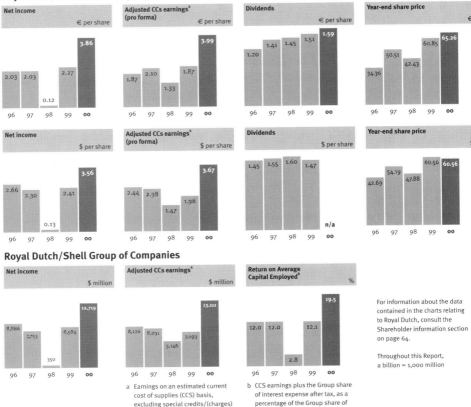

Fig 8.1 Financial highlights

Contents

Royal Dutch Petroleum Company

N.V. Koninklijke Nederlandsche
Petroleum Maatschappij

Founded on June 16, 1890

Carel van Bylandtlaan 30
2596 HR The Hague
The Netherlands

Summary of Group Results

Financial Results			$ million
	2000	1999	1998
Net income	**12,719**	8,582	350
Change	**+48%**	*+2,353%*	*–95%*
Earnings on an estimated current cost of supplies (CCS) basis	**12,364**	7,561	901
Change	**+64%**	*+739%*	*–89%*
Special credits/(changes)	**(747)**	468	(4,245)
Adjusted CCS earningsa	**13,111**	7,093	5,146
Change	**+85%**	*+38%*	*–36%*

a Earning on an estimated CCS basis excluding special items.

On an estimated current cost of supplies (CCS) basis excluding special items, earnings for the year – at $ 13,111 million – were 85% higher than those achieved a year ago. Reported net income for the year was $12,719 million, 48% above the 1999 result.

The overall business environment was more favourable as the benefit of higher oil and gas prices and higher refining margins more than offset the effects of lower marketing and chemicals margins. There was also a strong underlying earnings increase due mainly to cost improvements.

The cost improvement target for the end of 2001 (relative to the 1998 baseline), which was increased to $4 billion a year in December 1999, has been reached a full year ahead of schedule. The $4.0 billion achieved comprises $ 1.9 billion for Exploration and Production (of which $840 million was from exploration expense savings), $1.4 billion for Oil Products, $550 million for Chemicals and $130 million for other businesses. The new cost improvement target of $5 billion a year by the end of 2001, was announced in December 2000.

Capital investment for 2000 totalled $8.5 billion, 10% down from the 1999 figure. The return on average capital employed on a CCS earnings basis for the year was 19.5%; in 1999 it was 12.1%.

The total debt ratio at the end of the year was 11.0%; cash, cash equivalents and short-term securities amounted to $11.4 billion.

Underlying oil production growth for 2000 was 5%. Including the effects of divestments and production sharing contracts, oil volumes were essentially unchanged. Underlying gas production was 7% higher than in the previous year. Including the effects of divestments and production sharing contracts, gas volumes were 4% higher than last year.

Oil products sales volumes in 2000 were 4% higher than in 1999. Chemical sales volumes were lower than in 1999, however, excluding the effects of divestments and the formation of Basell, underlying chemicals business growth was 7%.

In 2000, Brent crude prices averaged $28.50 a barrel compared to $17.95 a barrel in 1999. Oil prices climbed steadily during much of the year due to production restraints by the major oil exporting countries. These restraints prevented global oil stocks from recovering to normal seasonal levels. Uncertainties over both economic growth and oil supply mean that crude prices are expected to remain volatile in 2001.

Industry refining margins recovered in all markets from the record low levels of 1999 as product stocks remained low throughout the year. Tighter product specifications and limited spare capacity in the USA and Europe are likely to support margins in these regions during 2001. In the Asia-Pacific region, margins are likely to be under pressure due to the regional over-capacity.

Chemicals trading conditions were particularly challenging. Towards the end of the year, cracker margins fell sharply to below the levels seen at the same time in 1999, and very difficult conditions prevailed in businesses downstream of the cracker. The outlook for Chemicals remains unsettled, especially in the USA, where there are uncertainties over economic growth and the cost of feedstocks and energy.

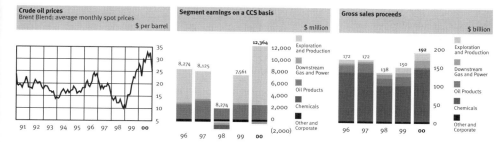

Fig 8.2 Operational and Financial Review

Exploration and Production

	2000	1999	1998
			$ million
Segment earnings	9,880	4,519	(247)
Special credits/(charges)	623	164	(2,221)
Adjusted segment earnings	9,257	4,355	1,974
Change	+ 113%	+121%	–57%

Earnings
Excluding special items, record adjusted earnings of $9,257 million were more than double the $4,355 million reported in 1999. The main reasons were higher oil prices (Brent was up 59%), higher gas realisations and volumes and lower operating and exploration expenses. Compared to the 1998 baseline, cost improvements reached $1.9 billion a year. This includes $840 million lower exploration expense.

Including a net special gain of $623 million, reported earnings amounted to $9,880 million. Special items comprised mainly the profits on sale of a number of assets in the USA, the UK and Australia.

Crude oil prices
Brent crude prices averaged $28.50 a barrel compared to $17.95 a barrel in 1999. Oil prices rose throughout much of the year due to production restraints by the major oil exporting countries which prevented global oil stocks from recovering to normal seasonal levels. Crude prices are expected to remain volatile in 2001.

Oil and gas production
Underlying oil production growth for the year was 5% as the benefits of new fields in the UK, USA, Oman and Canada and a lower impact from community disturbances in Nigeria were partly offset by normal field declines. Including the effects of divestments and production sharing contracts, oil volumes were essentially unchanged.

Underlying gas production for the year was 7% higher than in the previous year as increases in Oman, USA, UK, Egypt and Nigeria more than offset decreases in the Netherlands and Germany. Including the effects of divestments and production sharing contracts, gas volumes were 4% higher than last year.

Combined oil and gas production between 2000 and 2005 is expected to grow at an average annual rate of 5%. This growth rate is based on a diverse global portfolio which includes onshore and both deep and shallow offshore locations. These planned increases may be impacted by further portfolio actions and price conditions prevailing in the coming years.

Portfolio actions
The exchange of certain of the Group's interests in the UK North Sea and in the Gulf of Mexico for Marathon's interest in Sakhalin Energy in Russia was completed. A 7.5% interest in Sakhalin Energy was subsequently sold to Mitsubishi, resulting in a Group share of 55% and the lead role in the development and operation of the Sakholin project.

An offer was made for all of the shares in Woodside Petroleum Ltd, a company listed on the Australian stock exchange in which the Group currently has a 34% interest. The offer per share comprises A$14.80 plus a call option over one Woodside share, exercisable if a proposal to merge certain Group assets with Woodside is approved by Woodside shareholders. The offer is conditional on approval by the Foreign Investment Review Board in Australia.

The New Zealand Commerce Commission approved the Group's application to acquire Fletcher Challenge Energy (FCE). In early March 2001 the Group's offer was approved by FCE shareholders. It is anticipated that the acquisition will be finalised in the first quarter of the year.

In March 2001 a tender offer was made for all outstanding shares of Barrett Resources in the USA at $55 per share in cash, conditional upon, amongst other things, the acquistion of at least a majority of the outstanding shares.

In April 2000 the Group's 36% common interest in Altura – an associated company in the USA – was sold. The Group share of Altura's production in 1999 represented approximately 54,000 barrels of oil equivalent per day.

In Australia, the Group's interest in the Barrow and Thevenard Island (Carnarvon Basin) concessions was divested. In the UK, the divestment of the Group's interest in the Elgin and Franklin fields was concluded.

A letter of intent was signed to participate in the Saudi Natural Gas Initiative.

Capital investment
Capital investment of $5.0 billion was $0.4 billion lower than in 1999, reflecting continued investment discipline, stringent project selection, favourable exchange rate impact rind project rephasing.

Reserves
The proved hydrocarbon reserves replacement ratio for 2000 was 105% (before the effects of a significant divestment and acquisition programme). Therefore production during the year of 1.4 billion barrels of oil equivalent was more thon replaced. Including the net effect of divestments and acquisitions the replacement ratio was 69%.

The three-year rolling average proved hydrocarbon reserves replacement ratio (including oil sands and portfolio activities) stands at 117%.

The three-year rolling average oil and natural gas proved reserves replacement ratio (excluding oil sands) stands at 102%.

The additions to proved reserves arose mainly from discoveries and extensions in the USA and West Africa, improved recovery in Oman and Canada and revisions in existing fields in Oman and Venezuela, offset by the divestment of the Altura interest in the USA.

Statement of Income

$ million

	Note	2000	1999	1998
Sales proceeds		191,511	149,706	138,274
Sales taxes, excise duties and similar levies		42,365	44,340	44,582
Net proceeds		149,146	105,366	93,692
Cost of sales		118,328	81,839	76,674
Gross profit		30,818	23,527	17,018
Selling and distribution expenses		7,896	8,195	9,342
Administrative expenses		1,137	830	1,414
Exploration		755	1,086	1,603
Research and development		389	505	799
Operating profit of Group companies		20,641	12,911	3,860
Share of operating profit/(loss) of associated companies	6	3,859	2,321	(756)
Operating profit		24,500	15,232	3,104
Interest and other income	7	974	541	629
Interest expense	8	1,324	1,253	1,333
Currency exchange gains/(losses)		(114)	1	5
Income before taxation		24,036	14,521	2,405
Taxation	9	11,273	5,696	1,913
Income after taxation		12,763	8,825	492
Income applicable to minority interests		44	241	142
Net income		12,719	8,584	350

Statement of Comprehensive Income and Parent Companies' Interest in Group Net Assets

$million

	Note	2000	1999	1998
Net income	3	12,719	8,584	350
Other comprehensive income, net of tax:	5			
currency translation differences	19	(2,717)	(1,443)	482
unrealised gains/(losses) on securities		(238)	205	169
minimum pension liability adjustments		(70)	(95)	(13)
Comprehensive income		9,694	7,251	988
Net distributions to Parent Companies	3	(8,579)	(5,631)	(5,712)
Parent Companies' shares held by Group companies at January 1, 1998	22			(490)
Increase in Parent Companies' shares held by Group companies	22	(200)	(411)	(210)
Parent Companies' interest in Group net assets at January 1		56,171	54,962	60,386
Parent Companies' interest in Group net assets at December 31	4	57,086	56,171	54,962
Applicable to:				
Royal Dutch (60%)		34,252	33,703	32,977
Shell Transport (40%)		22,834	22,468	21,985
		57,086	56,171	54,962

Fig 8.3 Financial Statements

dividends are trailing downwards? I guess it must be because this is the trend in the US nowadays, but I'm no expert so I make a mental note to ask someone who is. Justin Urquhart-Stewart will know the answer, and if he doesn't I will get on to the Shell Company Secretary's department. I know the number will be at the end of the annual report.

The Financial Highlights appear on page 3 of the report so they immediately catch my eye. I examine them and they give me the warm glow that comes when I see things are going well. Now I slip into the routine procedure I adopt for reading all reports. They come in all shapes and sizes, whole forests are taken up with pretty pictures and flowery phrases, but I haven't got time to waste with such distractions so I have to cut through the frippery and get down to the facts. (Incidentally, here's a message for all those involved in producing these reports: study the Shell publication. It's a masterly interpretation of a complex organization and contains virtually everything the private or institutional shareholder wants to know.)

The first act of my routine is rather unusual. It is a tip I learned from Jim Slater. Look at the auditor's report. 'Always check the auditor's report first to make sure that the information has not been qualified in any way and confirms that the accounts give a true and fair view of the financial position of the company,' says Jim. 'The slightest qualification should be enough to encourage you to dispose of your shares immediately.' Auditors are usually independent

accountants who check the company's accounts to see they present a true and correct record. In Shell's case this will involve dozens of staff from KPMG and PricewaterhouseCoopers spending weeks checking and rechecking figures at Shell bases around the world. On page 36 of the annual report their findings are unequivocal: 'In our opinion the Financial Statements ... present fairly, in all material respects, the financial position of the Royal Dutch/Shell Group of Companies.' That's good enough for me.

Next stop is the Chairman's Statement. What I'm looking for here is very specific. I want a feel, an impression, of what has happened to the company during the year and what the big boss thinks is going to happen in the future. Chairmen (or chairwomen) are high profile, particularly in companies as big as Shell. They can't afford to hide anything under the carpet because truth will out, and when they look into their crystal balls the picture must be absolutely clear, otherwise the annual report will come back to haunt them. Honour can and does hang on the accuracy of a chairman's statement.

Despite this, of course, there are plenty of examples of company leaders who have got it wrong in their statements or at least furred the edges of the facts by using weasel words. From experience I know I'm safe with the Shell chairman. In two short pages, about 1,000 words, Sir Mark Moody-Stuart has to convey a complete picture of a huge and complicated world-wide operation so there's no room for flowery phrases or superfluous adjectives. Besides, my long-term interest in the business and my overall view of the financial highlights mean I am already aware he has a good story to tell. Petrol prices and the high cost of fuel generally might have been getting up the consumer's nose but it has meant a super bottom line for the oil companies.

Predictably, the statement is confident and I am relaxed. I notice though that it is Sir Mark's swansong as chairman. He's retiring later this year. How old is he? I check in the report. Just over 60, that's a bit young for retirement, I wonder why he is going? A note at the end of the Directors' Report tells me that he is staying as a non-executive director so that seems OK, but I will check what the word on the street is. More important though, who's taking over? I don't want some professional chairman who will just turn up at board meetings and chair the meetings like an automaton. Philip Watts is the new man at Shell's top and I am reassured. He's a man out of the Mark Moody-Stuart mould, been with the company since he was a lad, worked for Shell around the world. He's being elevated from chief executive and the picture in the annual report shows him in overalls and a hard hat. He's in his middle 50s so with luck he will steer the ship for a few years.

The financial facts

Now we come to the part of the examination exercise that those of us who are figuratively challenged would title Most Boring. And we would be wrong, wouldn't we? This is where the real story lies. And please, don't give me that creative accountancy argument and warn that if you look under the smooth stones you will find horrible wriggly things that have been hidden by the accountants. For goodness sake, life's too short, you have to trust somebody some time and I choose to accept the word of the Shell accountants, they are staff chosen because of their outstanding abilities and paid accordingly. I've been to Shell shareholder meetings, I know the pride in the company that is felt by the people who work there. That they have managed to condense the activities of tens of thousands of people at scores of bases around the world into three pages of easily comprehensible figures is nothing short of miraculous.

I'm not going to go through each of the headings and figures in the Financial Statements because they are mostly self-explanatory and in the annual report they are followed by 23 pages of explanatory notes and supplementary information which give much more financial detail of the group's separate activities. You should read them because they will increase your understanding of the business in which you own a share.

Along the way you will encounter jargon, language used by accountants, which is not deliberately created to make you feel small but does. Don't worry about it. People like us, who were not trusted with the chalk, should take time to understand the jargon and its significance by finding out the meanings and translating them into simple language.

Ever since I bought my first share I have kept a Little Black Book of words and phrases found in annual reports, which I have had to look up. Some, such as 'dividend' and 'turnover' seem so simple now that it is difficult to believe I didn't know what they meant but I can assure you it is true. Here is a list of terms, with explanations, that should help to get you started:

- **Acquisition.** No doubt about this word, it means one company has obtained control of another company lock, stock and barrel. It takes over everything – products, staff, buildings, debts, the lot. From this moment on, for business and reporting purposes, the two businesses are regarded as one. Incidentally, the purchase of the company that has been acquired need not necessarily be for cash. It could be a paper transaction involving shares of the parent company or a combination of cash and shares.

- **Assets.** Everything the company owns, from the stock in the warehouse to the cars in the car park.

- **Associated undertaking.** Nothing to do with a sideline in a funeral parlour. It means that Company A owns a large number of shares in Company B but not enough to have a controlling veto if Company B wants to do something Company A doesn't like.

- **Contingent liability.** Means we should be prepared, just in case something we think might happen, but we're not sure will happen, actually does happen.

- **Current assets.** Items which the company owns that will be used in the business during the current year. Things like cash in the bank, investments which can easily be cashed in, stocks of products, and debts that are owed to the company all come under this heading.

- **Current liabilities.** These are debts, amounts that have to be paid within a year. Could be taxes, loans, bank overdrafts, money for raw materials, dividends not yet paid to shareholders, anything that has to be paid out in the normal course of business.

- **Dividend.** This is the amount paid out to ordinary shareholders – that's you and me – during the year and usually comes in two parts at six-monthly intervals. It's our share of the profits but don't confuse it with earnings per share (see below). Our divvy is at the discretion of the directors. That's fair really because they are driving the bus and therefore should know how much of the earnings they need to retain for running the business. And if we don't think they're giving us enough we can always attend the annual general meeting and rattle their cage. The dividend is usually declared as an amount per share, so if you multiply the figure by the number of shares you hold you will know how much to expect. And remember, dividends are liable to income tax. An amount is deducted before you are paid so make sure each club member knows how much has been retained and how much his or her liability is.

- **Earnings per share.** Even someone who's no good with the chalk can work this one out.

EVER SINCE I BOUGHT MY FIRST SHARE I HAVE KEPT A LITTLE BLACK BOOK OF WORDS AND PHRASES FOUND IN ANNUAL REPORTS, WHICH I HAVE HAD TO LOOK UP. SOME, SUCH AS 'DIVIDEND' AND 'TURNOVER' SEEM SO SIMPLE NOW THAT IT IS DIFFICULT TO BELIEVE I DIDN'T KNOW WHAT THEY MEANT.

Take the company's annual profit figure after tax has been deducted. Divide it by the number of ordinary shares issued by the company. The result of doing the sum is the earnings per share (also explained in Chapter 7).

- **Exceptional items.** Most of the investment books that purport to be for beginners, and even those that are used by our more learned investors, fail to attempt a definition of this phrase, yet you will find it on most balance sheets. I interpret it as one-off changes or happenings in a business that have an impact on the year's results.

- **Extraordinary items.** Similar to the preceding item but more to do with actual profits or losses. Money items that are not part of the normal business of the company.

- **Financial instruments.** I'm happy to tell you this does not refer to a fiddle. Ho-ho. These instruments are things like bonds, loans and deposits and can be assets or liabilities. In some instances they do not appear in the main balance sheet but it is a fair bet they will be in the notes to the accounts.

- **Fixed assets.** Items or interests the company has which are used for running the business. Always check back on the previous year's fixed assets to see whether there have been any big changes. If so, find out why.

- **Gearing.** I explained this in the section on reading *REFS*, but to refresh your memory gearing is the comparison between what the company owes and what it owns. It is the ratio between the capitalization – the value of the shareholders' funds – and the amount it has currently borrowed to run the business. As a very general rule, if a company is geared at more than 50 per cent I want to know why, but much depends on the kind of business it is.

- **Going concern.** Good news. It means the business is expected to carry on trading.

- **Goodwill.** A hot potato subject. It's the good name and reputation of the company. But how do you value it? In takeover situations it is the difference between the price paid and the value of the assets and liabilities. Because I'm a simple soul, when I look at a company and try to assess its value I ignore goodwill, that way I make a conservative valuation and I'm consistent.

- **Group accounts.** This means that the parent company and all its subsidiaries are treated as a single entity. It also means that transactions between companies in the group are not included.

- **Intangible assets.** Things of value that are not touchy-feely. Royalties, patents, intellectual property, copyrights, brand names, trade marks and the ubiquitous goodwill.

- **Liabilities.** What the company owes to everyone.

- **Non-current liabilities.** Debts owed but it doesn't matter if they don't get paid off within the next 12 months.

- **Merger.** When two companies decide to join together, but no money moves out of the companies and no one has overall control after the deed is done, it's called a merger. When it is settled the balance sheets and profit and loss accounts are treated as one.

- **Minority interest.** Shareholders who own less than 50 per cent of the total equity.

- **Net current assets.** Another sum for the non-chalk-holders. Take the current liabilities away from the current assets and you are left with the net current assets.

- **Ordinary shares.** The best definition I have heard for this – for all I know it might be the official definition – is 'shares where the dividend can change with the level of profits'.

- **Preference shares.** If you hold these you are among the first in the queue when it comes to dividend payments, certainly you get yours before the ordinary shareholders. Preference shares usually have a fixed dividend rate too.

- **Provision.** It's the better-be-safe-than-sorry amount set aside to cover an expected loss or a liability than can't yet be properly quantified.

- **Proxy form.** Lets you pass your vote to someone else who can then vote on your behalf at the annual meeting.

- **Related party.** If Company A controls or has a significant influence over Company B, or if both of them are controlled or significantly influenced by another company or indeed one person, they are deemed to be related.

- **Reserves.** The parts of the profits that are kept in the share premium account just in case. If push came to shove these reserved funds would belong to the shareholders.

- **Revaluation reserve.** If an asset such as an office is revalued but not actually sold the gain is the revaluation reserve.

- **Rights issue.** Very popular way for a company to raise more money from its shareholders – remember how BT started to dig its way out of trouble in the summer of 2001? New shares are offered, usually at an attractive discount to the current price. Problem is that this results in more shares on the market which more often than not reduces the share price.

- **Scrip dividend.** You don't get a cheque you can cash, just more shares instead.

- **Share capital.** The money we shareholders put into the company.

- **Shareholders' funds.** Our funds plus those reserves I told you about.

- **Share premium account.** This is the amount of money paid for the shares over and above their face value at the time they are issued.

- **Subsidiary undertaking.** A grandiose phrase used to describe a business that is owned or controlled by the company.

- **Tangible assets.** Things the company owns that you can touch – land, buildings, equipment, cars, fixtures, fittings and so on.

- **Turnover.** The total value of all the sales made by the company during the year.

- **Working capital.** The money needed to run the business on a day-to-day basis. Basically it is the current assets minus the current liabilities.

Does this list clear up a few mysteries for you? Good. There is really no need to be frightened of the annual report and accounts, as long as you know the basics you should be able to understand most of what is inside those glossy covers and if you have a reasonably disciplined approach you will not be confused or wooed by the load of bumf that often surrounds the essential information. Tackle the job with a notebook beside you to write your comments and queries and do it in this order:

1. Check the independent auditors' report to see that they are totally happy with everything they have seen and have no reservations in approving the figures.

2. Read the chairman's statement. Is it full of superfluous phrases and clichés designed to pacify you? Does it go on and on thanking old and decrepit directors you've never heard of who are retiring? Or is it, like Mark Moody-Stuart's statement, a clear and concise account of what happened during the relevant year together with an outline of the company's approach to future market challenges and an informed prediction of how the company will perform against its peers?

3. If the company or group is large enough there will most probably be other statements from top people too, the chief executive officer and managing directors of the various divisions. Read these with the same dispassionate eye. You want facts and expert opinion, not platitudes.

4. Now study the financial summary. Compare the performance with previous years – in properly constructed reports all such facts will be included – to see whether the company is expanding, contracting or just lying fallow.

5. Look at the balance sheet, the profit and loss account and the cash flow statement. This will give you a feel for the company's size and will tell you how profitable it is. You will also

IF YOU HAVE A REASONABLY

DISCIPLINED APPROACH

YOU WILL NOT BE CONFUSED OR WOOED

BY THE LOAD OF BUMF THAT OFTEN SURROUNDS

THE ESSENTIAL INFORMATION.

be able to assess its ability to generate cash, which is the lifeblood of the business.

6. Turn to the notes to the accounts. Read them carefully and take time to understand them because this is the flesh on the balance sheet bones. It is detailed information about the sales and profits, showing which areas produce the best returns. You will learn more about the assets and liabilities of the business.

7. Now look at the things that particularly interest you. Directors' remuneration is one item that seems to annoy some investors, they get all huffy if they see that top management are getting huge salaries and big bonuses. Personally, I don't give a damn so long as the company is doing well for us shareholders. There's a lot of competition out there to attract the best people and I want them working for the companies I own. If we have to pay top dollar for their loyalty, so be it. Far more important as far as I am concerned are the shareholdings of the directors. I want them all to have a substantial stake in the company so that when it comes to making difficult decisions in the board room they have their own pockets in mind as well as ours.

8. Finally, look at the pretty pictures as long as they relate to the business and are not simply library shots of sunsets and beautiful people. Someone once told me to beware of companies that used sandy beach photographs in their annual reports, they would be bust within five years. I'm not sure whether it is true but it sounds very likely.

ANNUAL REPORTS AND ACCOUNTS SHOULD NEVER BE THE BE ALL AND END ALL OF YOUR RESEARCH. THEY HAVE THE OBVIOUS DRAWBACK THAT THEY ARE OUT OF DATE WHEN THEY REACH YOU AND BECAUSE THEY ARE PRODUCED BY THE COMPANIES THEMSELVES THEY WILL INEVITABLY ATTEMPT TO PRESENT THE BEST POSSIBLE SPIN ON THE FACTS.

Annual reports and accounts should never be the be all and end all of your research. They have the obvious drawback that they are out of date when they reach you and because they are produced by the companies themselves they will inevitably attempt to present the best possible spin on the facts. But I contend that the documents are essential if you are to get to know the company and its activities. You should not contemplate an investment without first having read and digested a company's annual offering to its shareholders.

Well done, Little One. You've passed all your exams and it's time to go out into the big world. You're going to earn a lot of money and it's going to make the whole family very happy. What is it Woody Allen said? 'Money beats poverty, if only for financial reasons.' You listen to your Uncle Woody. And be sensible, don't be in too much of a hurry to get rich. You might think you know it all, but you don't. There's still a lot to learn. Watch out for the baddies and don't listen to those people who say they can turn water into wine. Come and sit up here with Daddy and I'll tell you some stories that might help.

Concerned Parent

PART

3

THE FACTS OF LIFE

When the stock doubles, sell it.

If it doesn't double, don't buy it.

Will Rogers

CHAPTER

WHO'S LOOKING
AFTER THE
SHOP?

Examining directors' dealings is now accepted as a good yardstick by which to judge any company. Many of the specialist investor publications and websites list them on a regular basis and they are a good indicator of the present state of the company. After all, if the people who run the joint are buying shares it must be telling us something, mustn't it? Conversely, if they are dumping their holdings, we would be daft not to take note and consider jumping ship too, wouldn't we? Well ... yes and no. Like all investing rules it ain't always the case, so let me give you a more detailed explanation of what you should be looking for and also a much more relevant test I use to assess the dedication and beliefs of directors.

There's a general misconception that a single director buying or selling is not particularly significant. The reasoning is that in the case of a purchase he or she might have had a windfall and so wants to park the money, or if there's a share sale involved it could be because the cash is needed for an unrelated expenditure such as a wedding or school fees. I don't subscribe to the view that these are unrelated personal financial decisions and therefore irrelevant, in fact, particularly if the amount is significant, I take more notice if just one member of the board is making a move. If lucky Joe or Jill has come into a few bob and opts to buy shares in the company, surely that's a good sign? The money could have gone to purchase another organization's equity or a new car or a cruise, but no – our director has

enough faith in the future of his or her company to plant more seed money there. On the other hand if there is a sudden need for cash, why sell shares? There are plenty of other ways to raise readies including the most obvious, a bank overdraft. Selling shares tips me off that the director is not expecting much upward movement in the share price in the immediate future.

Most analysts will tell you that a cluster of directors buying is a good thing. I'm not convinced. It's not difficult to imagine a board room scene with the chairperson saying, 'Now pay attention, lads and lasses, we've got to do something to bump this share price up. If we all buy a few quid's worth of shares the market will think there's something up and we'll create a demand.'

So my advice is, when you are looking at directors' dealings, pay attention to the size of the deal. If it is relatively small (and I suppose I am thinking of anything below £10,000) then don't take too much notice, whether it is a single transaction or a whole group of them. Look too at the price paid, make sure it relates to the price you see quoted, because if it is simply a director realizing an option then it is not necessarily significant.

And mention of the size of the deal brings me to the yardstick relating to directors' holdings that I always consider when I am researching a company. I want each and every director, whether he or she works full-time for the company or is there in a non-executive capacity, to have a meaningful shareholding. Again, this can't be a rule set in stone because I realize that young directors may not have had time to accrue many shares, so I try to find out how long each person has been on the board. If they have sat there for more than three years then, in the case of employee directors, they should hold shares equivalent in value to at least one year's salary. And if they are non-executive their holding should be at least equivalent to one year's fees. In this way I will feel comfortable that the people who are running the show are just as keen as I am to see the share price rise.

Learn from the golfers

If memory serves me well – though it rarely does nowadays – it was the South African golfer Gary Player who said, 'The more I practise, the luckier I get.' This can be applied to almost every activity but it is particularly apt in the case of investment clubs. However, before you rush off and start buying and selling shares like billy-oh in the hope that your members will become better investors, that isn't exactly what Mr Player meant. He was referring to the countless hours he spent on the golf driving range examining, testing, altering, and tweaking his golf swing in an effort to ensure that when he went out on to the golf course to pit his abilities against his fellow professionals, that little golf ball would do what he wanted it to do. He was aiming to hit the perfect shot every time and the only way he could get anywhere near that ambition was to make sure that the routine he went through to hit the ball was replicated on each occasion. Equally important, if the shot was not perfect he would immediately examine his swing to find out what he had done wrong. In other words, he learned from his mistakes and made sure he did not repeat them.

Selecting shares that win is not down to luck, it is about routine and practice. I may sound like a gramophone record but it is imperative that your club has an aim (presumably, like Gary Player's perfect golf shot, it is to consistently choose winning shares) and that you establish a system that gives you a better-than-even chance of reaping profits. So here's a little prayer you can chant in unison before the start of every meeting:

'THE MORE I PRACTISE, THE LUCKIER I GET.' THIS CAN BE APPLIED TO ALMOST EVERY ACTIVITY BUT IT IS PARTICULARLY APT IN THE CASE OF INVESTMENT CLUBS.

We're going to research every share suggestion before we make the decision to purchase. We're going to completely understand the company we are considering – what it does to make its profits, its track record over the last five years, the standard of its management. We're going to be absolutely sure that every member present feels informed enough to make a decision before we vote. Amen.

Learn from those mistakes

Here's another tip I have cribbed from Mr Player's description of his routine. After he had hit a poor shot he immediately examined his actions to see what he had done wrong. So your club should take time to look back over recent months, identify loss makers – those you have sold or ones you still hold that are showing a paper deficit – and find out what went wrong. Why didn't these disappointments perform as you had expected? Was the company over-optimistic in its forecasts? Was your decision to buy built on half-hopes rather than hard financial facts? When you bought the shares you were convinced they were winners. If you did your research properly and the indicators that persuaded you to buy still hold good then it might only be a matter of time before other investors spot the opportunity and confirm what a clever club yours is. But if you made a mistake, or indeed several

mistakes, then be big enough to admit it. As long as you learn from the errors and don't repeat them the learning experience will stand you in good stead.

The club that never sells

On occasion I spread my writing talents to locations various national newspapers and financial magazines. In ProShare's *Dividend* magazine I make a regular appearance under the pseudonym of Portfolio Doctor. Investment clubs are invited to submit information about their portfolios: names of shares, when they were purchased, prices paid and so on. From all the portfolios sent in I select one and analyze it in detail then give my honest opinion about the individual holdings as well as my thoughts on the balance of the portfolio. I also suggest any changes I think the club could advantageously make to benefit its overall position. My diagnosis is published in the magazine in the hope that it will help other clubs as well as the one that was put under my microscope.

So what qualifies me to give such advice? Well, not a lot really. I'm not an Independent Financial Adviser or a stockbroker, just a professional private investor who has been learning and earning his living from the stock market for more than a decade and who believes that being a member of several investment clubs has increased his ability to make a profit. And of course the clubs are under no obligation to heed my words of wisdom.

In medical terms I am a GP rather than a specialist so in the course of a year I see dozens of portfolio problems but every now and again I see something that beggars belief. It happened when I received an e-mail from a club in the north of England (I will save the members' blushes by withholding the name of the club) which had been formed about two years ago. The members were concerned about the club's poor performance and felt a visit to the doctor was necessary.

I examined the list of purchases since formation and overall the balance of the portfolio was not too bad. Roughly about a third of the £20,000 income had been spend on FTSE 100 blue chips, about 40 per cent on middle-market stocks and the balance on what I would call 'hope' shares. Admittedly this latter bunch had no track record (indeed, a couple were so obscure that I must confess I had never heard of them) and I suppose the club could be criticized for taking such risks. However, it would be a boring old club that never had the occasional flutter on a rank outsider. Anyway, it was not that aspect of the portfolio that caused my anxiety. Nor was it the fact that the club seemed to have been unlucky enough to make its purchases when each share price was at its zenith so that all bar one of the investments had shown a loss to date. No, the really amazing and worrying feature of the portfolio was that during the two years of its existence *the club had bought 25 different shares and never sold a single one of them!* Can you believe that? From the balance sheet I deduce that each month the club receives subscriptions of about £800 and at the monthly meeting members vote to buy a different share. They have over two dozen shares now, almost all of them losing money (the total value of the portfolio is under £13,000 which means they are showing a loss of more than 30 per cent) and yet the club has never voted to sell a loser.

Here's a copy of my advice to this misguided club:

1. **Has your club never heard of selling shares? I've been involved with investment clubs for eight years now and I have never come across a club that has so many stocks in its portfolio.**

2. **Establish a maximum number, say 12, and ruthlessly prune the size of your portfolio.**

3. **Get rid of the dross. Some of your holdings are OK but there are a few strange shares in your list. These hope tiddlers were bought for a reason – maybe a sure-fire tip which you were so enthusiastic about that you did not bother to research it properly – but you have had them long enough to realize that the hope is never going to be realized. Cut your losses and don't look back.**

4. **Become enthusiastic and active investors. Appoint a 'champion' for each of your shares. The champion's job is to monitor his or her share on a daily basis and if there is a price movement or some news find out what it is all about. Then, in**

consultation with only the chairman, the champion has the power to authorize a sell decision.

5.   Establish a stop-loss policy and stick to it rigidly.

6.   Don't despair. Like many young clubs you have had teething troubles but if you do your research carefully, stick to reliable growth shares and ignore penny poopers that promise so much but rarely deliver, you will get rich steadily but surely.

··

I had a dream

One of the first investment clubs I ever joined – it must be more than a decade ago now – was formed with a specific aim. There were just a dozen members, we were each going to put in £50 a month, buy shares, and when we had a large and profitable portfolio we were going to sell a considerable proportion of the shares and purchase a château in France. Each member would be entitled to a month's occupancy (he or she could use it themselves or let it out) and the months would be allocated on a rotational basis so that every member got his or her share of the summertime. This was to be timesharing between friends and after we had bought the property we would continue to contribute £50 a month to buy shares so that our small portfolio would provide enough profit to cover the maintenance.

It was a great notion, a way to make a dream come true. After all, where does it say in the rules that your club investments should be restricted to shares? Why not a property in France? Or Lanzarote? Or Rhyl? (No, perhaps not Rhyl. But you get the general idea.)

The only drawback to the club's plan was our approach to selecting the shares that were going to do so well they would

MAYBE IT WAS A COMBINATION OF INEXPERIENCE, LAZINESS, DRINK AND INCOMPETENCE

BUT OUR PORTFOLIO WAS

A HOUSE OF CARDS BUILT ON PENNY-SHARE TIPS, WHISPERS HEARD IN THE BACKS OF TAXIS AND NOD-NOD, WINK-WINKS FROM PEOPLE WHO THOUGHT THEY KNEW BUT DIDN'T.

make our dream come true. We didn't get that quite right. Indeed, not to put too fine a point on it, we got it horribly wrong. We were young, headstrong and thirsty and we met in a West End pub after work. Maybe it was a combination of inexperience, laziness, drink and incompetence but our portfolio was a house of cards built on penny-share tips, whispers heard in the backs of taxis and nod-nod, wink-winks from people who thought they knew but didn't.

Our portfolio withered on the vine and our château became a *gite*, then the *gite* became a pigsty that would need extensive refurbishment. The dream was shattered and the members became dispirited. We disbanded.

However, there are two principles here that are worthy of examination. The first is that there's nothing wrong in a club having an aim in life other than money. Working towards a pot of gold that is to be used for a specific purpose – in this case a glorious holiday home – means that there is a tangible result for success. It might be a river cruiser, or an annual club visit to exotic climes for members and their families. It could just be a way of raising money to make a large collective charitable donation. Be careful though, make sure that everyone shares the enthusiasm for the end game.

The second point of principle is more crucial and perhaps was at the root of our club's failure. The main aim of our club when it started was not to learn how to invest in shares wisely. Not a bit of it, our desire was to have a holiday home on the other side of the Channel. We didn't want to waste our evenings doing boring things like researching companies, reading annual reports, checking on news about specific businesses and comparing historical prices. Long-term investing was not on our agenda. We were going to shoot for the sky, have a gamble on a bunch of outsiders, pick some big money winners and quit while we were ahead. Believe me, it never works like that. Sure, you may have beginner's luck and pick a penny share that becomes a pound. Maybe you can do it a second time. But it is a philosophy that will end in tears.

By all means have a dream, an aim, a goal for your club. But first you must make sure you have the means and the ability to get there. You must become accomplished investors, confident and knowledgeable enough to build a strong portfolio. That's the way to make dreams come true.

Day traders

Once upon a long time ago, as a yearling reporter on a Sunday tabloid newspaper, I was sent to cover the auditions for the auditions of a television programme called *Opportunity Knocks*. Hosted by a bad-tempered Canadian called Hughie Green (remember him?), it was the equivalent of today's *Stars in Their Eyes* and the pre-audition auditions involved

an endless stream of wannabe Beatles, Cilla Blacks and Tony Hancockses strutting their stuff early one morning in a cold warehouse in West Bromwich. For me it was a rather uncomfortable experience. I remember thinking of Robbie Burns's famous line 'Oh Lordie, would the gift thee gi'e us – to see ourselves as others see us.' The singers, nervous and some without music, were often tone deaf. The comedians used material recycled from the school playground and thought timing meant how quickly they could gabble their lines.

These hopefuls were dreaming the dream but sadly there was no possibility that any of them would ever make it on to the professional stage or screen. They were ill prepared and amateurish and were doomed to devastation when they received the inevitable 'We regret your audition was not successful' letter. Thankfully the only thing that would be hurt was their pride, but that is not the case with those foolish folk, either individually or as members of investment clubs, who have been lured by the temptation of day trading on the stock market. Day traders put themselves in real danger of losing their savings, homes, friends and even families as they chase the dragon of easy and instant profits.

Like the would-be singers and funny men and women, the day trader has a dream. After a hearty breakfast he or she wanders into the study, switches on the computer and looks to see which shares are increasing in value, gives the broker a call and buys a fistful, waits a couple of hours until the prices have gone up

SOME DAY TRADERS DO MAKE A GOOD LIVING

BY TAKING ADVANTAGE OF MARKET VOLATILITY

RATHER THAN LONG-TERM TRENDS.

NOTICE I SAY 'SOME' TRADERS.

THE EXACT FIGURE, OUT OF 10 DAY TRADERS,

IS TWO.

further, sells at a nice profit, repeats the exercise a couple more times before lunch then takes the afternoon off. Nice work if you can get it, and there is no doubt that some day traders do make a good living by taking advantage of market volatility rather than long-term trends. Notice I say 'some' traders. The exact figure, out of 10 day traders, is two. The other eight lose money and most of them lose their shirts as well.

But perhaps you are on of the blessed 20 per cent? Well, here's a checklist to see whether you could be among the chosen few:

- **You must be rich already.** To gamble and win at this level you must be able to survive those times when the shares you choose fall completely out of bed for no discernible reason. Realistically I reckon you should have at least £100,000 of stake money to stand even the remotest chance of winning.

- **You must understand exactly what you are doing.** You have to be able to

place bets on a falling market as well as when prices rise. It is known as going short as opposed to long. So first you must have a thorough knowledge of the workings of the market and devise a method and a discipline which you must follow no matter what happens.

- **Be prepared to sit at your desk day and night.** Forget that game of golf or shopping spree. While you have money in the market you must keep your eyes riveted to the screen. And if you want to play the American market as well as London you will have to do a night shift.

- **You must be an automaton, a mathematics graduate, fit as a flea with nerves of steel.** You are swimming in shark-infested waters. There are others out there with much more money than you and they are trying to beat you. When you have decided your strategy, nothing must divert you; emotion must not enter into the equation. As the figures on the screen move you must be able to calculate in your head exactly what they mean to you. Your reaction when you hit that 'trade' button must be at the speed of light. And, when you see prices going against you, refrain from panic.

If, hand on heart and in the privacy of your own home, you honestly believe that these four bullet points epitomize your personal strengths then by all means consider taking up day trading for a living. And good luck to you.

Outsider information

In a later chapter you will find my rather eclectic suggestions for books you should read. Top of my list is *The Investors Guide to Selecting Shares That Perform* by Richard Koch. I've never met Mr K and don't know much about him other than the fact that a decade or so ago he masterminded the turnaround of the Filofax company and in four years increased its share value by 760 per cent. I also know he has written one of the easiest to understand investment books I have ever read. It's packed with wise words which provide food for investor thought. Typical is his explanation of 'Outsider Information':

'Outsider information' is information gathered on a company by outside research which can be used to inform share purchase or sale decision. 'Insider information' is used for the same

purpose. But outsider information is different in a number of ways:

1. Outsider information is not short-term, price-sensitive information obtained from a contact inside the company. Instead, it is your own market research from talking to a variety of sources including customers, competitors and suppliers of the company in question as well as industry observers and other outside experts. Outsider information can also include data gleaned from talking to employees of the company, provided that they are told honestly that you are a researcher or investor and do not divulge information of a price-sensitive nature.

2. Outsider information is concerned with the long-term market and competitive position of the company, not short-term 'secrets' regarding impending actions or deals.

3. Outsider information requires data gathering, analysis and reflection before making purchase or sale decisions.

4. Outsider information, correctly analyzed, is much more reliable than insider information, where the rumoured deal may never happen or the market reaction may be different from what was expected.

5.   **Most importantly, use of outsider information is completely legal, whereas insider information can land you inside one of HM's prisons.**

I can think of no better description of what a club is trying to find out when it sets about researching a potential investment.

Money beats poverty, if only for financial reasons.

Woody Allen

QUESTIONS,

QUESTIONS

One of my jobs at ProShare is to help the excellent team there to answer letters and e-mails from some of the 150,000 people who are members of investments clubs around the country.

I have dipped into the postbag for a handful that I think will help clubs generally.

Q *Our club wants to use share dividends to buy premium bonds. Is that permissible? And can we buy them in the name of the club?*

A The short answer is 'No'. Premium bonds have to be bought in the name of an individual. I suppose if you want to buy bonds – and remember, there's a minimum amount which I believe as I write is £100 – one of your members could buy them in his or her name. But if you do go down this route make sure that you get a solicitor to draw up a legal agreement, signed by the premium bonds' owner, saying that any amount won by the bond will go immediately into club funds to be divided equally between the members. Warning: Don't rely on an amateur wording for the agreement that you have decided between yourselves. It has to be legal and watertight – suppose you won £250,000?

Q *I want to start an investment club but I'm having difficulty explaining the basic concept to my friends. Is there any literature that puts it all in a nutshell?*

A There is. A leaflet entitled 'A Way to Earn, A Way to Learn' is available free from ProShare. It gives you all the basic information about what a club is and how easy it is to start one. (Incidentally, the leaflet is beautifully written – I did it.) Ring 020 7220 1750 and tell them how many copies you require.

Q *One of our members is paranoid about the possibility of someone defrauding the club and the fact that, as partners, we would all be responsible. Is there any way of insuring against such an eventuality?*

A Your member is right in that your club is regarded as a partnership and in all probability you would all suffer if any member perpetrated fraud in the name of the club. It is a responsibility of which you should be mindful. Having said that, the rules of your club should be pretty fraud-proof and the agreement you have with your stockbroker is an added safeguard. Touch wood, I do not know of a case of fraud involving properly constituted investment clubs in Britain, although I seem to recall something rather iffy in Australia a while back. A couple of years ago we asked clubs if they were interested in taking out a fraud insurance policy but there was not enough interest then to make it viable.

Q *We're a group of friends, near neighbours actually, we formed our club a year ago. Because none of us knew much about the stock market we determined that we would minimize risk and stick to blue chip shares to start with so our first investments have been long-*

term FTSE 100 companies with the exception of one share on which we had 'insider information' because one of our members had worked for the company concerned for over 20 years and told us that the order books were full. The trouble is that the share prices have been going down! What are we doing wrong and how do we avoid risk?

A Let's get one thing straight from the start. Buying shares is a risky business. You can't avoid risk altogether because, no matter how carefully you select your investment, there are matters that can affect the share price and over which you have no control. Here are a few:

- World events. Who could have foreseen America's presidential pantomime. Or the Twin Towers horror? Or the rail chaos and floods here at home? These situations can and do cause havoc on global markets.

- The general economy. Inflation and interest rates are constantly on the move and can affect the price of individual stocks and/or sectors.

- Currency changes. A company which relies on overseas dealings for its sales or purchases knows that a change in the currency rates can have an adverse or advantageous effect on its bottom line. The company can take precautions by buying or selling currencies ahead but this adds to the risk.

- Management changes. The head honcho of a company can retire or simply walk out because he or she has had a better offer. In some instances entire management teams are poached by opposition companies, leaving a serious hole to be filled.

- Fashion. Investor fads are created overnight and disappear with the same rapidity.

There is nothing you can do about these things and they cannot figure in your initial assessment of the company because, although you can take intelligent guesses, they are largely unpredictable.

So, if shares are risky investments because their prices can fluctuate wildly, what can you do? The answer is straightforward and simple. You minimize the risk to insignificance by creating a well-diversified portfolio of high-quality stocks. Monitor the portfolio carefully, sell those shares that become dangerously over-popular and have a stop-loss policy that will weed out those that are not living up to your expectations.

And, as far as your present predicament is concerned, let me offer you two crumbs of comfort. The effects created by the types of happenings listed above are usually short-lived. As my friend and colleague Jim Slater is so fond of saying, 'Excesses usually regress to the norm.' (Incidentally, that is why he is wary of companies with very high PERs.) So in the long term your safety-first

approach, selecting shares that have already proved their worth as long-term occupants of a FTSE 100 place, should show you positive results. Another truism is that today's winners are invariably tomorrow's winners. Conversely, today's losers are usually tomorrow's losers.

So examine your portfolio carefully. Check the results for the past five years. Look for growth in revenues and earnings per share, pretax profit margins and the percentage earned on invested capital. If they all look good then hang on in there. Say your prayers, don't kick the cat and everything should be alright.

Q *I can't make up my mind whether to start a club among my friends or go for one that has members who are relative strangers but have a wide range of experience and skills. What do you think?*

A No contest. Go for friends every time. The Americans have done research in this area and, while a range of experience and skills is important, your club has a much greater chance of success if its members are friends beforehand and feel comfortable in each other's company. It's about looking forward to being together. Trust me, I have been to dozens of club meetings and those that comprise people who were strangers before the club formed stick out like a sore thumb. You just can't put a handful of strangers in a room and expect them to like each other so much they want to do it all again next month.

Q *Our club meets in the private room of a local pub. We don't pay for the room hire; the pub makes its profit from us in*

YOU JUST CAN'T PUT A HANDFUL OF STRANGERS IN A ROOM AND EXPECT THEM TO LIKE EACH OTHER SO MUCH THEY WANT TO DO IT ALL AGAIN NEXT MONTH.

drinks and the basket meals we have. The problem is the meals, I'm the treasurer and have to order the food two days before the meeting. I have difficulty in collecting the money, typically £7 to £10 a head, and people who apologize late or just don't turn up – admittedly they usually have a good excuse – are particularly unhappy about paying at all.

A Increase the monthly subscription by £10 to cover the cost of the meal. You will find your average attendance will shoot up and there will be a residue in the kitty at the end of the year to pay for the Christmas party.

Q *How do I calculate investment growth? I like to know how individual shares are doing, not just since we bought them (which our treasurer's report gives us) but in the current year. It gives me a feel for what's happening now rather than over the years. Trouble is, I am pretty hopeless at maths.*

A I am hopeless at sums too. I turned the sums teacher at Tettenhall College, Miss Pond, grey. Unsurprisingly I have never been asked to do the treasurer's job for an investment club but, because

basic maths is an essential requisite if you are to be a private investor, I have taught myself the rudiments of the game.

Here's how to work out your percentage growth for the current year. Find out the value of the share at the beginning of the year. Find out the value today. Take the first figure away from the second figure, divide the result by the first figure and multiply by 100.

Confused? I don't blame you, so let's do it with actual figures.

The share's mid-price valuation meant at the beginning of the year your holding totalled £5,000. A month or so has passed and today it is worth £6,000. Your paper profit this year is therefore £1,000. Divide that £1,000 by the £5,000 value at the beginning of the year (use a calculator, it's quicker). The result is 0.20. Multiply that by 100 to give you the percentage – i.e. 20 per cent.

Q *One member of our club is a share genius. He was in insurance but was made redundant and now he studies the markets all day. He subscribes to REFS and Updata and is becoming something of a local guru because he writes an investment column in the weekly* *newspaper. Some of us have talked about asking him to do the share picking for the club and produce a list of recommendations each month for the club to consider. We think it would give us a much better chance of picking winners than asking inexperienced members who haven't got his available time or knowledge to do the job half as well. What do you think?*

A I hope he tells you to get knotted. If he's got any sense he will because the burden you are putting on him is unacceptable. Suppose he picks a bag of nails? You little lemmings will follow him over the cliff and I can just hear your accusatory squeals as you plunge towards the rocks: 'But Sidney, you told us ...'

By all means get this special chap to give you guidance, but it must be with a view to making you competent investors too. Ask him to talk for five minutes at each meeting on a different aspect of investing. Get him to explain the systems and sieves he uses. Reprint copies of his newspaper column and give them to any new members. Make him a star of your club, be proud of his abilities, offer to help him with his researches, covet him but never put the onus on his shoulders of being the one member responsible for selecting your shares. Trust me, unless your club is democratic it will die.

Q *I'm in the process of approaching friends at work who I think might want to join a new club. While there's a general interest I sense they are worried about the commitment because the question I keep being asked is 'How much of my spare time will it take up?'*

A At first sight this is a 'How long is a piece of string?' question and the temptation is to say 'Don't worry. We only meet once a month.' That would be wrong. An investment club is a commitment and it does take time. It is difficult to be specific but your potential members should understand that in addition to the monthly meetings, which will take up about three hours plus travelling time, they will be expected to do their share of the research. I estimate this might add up to a total of four hours per month. Be on the safe side and say an average of two hours a week. This may put a few people off but it is better to be clear from the outset that members will be expected to play their part rather than leave all the work to the chosen few. Incidentally, officers of the club should add a further couple of hours to their monthly time commitment.

Q *I guess you would call our club unusual. There are just four of us, all housewives and mothers, and when we have dropped off the kids at school we drive to my house for a cup of tea and an investment club meeting (we started off as a slimmers' club but that didn't work). Anyway, we meet five days a week during term time, I've got a computer which gives real-time prices via the Market Eye service, and we feel we are ideally placed to do a bit of day trading. Are there any rules that say we can't do this?*

A Not that I'm aware of. By all means day trade if you want to. At this point I

I HAVE MET A TOTAL OF NINE DAY TRADERS IN THE PAST YEAR, ALL OF THEM HAVE SUFFERED SUBSTANTIAL LOSSES AND TWO ARE ON THE VERGE OF BANKRUPTCY.

could put my Old Woman hat on and bang on about the dangers of this kind of investing, but I take the Samaritans approach, which is that if a stranger makes contact and asks you a question, they have already decided, albeit subconsciously, what they are going to do. So, rather than give you advice about making sure you know what you are doing and warnings about the stamp duty which is payable on each transaction and the spread between buying and selling prices, let me pass on one fact. I have met a total of nine day traders in the past year, all of them have suffered substantial losses and two are on the verge of bankruptcy.

Q *A group of us, all neighbours, have just had a meeting to discuss forming a club and – would you believe it? – we've had our first disagreement. We can't get unanimous approval for the name. One faction want the Coniston Investment Club (that's the name of our road) and the others are keen on the FISS Investment Club, which is an acronym for mentally challenged people selecting shares. Are there any rules about this? And which one do you like?*

A You're not going to believe me, but this is important. A name is something you are going to have to live with. I grew up in the era when tuberculosis was rife and I could have cursed my parents for landing me with the initials TB. I also know at least one club that has become extremely successful with members who are such sensible investors that they are in demand for television and radio appearances and interviews with the press. The core of the club is a group of police officers who chose the name Elizabeth Swalocs for their club. For those who don't know – and I must confess I didn't until someone explained it to me – that's a fairly well-known joke involving the short form of the Christian name and the juxtaposition of the initial letters that results in a rude expression. Work it out for yourself, it will make you smile. Certainly it's funny to an adult audience but on two occasions I have had television programmes turn them down, for an interview and a panel game, because the name would have to be explained. The same problem applies to another of ProShare's members, the Acquisition of Random Shares and Equities club. The BBC won't have them on before the watershed 9 p.m.

I wouldn't presume to adjudicate between Coniston and FISS. To be honest, I don't think much of either of them, the first one's boring and the other, if I have worked it out correctly, would be embarrassing to explain in mixed company. My advice is to find a name that gives you a smile and not a snigger. Here's just a few from ProShare's database of over 10,000 that appealed to me.

Common Cents	Relief of the Poor
Canny Wee	Relentless Tortoise
Peeny Pichers and Skinflints	Inn Cider Dealers
	Stinking Bishops
Willy Chuff Chuff	Aberdabadoo
Quidsin	Profits of Boom
Bullish Lambs	Leaping Spiders
Unusual Pigs Delight	Nowt to do with me pal
Great Expectations	E.Buggers!
The Mole in the Wall Gang	Whoshareswins
Bucket and Plunger	Pile High Club
	Fat Cigars
Wires and Pliers	Nervous Tics

There are also over 70 Midas Investment Clubs, several dozen Millennium Millionaires, and so many Golden Girls we've lost count. So do try to be original.

Q *One of the ways we want to improve our investment knowledge it is get some hands-on experience by visiting a quoted company and talking to the people who run it. How do we go about making the arrangements, and could we go as a club or should we send just one or two people as our representatives?*

A First, let me say this is a great idea and I would recommend it to any club. Company visits are common practice for clubs in countries like the USA and Sweden, and here the idea is catching on. Certainly the vast majority of quoted companies will welcome you.

Ideally you should start your visit programme with a company local to your area and if possible choose one where there's something to see as well as talk about. One of the utilities – water, power, that sort of thing – would be perfect. In these cases you should ring up and ask for the Investor Relations Department. Explain that you are an investment club and that you are considering an investment in the business so you would like to look around and ask some questions. If they are any good at their job (and most of them are) you will be welcomed with open arms. This is what they are there for. There is probably a standard tour, but my advice is to say that's all very nice but it does not quite satisfy your needs. Is there a chance of talking to the finance director or, better still, the chief executive? Make it plain you are not planning to ask any difficult or complicated questions, it is just that you genuinely would like to invest in local businesses so you want to find out more about them. Pound to a penny they will welcome you with open arms, lay on refreshments for you and turn out the top brass. I have done it dozens of times and I know it works.

IDEALLY YOU SHOULD START YOUR VISIT PROGRAMME WITH A COMPANY LOCAL TO YOUR AREA AND IF POSSIBLE CHOOSE ONE WHERE THERE'S SOMETHING TO SEE AS WELL AS TALK ABOUT. ONE OF THE UTILITIES – WATER, POWER, THAT SORT OF THING – WOULD BE PERFECT.

If the company you want to visit is comparatively small and doesn't have such visits as a matter of course you will probably have to persevere. When you ring up – my experience is that a conversation is better than a letter – ask for the chief executive or one of the directors by name. If there are none available ask for the company secretary. Keep at it, don't be put off, and if the switchboard person says, 'Can you tell me what it's about please?' simply say, 'Yes, of course. We are thinking of investing a substantial amount of money in your business. Are you the right person to talk to?' Don't be worried about this, remember you are seriously considering investing in this company and if they have any sense they will want your money and support. When you get through to the right person explain clearly who you are and what you want.

If the company has never arranged this sort of event before it may be necessary for one of your members to call at the company beforehand to discuss the format of the visit.

One of the problems you might encounter is the time of your visit. Remember, companies generally work office hours and that means day time Monday to Friday. For the personnel concerned, your visit, welcome though it may be, will be part of their work. They will want it to be part of their working day and not eat into their leisure time. Also, there's not much to see in a company outside office hours.

Q *I am the founder and chairman of a club in Essex and I am having trouble with the membership. At the meetings I allocate research work to everyone to find out information about companies I* *have chosen to look at. I have told them where to find out the information and how I want it presented. The problem is that some of them do not do the work properly or do not turn up at the meetings. I am thinking of establishing a system of fines and possible expulsions as an example to the others. What is your opinion?*

A   My opinion? It sounds like the investment club from hell. Fines? Expulsions? Companies you have chosen to look at? It's a wonder anyone turns up to the meetings. This is supposed to be fun. If I were you I would wind the club up tomorrow, admit that you are useless as a chairman and go and get yourself a life.

Q   *There's a rumour going round that all-women clubs are more successful than all-male clubs. Is that true?*

A   Sadly, yes. At first I could dismiss it as a statistic from America. But the Yanks have done their research and come up with the fact that all-female clubs are just under 5 per cent more profitable than all-male clubs. They put it down to the fact that women are more prepared to find out all the facts about a company and less subject to knee-jerk reaction. Also, in America women wear the financial pants in a family. Shockingly, recent research in the UK has produced a similar result. I am speechless.

Q   *We're neighbours who are starting a club amongst ourselves and can't decide on whether to put in a lump sum at the beginning and how much the monthly*

subscription should be. Half of us feel we should forget the lump sum and practise by picking pretend shares while we build up enough money to make a purchase. There's also a suggestion that we each subscribe £50 a month instead of the £25 I originally planned. The argument is that the smaller sum would mean we could not invest every month. There are 14 of us altogether.

A   It's important that you sort this out right at the start. At the next get-together read the following sage advice out loud. *You should regard the money that you put into the investment club as 'lost' money. Treat it as if you are never going to get a penny of it back.* One of the great temptations when you are caught up in the euphoria of starting a club is that you see it as an answer to your dreams of riches. It isn't. An investment club is merely a stepping stone on your road to riches, there to provide you with the knowledge and the confidence to build your own personal portfolio of winners. If you like the shares that your club picks then buy them for yourself, take advantage of the tax breaks and profits that personal equity investment can bring. Tax shelters such as ISAs (Individual Savings Accounts) and capital gains tax allowances are available to you as an individual but not as a club.

To give you a more specific answer, I would seriously consider a lump sum contribution at the start. These fantasy share games are all very well but there's nothing like the real thing and your members will be itching to dip their toes in the water. If you don't want to contribute more than £25 a month then say so and do it forcibly. If you can't get complete agreement then suggest a variety of contributions, there's no reason why your moneybags neighbour should not contribute twice as much as you every month, he will take twice your share of the profits or suffer twice the pain of the losses. But if you go down this road remember that he or she does not get twice the say in which investments are chosen. An investment club is a democratic one-member-one-vote organization. There cannot be second-class citizens.

If no one ever took risks Michelangelo would

have painted the Sistine floor.

Neil Simon

11

THE GOOD LIFE

I visit a lot of investment clubs and talk at quite a few investor conferences so I know there is an impression around that I've got best job in the world. A professional private investor. It's a relaxing, comfortable way to earn a crust. Of course there's a bit of work involved but nowadays, with so much analysts' information available, and modern research methods accessed at the touch of a button, it must be a doddle. Work from home, answerable to no one but yourself, fingers in a dozen pies and if one starts to go wrong all you have to do is take your finger out and put it in another warm pie. I hate to disillusion you, but in my case anyway, it ain't quite that easy. There's one hell of a difference between the dream and the reality. I must not mislead you, I enjoy every moment of my life, I have never had so much fun or satisfaction, but relaxing? A doddle? I can think of more appropriate descriptions. Frustrating, exhilarating, exciting, frightening, annoying, tiring – these adjectives fit the bill better.

So here, for the first time, is the difference between the perception and the reality of a typical week in the life of a professional private investor.

The perception

Monday

Wife wakes me up at around 10 a.m. with orange juice, a cup of tea and the papers. Don't bother with the *FT* because the markets haven't been open for a couple of days. Read the sleaze in the *Sun*. Leisurely shower then, because it is a nice day, wife and I take the dogs for a long walk.

Snack lunch at the local pub, couple of pints then back home for a snooze. Around 4 p.m. check the share prices on teletext. The FTSE's up a few points and I've got a couple of stocks in the Biggest Winners list and none in the Biggest Losers, so that's OK. My stockbroker calls to give me the good news that my portfolio is worth a few hundred more than it was on Friday and my American investments are on the up too.

In the evening dinner, a bit of television, and bed.

Tuesday

Pretty much the same, except that because the markets were open yesterday I turn to the prices page of the *FT* and check the detail of my stocks. I see that little AIM baby I was tipped by an insider source is starting to perform. Gone from 10p to 50p. I think I will dip my bread in this one, buy another slug of shares, because my contact reckons it will double again before the week is out. What is it the company does? Really must find out.

Dog walk, pub lunch, snooze.

In the evening Sid and Elsie come round for dinner. Sid's the chairman of a major plc, he's a bit of a bore really but I'm a big shareholder in his business and he can give me the inside track on what's happening. Elsie works in the Oxfam shop on Fridays. She's nice.

Boy, can Sid drink! Three bottles of the Gran Reserva Rioja, I only had one glass and the ladies drank white. Fortunately, Sid travels in the company's chauffeur-driven limo so we poured him into it at midnight. Before he got to the giggly stage Sid told me things were not so good business-wise. Take action tomorrow.

Wednesday

Lie in this morning. I don't like these late nights. Phone the broker and tell him to sell Sid's company's shares. Broker knows I had Sid round to dinner so the news will spread round the City like wildfire. I'm not bothered, my holding has gone.

Dog walk, then pub. Tone, the landlord at the pub, tells me that he's heard a whisper one of the Oxfordshire breweries is going to be taken over by a big Midlands group. The rep who told him wouldn't say who the buyer is. I must look into that. He knows a thing or two, does Tone. He also mentioned his girlfriend and her mates had been out for a pizza at that new place and it was packed. I happen to know the pizza parlour is part of a publicly quoted chain. News that it is busy puts me on red alert. Busy means profit. I buy the shares.

Television then bed.

Thursday

Up with the lark, around 9 a.m. Big day today. Wife will have to take the dogs by herself, I'm off to London. First-class rail from Didcot to Paddington then a taxi to the City. Lunch at the new Conran restaurant with the editor of a newspaper. What a nice man! Says he's so pleased with my column he's doubling my fee and putting me in for a national award. Also mentions in passing that one of the small magazine publishing groups is in trouble. It's this sort of insider info that keeps my portfolio healthy and I make a mental note not to buy the shares.

Afternoon watching some film or other at a cinema in Leicester Square. Pay three times more than prices at the Regent, Wantage. Must remember to find out whether the London cinema is a quoted company and, if so, buy shares. Snooze in cinema.

Dinner at Brooks Club in St James's with investment guru friend. He knows much more about the business than I do and he's therefore much richer. He is very bearish about the future, thinks the market is in for a serious downturn.

Late train from Paddington to Didcot, taxi home because I've drunk too much with guru.

Friday

Wake with headache. Lie in bed until noon then totter down to pub. Tone says it was his night off last night and he tried the new pizza place. It was rubbish, only him and his wife in there, the service was slow and the pizzas weren't crisp. Use the mobile to ring the broker and tell him to sell the pizza parlour shares. It's inside info like this that keeps me ahead of the game.

Home for a snooze. Suddenly remember guru's warning about impending market doom. Get on phone to broker and order him to sell entire portfolio. I'm in cash now and the market can do what it likes.

Sid and Elsie's for dinner. He's a bit gloomy. Apparently he's had the sack.

Saturday and Sunday

I don't work weekends.

....

The reality

(And I promise you this includes extracts from my actual diary and represents a typical week.)

Monday

Up at 6.30 a.m. Take my wife, Helen, a cuppa then spend an hour walking the dogs and thinking. Shower, breakfast; in the office (I have a separate building in my garden) by 9 a.m.

It's portfolio day. I turn on the computer and open first the Finsight then the Sharescope programs and update them via the Internet. These are the two services I use to keep track of my various portfolios, plus of course hemscott.net and online *REFS*.

Including my wife's portfolios I have 16 portfolios altogether and Monday

morning I go through them all with a fine tooth comb. Most of the portfolios are PEPs and ISAs going back several years. They mainly comprise blue-chip stocks and I rarely change them but it's worth keeping a weekly eye on their progress.

Here's my routine for this weekly health check. The 16 portfolios comprise a total of around 25 stocks and each one is subjected to the same scrutiny.

1. I check each share against a notebook in which I have recorded the original reasons why I bought it. This is my Manual, and it never leaves my office. I explained earlier that every investor and certainly every investment club should have a notebook of this sort because it is a factual reminder of what induced you to invest your money in the first place. I fill in the details just before I make the actual purchase and I choose this point in the purchasing process for two reasons: (a) it focuses my mind on why I am so excited about the share that I want it in my collection; and (b) it sometimes brings me up with a jolt. Am I really buying it simply because Jack said I should fill my boots? Or do I truly believe the rumour that Microsoft is about to pay millions for some technology it forgot to invent itself? If you haven't already adopted this final test technique I can thoroughly recommend it. For the rest of my weekly check I will have the original purchase reasons at the back of my mind. Have they been achieved yet? Is there a chance my

hopes will be realized soon or should I write this one off to experience? Have the hopes become reality and if so is it time to take the profits or is there more to come?

2. Now I look at the share's price progress during the week (I have watched it on a daily basis, sometimes three or four times a day but on Mondays I aim to see it in perspective). For this part of the check I use my Finsight program (it used to be called Infotrade but there was a management buyout). An icon at the top of the screen says 'Shares' and this takes me to the place where I can access the details of every quoted share. I type in the first three or four letters of the company's name and I can then get much of the information I need. It's all there, all the basic facts from the net asset value to the directors' dealings. What I'm looking for is the price history and I prefer to see it as actual figures rather than comparison graphs. That's because the closing prices for each day are listed and I can therefore spot a blip, up or down, and pinpoint it to an exact day. If there is a blip I'm straightaway off on a treasure hunt but I will explain that in a moment.

3. Assuming all is well – hopefully there's been a steady rise – I will move to the Internet where I open up the home page of my server, hemscott.net. Rather like our daily newspapers we all have our favourite financial information sites and Hemscott's is mine. I have had the service since I first had the Internet so know my way around it. Also the editor of Hemscott Analyst Tom Stevenson, is a top-class journalist and sensible investor. On my list of favourites I also have ft.com, iii, Investors Chronicle and yahoo finance. I find ft.com particularly good for breaking news stories. My Monday visit to the web is to check in the archives for any news stories I may have missed relating to the share I am examining. I also try to find out if there's been an analyst's report published that I can access.

4. I look at the company's own website. This is very much the pot luck part of the examination because the standards vary so much. My major gripe is that companies don't update their information fast enough, we all know this is the communications medium of the future so why not get organized now? It is a chance to present a modern, go-ahead image to shareholders but still businesses only pay lip service to it.

5. Finally, still on the Internet, I open up online *REFS* which is a shareholder miracle. (I'm sorry if you think I go over the top about this product, as I said before, they don't pay me a penny for saying this but as far as I am concerned it is as important to my working life as the telephone.) I print off the relevant page, which I know contains up-to-the-minute information, and spend 10 minutes studying it.

I do this health check on all my shares, anything between 20 and 30 depending on how heavily I am invested, and it takes time. While the majority will be routine examinations they can't be skimped and when there is a blip in the prices section I have to go off on a treasure hunt. Why the price change? Was it a general market movement or something specific? I will probably already know the answer. Neverthess I will check it out, scouring the news and feature archives of the newspapers and magazines looking for comment. I will talk to contacts, ring the company and pester them, keep at it until I find the answer. My money is riding on this horse, I'm a genuine part-owner and I want to know what's going on.

This portfolio examination takes until the early evening and my only break is a snack lunch in my office while I watch *Working Lunch* and the news headlines. The portfolio healthcheck requires concentration and by the time it is completed I am worn out. So at least the perception about television then bed is true.

Tuesday

First thing after walking the dogs I implement the decisions I made on Monday. I've had a chance for further contemplation overnight plus a ponder on the dog walk and before I take any action I will run over the situation again and re-examine the figures. This is not dithering, it is a deliberate delay because I know I have a streak in my nature that

will say jump when it may not be the prudent thing to do. That's why I can't sit at the computer screen all day watching share prices change, despite the fact that I know it's stupid to try to beat the market by day trading I admit I am tempted. I know the chief executive of a major plc who recognizes he has the same fault, a reckless gambling instinct, and therefore puts off any major decision for at least 48 hours. I'm not that bad but I do consciously wait a day between deciding to trade a share and actually doing the deed. It is a good discipline and I recommend it. You gain more times than you lose.

Nowadays I do most of my trading via the Internet. It's cheaper, but that is not the main reason I have moved from telephone dealing. I feel more relaxed, more comfortable doing it on screen. My conversion came about early in 2000 when we had that boom in technology stocks and the brokers' phone lines were jammed. It could sometimes take hours to get through and then you were faced with that infuriating 'Press 1 if you want … or 2 if you want …' disembodied voice. On the Internet I can take my time, regular usage has made me familiar with the process, it is just all very easy.

The remainder of Tuesday is taken up with reading the heavy newspapers and magazines that have been around since the weekend.

Wednesday

London day. The whole journey – car from home to Didcot, train from Paddington, tube or taxi to the City – takes two hours. I try to catch a train around 7 a.m. because it gives me a full day in town to see all the people I want to see. It's amazing how the diary gets crammed when you try to fit everything into a single day.

Picking one recent Wednesday at random I have an early meeting with Diane Hay, the chief executive of ProShare. We spend an hour talking about the website content (it's exciting, take a look at www.proshare.org.) and various other aspects of the business.

Then I have a meeting with James Hanbury, the publisher of *Investors' Week* magazine, who is planning a regular investment club supplement and wants my advice and opinion on the content.

Lunch is with Declan Curry, the BBC's man at the Stock Exchange who has brought a breathe of fresh air to the world of finance on our television screens. He's on BBC One's breakfast show and the News 24 channel. We eat at the Fish restaurant near London Bridge. Although I have only been there twice it has fast become a favourite because the first time I went there I was so impressed I bought a tranche of their shares and sold them two weeks later at a 30 per cent profit.

After lunch I have a change of hat and become chairman of BioProjects International, an investment company which specializes in financing and advising early-stage biotechnology companies. We have offices in Cornhill and I visit my colleague Julian Viggars there. We have lots to talk about because our company, which has raised and invested several million pounds since it was formed less than a year ago, has some excellent new investment propositions to consider.

In the evening I attend the regular monthly meeting of the Mashed Pesetas Investment Club. I know my other clubs will forgive me if I say this is the best investment club I have ever belonged to, but it is certainly not the most successful.

Mashed Pesetas began life in the mid-1990s as the Deep Groat Investment Club. Its origins are rather obscure. I notice that some of the members also belong to a motor cycle club and come to the meetings on their Harleys so that could be the bond that brought the founder members together. On the other hand some of us, including me, wouldn't be seen dead on a motor bike. Suffice to say we are an eclectic collection, a dozen men and one lady, who have run the gamut of investment club experiences. We began with a boom and within months had doubled the value of our portfolio. We crashed in the technology-media-telecommunications débâcle and became so disillusioned that the club disbanded. A hard core of original members missed the craque more than anything else so we reformed as Mashed Pesetas. We now have a disciplined approach to our investing and we are doing fine, learning from our mistakes and enjoying the meetings.

I catch the 11 p.m. from Paddington to Didcot by the skin of my teeth. I imbibed too much at the Mashed Pesetas meeting so I take a taxi home. I'll pick my car up from the station park in the morning. It's been a long day.

Thursday

Writing and contacts. I write because I thoroughly enjoy it. I have regular commitments in newspapers, magazines and on the internet. They're all fun to do, nobody dictates what the subjects of the columns should be, but collectively they take quite a while to complete. I dabble at them during spare moments on other days but Thursday is mainly occupied with writing.

I mention contacts because the two activities are inexorably linked. I get the ideas, opinions and expertise for my columns by talking, usually on the telephone, to people who are faster guns than me when it comes to almost any subject. Elsewhere in the book I have written about the people who have an influence on my investment decisions but there are many others whose thoughts and knowledge I respect. Jeremy King at MoneyWise, Tom Stevenson and Graham Quick at Hemscott, Jack Murdoch in Glasgow, Mac Scott in Wolverhampton, David Holland, Mark Slater, Jean Hicks, Emma Kane – the list is endless. They may not get a call from me for weeks but when they do they can be sure it is usually to pick their brains.

Friday

One of the unwritten rules of the City of London is that not much happens on Fridays. From 9 a.m. onwards everyone seems to be winding down for the weekend. That's suits me fine because Friday is research day. A time to explore new avenues, perhaps shares, maybe a new business venture, or merely reading the writings of the great investors and businessmen. Whatever it is, the approach must be disciplined because this is work, not pleasure. Therefore I go into the office at 9 a.m., break for a snack lunch, and don't leave until late afternoon. This is not being a goody-goody swot, it is simply that the only way I can train myself to work

FRIDAY IS RESEARCH DAY. A TIME TO EXPLORE NEW AVENUES, PERHAPS SHARES, MAYBE A NEW BUSINESS VENTURE, OR MERELY READING THE WRITINGS OF THE GREAT INVESTORS AND BUSINESSMEN.

efficiently is to establish a routine which must not be broken.

Saturday and Sunday

Sacrosanct. Lawn cutting, walking, talking to friends and neighbours, visiting family, going to the pub, writing private letters and e-mails, reading – I soak up well-written fiction.

> You may be wondering where writing this book features in this list of daily activities. I can tell you that for three months I stole an extra hour from each day by getting up at 5.30 a.m. I do not recommend it, except as a near-certain formula for divorce.

Weekends are for anything but thinking and talking about stocks and shares. The only exceptions to this are the 15 weekend days in the year, usually Sundays, when I talk at seminars or conferences for investors and investment clubs.

....
Rather personal

My best investment

Every investor dreams of a true 10-bagger. For the uninitiated that is a share that goes up to 10 times what you paid for it and then you sell it. It's those last five words that sort the men from the boys – *and then you sell it*. A 10-bagger is only true if you take the profit. During the dot.com and technology stock booms there were plenty of 10-bagger situations, shares going from nothing to

EVERY INVESTOR DREAMS OF A TRUE 10-BAGGER. FOR THE UNINITIATED THAT IS A SHARE THAT GOES UP TO 10 TIMES WHAT YOU PAID FOR IT AND THEN YOU SELL IT. IT'S THOSE LAST FIVE WORDS THAT SORT THE MEN FROM THE BOYS – *AND THEN YOU SELL IT.*

sky-high overnight as investors, like lemmings, scrambled to get in on the rich pickings.

Many of my friends who are, like me, serious investors made huge killings. At least, that's what they say, but long ago I learned to take a pocketful of pinches of salt with me when I talk to investor friends. Like fishermen and golfers they remember the big fish and the sweet shots and they tend to get bigger and sweeter in the telling. I too made a lot of money in that balmy six months between October 1999 and March 2000, I paid an enormous capital gains tax bill and didn't regret a penny of it. But in 10 years of investing the true 10-bagger had always eluded me.

Then along came the Money Channel. Wall-to-wall financial news on satellite television, good journalists and presenters, informed opinion, tips, chat about shares. I thought it was a great concept. Adam Faith (real name Terry Nelhams-Wright, but who cares?), who has a quirky investment technique but has made – and probably lost – a stock market fortune or two along the way, had 10 per cent of the Money Channel action. And the two top guys at respected stockbrokers Killicks, Paul Killick and Matthew Orr, had substantial stakes.

On 17 August 1999 I bought Money Channel shares at 44.25p per share on my Charles Schwab Frequent Trader account. Slightly less than five months later, on 8 February 2000, I sold my Money Channel shares at £4.80p per share.

My first-ever 10-bagger.

My worst investment

Even though you sell a share and take a reasonable profit – in the case of Money Channel my profit was more than reasonable – you are slightly piqued when the share's price continues to rise. Money Channel went up to £5.22 before it began to fall.

I still liked the concept and in the spring of 2000 I appeared on a couple of the station's programmes and was impressed by the professionalism of the staff and the state-of-the-art equipment and smart premises. When my friend Tony Hobman, who I knew from personal experience was an excellent manager of people and good business thinker, joined as chief executive officer I felt it was time to go back in. On 6 June 2000 I bought Money Channel shares again. My outlay was exactly the same as when I became a shareholder the first time but of course it bought substantially fewer shares.

As I write the shares are suspended from the Alternative Investment Market and the receivers are in at the company. Although several months has passed since they put the shutters up I have so far not received any communication from the receivers – I don't even know who they are – but why am I not surprised? I'm not sure how these buzzards go about their work but obviously their priority is not to tell the owners of the company (us) that they have been called in to sort things out. Anyway, I'm not holding my breath for the payout because I guess there will be little or nothing left in the kitty for us.

What went wrong at Money Channel? Goodness knows, I would not presume on personal friendships by asking any of the directors because it would be embarrassing for them to be put in a position where they would have to refuse to pass on confidential information during the receivers' enquiry.

My guess is that the Money Channel seemed like a good idea, but wasn't in the long run. A television channel devoted to finance might be appealing to anoraks like me but let's face it, to the majority of people it would be like watching paint dry. How many times have you been talking excitedly about the fact that your favourite share has moved upwards by 4 per cent in the last month, only to find that your audience of one is looking glazed? Even I get bored with constantly thinking, talking and reading about shares.

If the audience for a television channel is not big enough it will not attract advertisers, and if the advertisers stay away there is no financial future for the business.

Incidentally, I did have a reasonably substantial investment in another company that went bust on me but it was a few years ago and I can't for the life of me remember the company's name. The brain is like that, it has the ability to forget the bad things in life. I do know the share was recommended to me by my brokers at the time, Branston & Gothard, but as they too had the receivers in shortly afterwards I can't ask them for details.

Research – I do it my way

For several months recently, when I have not been slaving over a hot computer to produce this book, I have been part of a team examining companies with a view to investing large amounts of money, usually hundreds of thousands of pounds. Needless to say these big bucks are not all mine and the fact that other folk place their faith in my ability to sort wheat from chaff certainly focuses the mind. (Before the Financial Services Authority come knocking at my door I hasten to point out that I am not a qualified adviser and therefore the final investment decision on this research is not made solely by me, neither do I receive any commission or similar remuneration for my efforts.) Other members of the research team are specialists, highly qualified and experienced in the areas in which each company is involved. I'm there, I guess, to bring a layman's perspective to the situation.

At first sight this kind of research has little to do with investment clubs but I think you will be interested to know how I approach my part of the operation because our team as a whole exactly mirrors the principles of a club.

Each company under our microscope presents its own set of circumstances – is it well established or a start-up? – so it is not possible to create a standard list of questions. However, for me there is a set of searches that are common to almost every business.

The company

Hopefully there is a company history going back several years because this means we can base decisions on facts rather than hopes. In a perfect world it will be an established leader in its sector with a good profit record. One if the truest sayings is (I know, you've heard it before): 'Yesterday's winners are tomorrow's winners. Yesterday's losers are tomorrow's losers.'

In our team there are financial experts who can skim through a set of accounts in seconds but if I ask them to explain and summarize they lose me. So, in the comfort of my own home, I get the financial facts down to a level I can understand by drawing little graphs of turnover, profits and earnings per share. If they show a steady increase I go to bed and sleep soundly. If there are blips I sit up half the night trying to find out why.

Bigger companies often have a variety of income streams so I want to know that each source is properly profitable and if not, why not?

If it is a start-up business it must have a good business plan and I will examine this in great detail and with a good deal of scepticism. If it is a highly technical product, and I regret to say many of them are, this is the hardest part of the job. I hate it. I have to make myself read and re-read sentences, sometimes taking it one word at a time in order to understand what it is all about. I am constantly on the phone to the expert members of the team asking what this or that means and I can sense their exasperation as they explain things again and again. I don't care. I have long ago ceased to be embarrassed by my ignorance.

The product's USP

When I was a copywriter with an advertising agency and we secured a new client we always started our creative head-banging sessions by trying to identify the new product's USP – its unique selling point. What made it different? Cheaper, more sophisticated, smaller, bigger, more powerful, there was always something to major on. As a potential investor I am comforted if a business has an outstanding USP.

The market

It must be big, no point in having a product or service which is wonderful but for which there is limited demand. Is the market saturated or is there some way to go? If the market is expanding how is the company going to secure more than its fair share, and if its potential is fully realized how is the company going to steal business from its competitors?

The customers

The number of customers matters. A wide customer base usually means greater management and sales effort but the risk is reduced. A company is exposed if it relies on a single-figure list of customers because the loss of one can have a serious adverse affect. I talk to the customers to gauge their satisfaction.

The suppliers

When a company has a product it invariably buys in materials. I talk to the suppliers because this is an effective way to assess how the company does business. The suppliers must be content. I learned the lesson many years ago when I investigated a West Midlands engineering company that deliberately chose small suppliers, filled their production capacity by giving them big orders, then squeezed them dry by dictating price and paying late.

The competition

This is one of the best ways to establish the standing and potential of a business. First, I draw up a list of competitive companies. Then, based on information I glean from talking with customers, end users, suppliers and independent sources such as analysts and journalists, I create a league table based on turnover, profitability and market perception. If the company under the spotlight is the league leader how is it going to retain the position? If it is not ahead of the field I want to know why other businesses are better and how we can topple them.

The management

Experience. That's the essential ingredient in any management team and, make no mistake, teamwork is what it is all about. Certainly the man or woman at the top must be seen to be the leader but a chief executive is only as good as those who work below him or her. CEOs tend to fall into two categories, those who are professional businesspeople, guiding the company through a business jungle of wheels and deals, and those who are there because they know the company and its products. A combination of both is ideal but a rarity so I prefer the latter. I like a leader who knows the product, its customers and its competitors and has been around for a reasonable length of

I CREATE A LEAGUE TABLE BASED ON TURNOVER, PROFITABILITY AND MARKET PERCEPTION. IF THE COMPANY UNDER THE SPOTLIGHT IS THE LEAGUE LEADER HOW IS IT GOING TO RETAIN THE POSITION? IF IT IS NOT AHEAD OF THE FIELD I WANT TO KNOW WHY OTHER BUSINESSES ARE BETTER AND HOW WE CAN TOPPLE THEM.

time. In other words he or she has a feel for the environment in which the company operates.

Of equal importance is the finance director, particularly if the chief executive is a product rather than a figures person. The money man or woman need not necessarily have been with the company long but his or her track record must stand careful scrutiny. We are considering giving our money to this outfit and we must be sure it will be nurtured efficiently.

I check the salaries, the shareholdings and the warrants because I want to know the senior personnel are well paid and that their carrots, in the form of bonuses, options and/or warrants, are attractive enough to make them want to stay. I cannot overemphasize the importance of a settled and reliable management. It can make or break a company.

Make-weights

I take a look at the non-executive directors. Why are they on the board? If they are able to contribute opinion and expertise, fine. If they are there simply because they will say 'yes' and not make waves I get suspicious. And if any of them holds an insignifancant number of shares in the company I am uncomfortable.

Achilles heel

There has to be a snag, there always is. I don't kid myself, saints are not appointed CEOs, so they cannot be blamed for sticking to the good news. On the other hand it is my job to get the full picture so I have to discover the warts and all. Looking under all the stones takes time but it is imperative. Here are just a few of the things to look out for: a shortage of skilled workers, high borrowings, an outstanding court case, unsecured patents, currency exposure, a poor order book, vulnerability to an unwanted takeover.

There are, of course, many other yardsticks by which to measure a company's worth. Dividends, liquidity, City opinion, interest being paid, gearing, they all play a part in painting the finished picture. It is an interesting and sometimes frustrating exercise but I enjoy doing the detective work because I know that if, in the end, we take a stake in the company it will be money well spent.

A sounding board

One of the main principles of an investment club is that you learn to listen and take on board the opinions and thoughts of other members. Inevitably, you listen more to some than others and all the decisions taken by the club are not necessarily applied to your own portfolio. Indeed, looking through my list of private holdings I notice that only about 50 per cent of the shares are mirrored in the portfolios of the clubs to which I belong. That's a good thing because only a small percentage of my capital is tied up in the clubs, I estimate about 0.5 per cent.

As far as my own share portfolio is concerned I make my own investment decisions so major mistakes will be mine but I do have sounding boards, individuals from whom I have learned and who play a significant if indirect part in my trading activities. I have therefore formed the Gang of Six Investment Club with a membership which is slightly unusual because until the individuals concerned read this they will have no idea that they are members. There are no subscriptions and no benefits to anyone else but me.

The aim of the club is simple. It acts as a sounding board for investment ideas. Blatantly I use the other five members for their knowledge, their experience, their expertise and their opinions. Here is a list of the other five members of the Gang of Six Investment Club:

Jim Slater

No surprise here. I consider Jim to be the best and wisest investor I know. When I first decided to invest I had difficulty in understanding the fundamentals of the business, there did not seem to be a Janet-and-John primer to explain in readable terms how the whole process worked. Then I came across Jim's two books, *Investment Made Easy* and *The Zulu Principle*, and the scales were lifted from my eyes. I met the man himself when we were both speakers at the first Sharelink Investors' Conference in Birmingham, some time in the mid-1990s. Since then we have become good friends, shared many a fine lunch together, and become involved in BioProjects International.

Jim is the voice of experience. A colossus who has strode the business stage of Britain for over half a century, he has experienced the highest of highs and the lowest of lows. A qualified accountant, he was Sir Donald Stokes's right-hand man in the heady days of British Leyland. He built up one of the most successful conglomerates in the land, Slater Walker, only to see it collapse in spectacular fashion. He reinvented himself as an author of children's books and then as a financier and investor. And, perhaps most pertinent to this book, Jim Slater became the unconscious champion of the private investor when he used his prodigious knowledge to devise *REFS*.

We talk, usually on a daily basis, and his advice is invaluable.

Peter Reynolds

Peter and I have been friends since we were seven years old in the first form at Tettenhall College. We lost touch for many years but he reappeared in my life at the end of the 1980s when I was living and working in Spain. Again, I value Peter's opinions because they are based on hands-on experience. Like Jim, he has thrived on making a difference to the businesses and industries in which he

has been involved. Since we left college he has headed a wide variety of industrial businesses, rarely as the chairman but invariably as the driving force that makes things happen. He has bought and sold more companies than I have owned cars and while they are in his ownership they never stand still. He develops them, hones their overheads, increases their bottom line, cuts off loss-making limbs and puts muscle into those with potential. He is a company doctor and an entrepreneur at the same time and, like me, he thrives on the buzz of equity investment. Peter is a brave and sensible shareholder on a grand scale in Britain and America. He has excellent contacts and advisers in many countries, and I listen when he talks.

Justin Urquhart-Stewart

Although we talk, often two or three times a week, Justin is likely to be surprised to find himself on my list. Despite his bouncy and bustling style – you will probably know him for his regular appearances in trademark red braces on such television programmes as *Working Lunch* and *GMTV* – he is a modest man. Until recently he was the public face of Barclays Stockbrokers but now he and his friend Tom Sheridan head a stockbroking business, Seven Investment Management which specializes in advising high-net-worth individuals. For me, Justin's strength is his overall grasp of stock markets around the world and his lateral thinking when it comes to assessing the impact of events on share prices. I am a member of two investment clubs where Justin is also part of the gang, and at each it has become part of the routine for him to spend 10 minutes giving his interpretation of the state of the market. If I have an idea, a glimmer of an investment thought, I will usually run it past Justin early in its life because he will invariably provide me with a fresh perspective on it.

Forbes Petrie

If any one of my 'investment club of six' will be gobsmacked to find himself as a member it will be Forbes. He is not a private investor and has resisted all my blandishments to become one. It's not that he is afraid of risk – on the contrary he thrives on it as long as he is comfortable with the levels – it is just that he is not in complete control, and, believe me, Forbes likes to be in control. He lives his leisure life to the full because he organizes it that way and in business he has the same drive and flair for planning. He was a leading light in the success of the Prontaprint instant print chain and had particular responsibility for spearheading its drive into Europe. He then started the Pirtek franchising business from scratch and took it to the top of the franchise league. His knowledge of early-stage businesses and the potential of blue-sky ideas is second to none and invaluable to me. Forbes is an entrepreneur with in-depth management ability which is a rare combination. He also tells it like it is, no pussy-footing around, and for me that is essential.

Let me give you an example. I recently had an investment opportunity, a new business in which I had complete faith as well as a seat on the board of directors, and I contacted friends and family to offer them a stake in the company. Everyone accepted, except Forbes. He rang and said, 'We're friends and we exchange opinions regularly. If I bought into your new business I would hesitate about picking up the phone in case you thought I was ringing to see how things in the company were going. You might hesitate to ring me because you would feel you had to brief me on my investment before we talked about anything else. If anything went wrong with the investment we would lose a friendship and I don't want that to happen.' That's being honest and that is Forbes.

Helen Bond

I can hear the more cynical of you saying 'creep'. Not true. Helen is my wife and, as you have probably guessed, a woman. She is also younger than me and has a number of talents which I do not possess in the same degree – style and common sense being among the most obvious. She looks at the world from a different viewpoint to me and forms opinions which often contrast totally with my perceptions. Time and events have taught me that she is more often right than wrong – aren't all women? – so her thoughts influence my investment decisions. I also use her as a filter to put the happenings of the day in perspective. As she prepares dinner I sit in the kitchen and tell her what has occurred. Most times she just listens while I babble on and get my mind into some sort of order, but occasionally she will interject with an opinion. It helps because, as I have said, private investing can be a lonely old business. Oh, and I nearly forgot, I want her in my gang of six because I love her very much. Go on, say it. 'Creep'.

No investor should be an island so I recommend you create your own circle of competence, your Gang of Six Investment Club which will exist outside the conventional club to which you belong and will provide you with a sounding board for your ideas and methods.

He's called a broker because, after dealing
with him, you are.

Anon

CHAPTER 12

THE
BROKER

Every investment club and every private investor needs a stockbroker. In each share transaction the broker is the essential ingredient, the go-between, the person who accepts, and sometimes initiates, investors' instructions and liaises between the club or the individual and the stock exchanges and the companies' registrars. Not so many years ago the stockbroker was perceived as a man of mystery, a rotund figure who operated from an oak-panelled office between 10 and midday then took himself and a favoured client or two off for a lunch of grouse and claret at the club. Whispered insider deals were clinched over the port then it was back to the office for an hour's snooze before catching the five o'clock home to Maidenhead.

If that was ever the case, the image and the reality have certainly changed in recent years. The explosion in the number of clubs and investors in Britain has brought increased pressure and competition to the cosy world of the stockbroking profession. It has also dramatically altered the range of services on offer. Now stockbrokers come in all shapes and sizes and the investor and the club are faced with a wide choice when they decide who should have the commission on their trades. The good news is that the range of brokers is as diverse as the client base it serves. For the club that wants to take an active interest in the stock market, do its own research and make its own investment decisions, the arrival of the execution-only broker has proved a boon.

Not so many years ago the phrase 'execution only' meant nothing other than a no-options sentence for first-degree murder. Today it is used to describe the revolution that changed the cocooned world of the stockbroker for ever.

David Jones, a Midlands-based entrepreneur, is generally acknowledged to have been at the vanguard of the execution-only system of buying and selling shares in Britain when he set up a new brokerage firm, Sharelink, in Birmingham. Almost single-handedly he buried the image of the stockbroker as a

NOW STOCKBROKERS COME IN ALL SHAPES AND SIZES AND THE INVESTOR AND THE CLUB ARE FACED WITH A WIDE CHOICE WHEN THEY DECIDE WHO SHOULD HAVE THE COMMISSION ON THEIR TRADES.

crusty old buffer whose mysterious and often dubious services were only available to the rather rich. Not for Mr Jones the swish oak offices, long lunches and high commissions. He recruited a young and enthusiastic staff whose only function was to buy and sell shares on the instruction of Sharelink clients. No advice, no opinion, simply a middleman function, and this no frills service was reflected in comparatively low commission charges.

Within a couple of years rumour had it that Sharelink was handling 10 per cent of the total number of deals being done on the London stock market. It was inevitable that such success would attract the attention of bigger brothers and sure enough one of America's largest brokers, Charles Schwab, bought Sharelink and changed its name.

So began the transatlantic invasion of this country's stockbroking business and today there are at least a dozen of Britain's execution-only brokers that have American parents.

On the telephone, by post, in regional offices and increasingly on the Internet, clubs transmit their own share-dealing decisions using brokers merely as order takers. Commissions for transacting the trades seem to get lower and lower. With more and more of these basic brokers chasing investors and clubs to join their customer base an astute club could find itself paying next to nothing in brokers' charges.

Another by-product of this increased competition for business means that the execution-only phrase has become something of a misnomer. In addition to carrying out clients' instructions the new breed of stockbroker offers a host of additional services to tempt you to join its database. Up-to-the-minute financial news displayed as it happens, portfolio management, administration of PEPs and ISAs, share tracking with prices only slightly delayed or in some cases instantaneous, nominee accounts, banking, share alerts, analysts' consensus opinions, overseas dealing, notification of new issues, and – that vital aid to successful investing – company information.

Information is lifeblood for the private investor and most, if not all, of these low-cost brokers provide links to enable individuals and clubs to obtain it via the Internet or the postal services. Invariably it comes from one or more of the major wire services or data providers but this is of no real concern to the customer because it is usually free of charge.

I have also noticed a welcome tendency to give a blanket opinion on certain stocks. Some of the bigger brokers, particularly those associated with large British banks, will, if asked, give to their execution-only clients an overall assessment of around 200 UK companies. It must be emphasized that this is not advice to individual investors or clubs, it is purely the broker's opinion on whether a stock is worth buying, selling or holding.

So how do you select an execution-only broker? The first thing to do is contact the Association of Private Client Investment Managers and

SOME OF THE BIGGER BROKERS, PARTICULARLY THOSE ASSOCIATED WITH LARGE BRITISH BANKS, WILL, IF ASKED, GIVE TO THEIR EXECUTION-ONLY CLIENTS AN OVERALL ASSESSMENT OF AROUND 200 UK COMPANIES.

Stockbrokers (020 7247 7080) and get their list of members.

As always, it is horses for courses. Each broker will have literature they will send detailing their services and charges and you must select one that suits your particular requirements. Several brokers, particularly the larger ones, have a service specially tailored to investment clubs (see the list at the end of this chapter). If I was in your position I would contact them all and ask for details, and as you examine the information here are a few points worth bearing in mind:

- If you intend to use the telephone for your dealing, ring up a selection of brokers' general enquiry numbers and note down how long it takes before you speak to a real person. A couple of years ago the boom in investor business caused overload in many offices. It took a while for them to gear up to the increase and even now there are still a few who have not got their acts together. There is nothing

worse than listening to a monotonous *burr-burr* or a recording of 'Pomp and Circumstance' for minutes on end while you wait. Check too that you are not going to waste an age pushing a series of buttons before you get through to a real person who can actually help you. Remember, you are thinking of using these people for your share trading and, in dealing, seconds might count.

- If you are one of those clubs that wants to hold actual share certificates rather than use the broker's nominee account, will you have to pay extra for each trade? (You may find that some firms will not want your business if you insist on certificates. It is therefore best to establish this at the outset.)

- What are the total costs of being a customer? The commission for carrying out a single instruction might be very low but what is the charge for managing the shares in the nominee account? Will the broker collect your dividends and reinvest them for you and, if so, is there an additional charge for that service?

- If there is cash in your broker account what interest rate will it accrue for you?

- How will you be expected to settle your account when you buy shares? Will the broker insist on a direct debit? Can you pay by cheque? Some brokers insist that you open bank accounts with a bank they nominate. If this is acceptable to you, make sure you have a cheque book with it so it can be operated like a normal account.

- Remember, even though they streamline the process of share trading, nominee accounts were introduced principally to make life easier for the stockbroker, So make sure you don't lose out. You want your rights – the annual report, the ability to attend and vote at AGMs and so on – and any perks that may be available to certificated shareholders.

- Make sure there are adequate insurance arrangements in place to safeguard your club against fraud. Also check on the compensation arrangements to cover the club if the broking business goes into liquidation or is wound up.

- Find out when you use the Internet or the phone for a buy or sell price, will it be real time or delayed? Is it the price you will be dealing at? Is it the best possible price or will the broker try to improve on it?

The execution-only dealers have brought a breath of fresh air into the élite world of stockbroking. Their main drawback seems to be that such low commission charges encourage investors to buy and sell frequently rather than stick to the conventional wisdom of buying for the long term.

There is another and rather worrying side-issue to consider too. These new kids on the block set up shop in Britain in response to the explosion of interest in stock market investing that accompanied the bull market at the turn of this century. Day trading was the talk of the town and barmy television shows like *Show Me The Money* – remember that? – encouraged inexperienced investors to trade on a daily basis. It was all too good to last and it didn't. The bubble burst and the short-term, get-rich-quick merchants left the market place in tears.

The investors who remain are in the main sensible, more experienced people who are in it for the long term. This means they choose stocks carefully and hang on until the story changes, which in turn means they pay out less commission to brokers. The result is that the takings in some brokers' tills are diminishing to the point where they are losing money and, I know the Americans, they will not put up with that for long.

Please don't think I am scare-mongering, as I write it hasn't happened yet, but mergers and takeovers in the execution-only broker business have already happened and I wouldn't be surprised if, in the near future, a number go to the wall. There's not much you can do about it and be assured that the regulatory authorities have put excellent

MERGERS AND TAKEOVERS IN THE EXECUTION-ONLY BROKER BUSINESS HAVE ALREADY HAPPENED AND I WOULDN'T BE SURPRISED IF, IN THE NEAR FUTURE, A NUMBER GO TO THE WALL.

safeguards in place to ensure your holdings are protected in the event of it happening to your broker, nevertheless it will be an aggravation. Be aware of it when you select your broker.

The advisers

It is a fact that there are investment clubs who have not got the time, the confidence or indeed the inclination to sort out share winners for themselves and therefore prefer to deal with advisory brokers. It is unusual, and personally I find it difficult to come to terms with because it seems to contradict the basic tenet of an investment club, but there's no law against it. The advisers, who must be fully qualified, seem to fall into two categories, reactive and proactive.

The reactive ones will be available on the end of a phone to offer an opinion on a share your club fancies. The opinion is usually well founded because it is based on professional research and admittedly this will save your members hours of delving into company histories, scouring news archives and assembling financial data. There's an increasing tendency for these reactive advisers to base their fees on a time basis, rather like a solicitor or an accountant. Thus you can have 10 minutes for £10 or a full half-hour for £25 and so on. It remains to be seen whether the idea catches on.

A club that wants advice should really seek out the proactive broker. He (or she) is the one who gives opinion as well as advice. He will say, 'Yes my friends, this is a good stock and it is worth buying but it is not for your club. It does not fit comfortably with your risk profile and it would make your portfolio overweight in that particular sector.' And he will ring you next day, or next week, and suggest an alternative investment. Equally important, he will monitor your shares for you and make recommendations for change when he considers it appropriate. To do this properly he must know a great deal about you so, when you open an account with a broker who is prepared to offer opinions as well as advice, expect to be quizzed. He will want to know whether the club is looking for safety or will tolerate a degree of risk, whether you

need income or capital growth, and so on.

The commission rates for these advisory brokers are understandably higher than those of the execution-only operator. Typically they will charge anything between 1 and 2 per cent. Some will charge a fee plus commission, others will want an annual lump sum against which your commissions are offset. And most advisory brokers will require a minimum value for a portfolio before they will agree to handle your business.

The discreet adviser

Frankly, I don't know a single club that uses a discretionary broker but, just to complete the stockbroker picture, you might as well know about them.

Investors who do not have the time or the inclination to study the stock market themselves use the discretionary broker. You entrust your money to him, or quite often her, and he or she creates and manages a portfolio for you, so again you will have to detail your circumstances and requirements. He or she will also make a note of any prejudices you have, for example, an aversion to investing in tobacco companies or weapons manufacturers.

When you have amassed a few hundred thousand quid, and you just want to stop and smell the flowers, that's the time to appoint a discretionary broker.

Whether you opt for an execution-only, advisory or a discretionary broker, it is advisable to check them thoroughly first. Go for a well-known and respected name and check their track record. Also, if you go for an advisory broker, create a rapport between yourself and an individual adviser. After all, my reading of the Financial Services Act makes it plain that anyone giving detailed financial advice should have an intimate knowledge of the client's profile and requirements.

A list of all three categories of broker can be obtained from their trade association, APCIMS (the Association of Private Client Investment Managers and Stockbrokers), on 020 7247 7080. Meanwhile, here is a list of those brokers who I know offer services to investment clubs.

Barclays Stockbrokers

ADDRESS:
Tay House
300 Bath St
Glasgow G2 4LH

TELEPHONE:
0845 777 7300

E-MAIL:
investmentclubs@barclays.co.uk

WEBSITE:
www.barclays-stockbrokers.co.uk

DEALING METHODS:
Telephone, Internet and WAP

TYPE OF ACCOUNT:
Nominee account only

Charles Schwab Europe

ADDRESS:
Cannon House
24 The Priory Queensway
Birmingham B4 6BS

TELEPHONE:
0870 601 8888

WEBSITE:
www.schwab-europe.com

DEALING METHODS:
Post, telephone, Internet and automated touchtone telephone

TYPE OF ACCOUNT:
Nominee account only

City Deal Services

ADDRESS:
Kingfisher House
Radford Way
Billericay
Essex CM12 0GZ

TELEPHONE:
0800 917 1119

WEBSITE:
www.citydeal.co.uk

DEALING METHODS:
Freephone telephone dealing

TYPE OF ACCOUNT:
Nominee with interest-bearing bank account

Comdirect

ADDRESS:
Boatman's House
2 Selsdon Way
London E14 9LA

TELEPHONE:
0870 600 6044

E-MAIL:
info@comdirect.co.uk

WEBSITE:
www.comdirect.co.uk

DEALING METHODS:
Telephone and Internet

TYPE OF ACCOUNT:
Nominee account only

DLJ Direct

ADDRESS:
Investment Clubs
Capstan House
One Clover Crescent
East India Dock
London E14 2BH

TELEPHONE:
0800 358 4477

WEBSITE:
www.dljdirect.co.uk

DEALING METHODS:
Internet and telephone

TYPE OF ACCOUNT:
Nominee account only

E*Trade UK Limited

ADDRESS:
Mount Pleasant House
2 Mount Pleasant
Cambridge CB3 0RN

TELEPHONE:
08000 52 50 50

WEBSITE:
www.wtrade.co.uk

DEALING METHODS:
Internet and telephone

TYPE OF ACCOUNT:
Nominee account only

Hargreaves Lansdown Stockbrokers

ADDRESS:
Kendal House
4 Brighton Mews
Clifton
Bristol BS8 2NX

TELEPHONE:
0117 900 9000

WEBSITE:
www.hargreaveslansdown.co.uk

DEALING METHODS:
Telephone, Internet and postal

TYPE OF ACCOUNT:
Nominee only for investment clubs

iDealing.com

ADDRESS:
Freepost Lon 3628
London E1 7BR

E-MAIL:
admin@idealing.com

WEBSITE:
www.iDealing.com

DEALING METHODS:
Internet only

TYPE OF ACCOUNT:
Nominee account only

NatWest Stockbrokers

ADDRESS:
55 Mansell St
London E1 8AN

TELEPHONE:
0870 600 40 80

FAX:
020 7895 5495

WEBSITE:
www.natweststockbrokers.co.uk

DEALING METHODS:
Telephone and Internet

TYPE OF ACCOUNT:
Certificated or nominee

Self Trade

ADDRESS:
New Priestgate House
57 Priestgate
Peterborough PE1 1JX

TELEPHONE:
0845 100 0210

WEBSITE:
www.selftrade.co.uk

DEALING METHODS:
Internet or telephone

TYPE OF ACCOUNT:
Nominee only

StockAcademy

ADDRESS:
Compass House
Vision Park
Chivers Way
Histon
Cambridge CB4 9AN

TELEPHONE:
01223 234 545

WEBSITE:
www.stockacademy.com

DEALING METHODS:
Telephone and Internet

TYPE OF ACCOUNT:
Nominee account

The Share Centre

ADDRESS:
PO Box 2000
Aylesbury
Buckinghamshire HP21 8ZB

TELEPHONE:
01296 41 41 41

FAX:
01296 41 41 40

WEBSITE:
www.share.com

DEALING METHODS:
Post, telephone and Internet

TYPE OF ACCOUNT:
Nominee or certified sales

TD Waterhouse

ADDRESS:
Exchange Court
Duncombe St
Leeds LS1 4AX

TELEPHONE:
0800 1698 899

WEBSITE:
www.tdwaterhouse.co.uk

DEALING METHODS:
Telephone, Internet and WAP mobile phone

TYPE OF ACCOUNT:
Certificated and nominee services
(nominee only for clubs using the Internet)

Men who don't take risks won't drink champagne.

Russian saying

SPREAD BETTING —
BOON OR
BUST?

He does not have the trappings of your average bookie. The beige check suit, greasy trilby and beer gut would look out of place on this spare, mild-mannered and bespectacled gentleman. His background too – Eton, Oxford, the Guards, and merchant banking – would not seem the ideal training for someone who was aiming to make a living by taking bets from Joe public.

Yet when I asked Stuart Wheeler how he would describe his occupation he had no hesitation: 'I'm a bookmaker and proud of it,' he smiled. 'In fact it is very important that you describe me as a bookmaker because we wouldn't want to be confused in any way with stockbrokers. Our clients are placing bets, not buying shares, so there is no tax to pay on their winnings.'

He's touched on one of the main reasons I am including details of the betting business in this book and why I visited the London offices of IG Index, Stuart's spread betting company. Any way of avoiding the iniquitous capital gains tax must be worthy of close examination, but I was wary on two counts: I wasn't exactly sure how the game is played and I know my gambling genes are dangerous and likely to run riot.

The Stuart Wheeler story is fascinating. In the merchant banking depression of the early 1970s he lost his job in a small merchant bank, but his blue-blood background stood him in good stead. He went to see Cyril Stein, legendary head of the Ladbrokes betting empire, and suggested Ladbrokes should compete with Coral Index, a subsidiary of the big Coral bookmaking business, which took bets on futures, options, derivatives and so on. Stein refused, though it could not have been such a crap idea because he later bought Coral Index himself. Stuart (I use his Christian name

ANY WAY OF AVOIDING THE INIQUITOUS CAPITAL GAINS TAX MUST BE WORTHY OF CLOSE EXAMINATION, BUT I WAS WARY ON TWO COUNTS: I WASN'T EXACTLY SURE HOW THE GAME IS PLAYED AND I KNOW MY GAMBLING GENES ARE DANGEROUS AND LIKELY TO RUN RIOT.

THE SPREAD-BET BOOKMAKER
IS DIFFERENT BECAUSE HE DOES NOT OFFER ODDS.
YOUR BET IS BASED ON YOUR OPINION OF
HOW MUCH A SHARE (OR INDEX OR WHATEVER) WILL
GO UP OR DOWN IN THE FUTURE.
IF YOU GUESS RIGHT YOU WIN,
GUESS WRONG AND YOU LOSE.

because everyone from the receptionist to the lady who brings the tea does) decided to start his own spread betting company in 1974.

The initial concept was to offer people the chance to speculate on the price of gold, which was a commodity very much in the public eye because exchange control regulations were being eased. It was an entrepreneurial business and, as with so many pioneering ventures, it had a rocky start. But Stuart persevered and, to cut a long story short, he now heads the biggest spread betting business in Britain. He recounts fascinating tales of big winners, such as the country GP who has made over £2 million, the Birmingham restauranteur who has turned £30,000 into £1.5 million and the gambler who placed 62 consecutive winning bets. And because he's a good chief executive he doesn't tell any stories about those who lost not just their shirts but their underpants too.

The financial arm of IG Index (they also have a sports betting division) offers you the chance to bet on anything to do with money. Shares in the UK and America, stock market indices, futures, derivatives, options – you name it and IG will probably take your bet.

Please note, I do not say they will give you odds. This, I believe, is the essential difference between Stuart and the conventional bookmaker you will meet at the racecourse or in the high street shop. The traditional bookie offers you odds on whether an animal will win a race. If he, the bookie, thinks it is five times more likely another horse will win the race he will offer you odds of 5–1 against your horse winning. The spread-bet bookmaker is different because he does not offer odds. Your bet is based on your opinion of how much a share (or index or whatever) will go up or down in the future. If you guess right you win, guess wrong and you lose. It is as uncomplicated as that, but as always the devil is in the detail and how

the bet works takes a bit of explaining. 'Indeed, some of my best friends are highly intelligent captains of industry and even they have difficulty in understanding at first,' admits Stuart. 'Then suddenly the penny drops and it's easy.'

To make matters worse there are two completely different ways of speculating on what is going to happen to the markets in the future. You can have a spread bet or buy a contract for difference (CFD). Let's look at the spread bet first. Remember, you can get a quote on almost anything financial from individual shares to international currency movements but I want to keep it simple so let's assume you or your club want a bet on what will happen to the FTSE 100 Index in the future.

A bet on the FTSE

Suppose the FTSE yesterday closed at 5915 (I know it didn't, this is only an example). You and the other club members believe that over the next few months it will go up. You contact the bookmakers, either by phone or via the Internet, and ask them what spread they are quoting for the FTSE 100 in September.

They will immediately quote something like 5940–5950. This is a statistical figure which provides a benchmark for your bet. It means they will 'sell' you the FTSE at 5950, the higher of the two prices. You decide you want to bet £20 a point, which means that, come September, every point the FTSE finishes over 5950 earns you £20. And you don't have to wait until September, if the

FTSE leaps up in the next few weeks or even days and you think it is high enough, you can close the bet at any time and take your winnings.

In fact, let's assume the FTSE does rise soon and in a month's time you contact the bookmakers and find they are now quoting a spread of 6030–6040 for September. You decide enough's enough and you close the bet, accepting the 'selling' price of 6030. That's an improvement of 80 points on what you paid, which at £20 a point is £1,600 profit.

Of course, if the unthinkable happens and the FTSE drops between now and September, you would lose £20 a point. You will also kick yourself for not having foreseen the market fall, in which case you would have 'sold' the FTSE at 5940 and watched gleefully as the barometer fell. But you didn't and that's life. Better luck next time.

....
Take out a contract

A Contract for Difference (CFD) is technically not a bet but a share transaction. It enables you to deal in a share at the current market price without having to outlay the full price of the share. IG Index acts as the principal in buying the share and allows you to secure the full profits (or losses) of the share but you only have to outlay one-fifth of the full purchase price. It's referred to in the jargon of the trade as 'dealing on margin' and enables you to acquire shares valued at up to five times what you are prepared to lay out. There will be a small transaction commission – typically 0.25 per cent – plus a reasonable amount of interest on the loaned money which is calculated and added to your bill at the end of each day. Here again you can go 'long', which means you believe the share price is going to go up, or 'short' which means you think the price is going to go down.

I should make it clear that at no time do you actually own the shares, although if a dividend is paid during the period your position is open you will be credited with it.

There is no closing time for these CFDs, you can keep them going as long as you want to, but remember you will be

A CFD IS TECHNICALLY NOT
A BET BUT A SHARE TRANSACTION.
IT ENABLES YOU TO DEAL IN A SHARE
AT THE CURRENT MARKET PRICE
WITHOUT HAVING TO OUTLAY
THE FULL PRICE OF THE SHARE.

paying the interest on the money loaned to you. I should also emphasize that, because a CFD is a share transaction and not a bet, the profits will be subject to consideration for capital gains tax.

The whole spread betting business is fascinating, but is it for you or your club? Before we decide let me give you another positive scenario. Your club has a long-term safe share portfolio of, say, £250,000, but an uncomfortable feeling that the market might be heading for a substantial fall. You can liquidate your portfolio now and wait until the markets turn and buy the shares back again. Depending on the kind of broker you use it could cost you up to 5 per cent in transaction costs plus a substantial capital gains tax liability because you have realized your profits.

Alternatively, you could take out a 'short' bet that would cover your losses if the market goes down. Transaction charges would be negligible and your would have no tax liabilities.

So it could be a protection for your portfolio. But does it open new investment doors for you? The answer, until you have a big enough portfolio to consider this form of protection, is almost certainly no. Neither in spread betting or purchasing CFDs are you actually buying shares, bets are pure gambles and, although you can use your investment knowledge to decide whether a share is undervalued or overvalued, you are not securing one iota of ownership of the underlying asset.

I believe too that, particularly in the case of spread betting, you are introducing an unacceptable extra ingredient into the equation. Time. It is difficult enough to find a share whose value is not properly reflected in the market (because, let's face it, that is all you are trying to do when you invest). When you do find an undervalued share you buy it in the hope and the expectation that it is going to go up as the rest of the market realizes how perspicacious you have been and other investors are prepared to pay you more than you paid in the first place. Trouble is, when you place a spread bet, you also have to take a guess as to how long it will take for it to dawn on the others that you were far-sighted and they were slow. A week? A month? A year? No matter how much research you have done, I defy you to predict the answer to that question with any certainty. But a spread bet has a finish date and in my book that's where the snag lies. CFDs don't have this imponderable, at least they don't as long as you are prepared to let the interest clock keep ticking, it's a relentless drip notching up a debt for you that grows daily. The rate seems reasonable, just a tiny bit above bank base rate, but the bottom line gets bigger and bigger.

However, if you are aware of these easily ignored snags and you and the whole club understand exactly what you are doing there is undoubtedly an upside to both these gambling systems. The greatest attraction of spread betting, for me particularly, is the total freedom from tax. No capital gains tax, no income tax, the spread betting firm even pays the betting duty for you and you don't have to declare details of any of the transactions to the taxman. (You will understand that this is the situation as I write so I apologize if by the time you read this, the chancellor has found a way to shaft us. On the other hand he might have seen the light and abolished capital gains tax. Dream on, Terry).

It almost certainly will not cost you as much to benefit from price rises as if you had bought the shares outright. Stuart makes the point that a £10 bet on a share is the equivalent of buying 1,000 shares. If a share is priced at, say, £5 you will have to outlay £5,000 to buy 1,000 shares. If the price goes up by 1p you will have made a profit of £10. If you place a spread bet at £10 a point on the same share and it goes by 1p you also make £10.

There are a couple of other things I like about the system. The bookmakers seem very accommodating when it comes to granting credit facilities to clients, at least they gave me an excellent limit. I realize it is putting temptation in the way of the unwary but if you are sensible it is a bonus, particularly if you spot an opportunity you can't afford to miss. The other attraction, which applies only to spread betting, is that there are no commission fees. The bookmakers make their profit from the dealing spread – the difference between the price they 'buy' and 'sell' a bet at.

The final plus point that should be emphasized is that you, the punter, have the opportunity to put an absolute limit on your loss, so that if the stop-loss is reached the bet will be closed.

Incidentally – and this makes little or no difference to you or me but it is interesting – the bookmaker takes little or no risk in this business. He acquires or sells the relevant shares from stockbrokers so his potential losses are covered. At the end of the day it comes down to how much of a gambler you are.

If you can place the bet and not feel your heart thumping,

Or send the blood pressure gauge off the scale,

If you can concentrate on other things

And resist the temptation to turn on the computer,

If you can tell yourself it's only money and really mean it,

Then yours will be the earth and everything in it.

And you will be a financial gambler, my son.

You'll also be a better man than I am, Gungha Din.

There are two times in a man's life when he should not speculate: when he can't afford it, and when he can.

Mark Twain

14

YOUR ANONYMOUS CLUB MEMBER

At first sight investment trusts and unit trusts would seem to be a waste of time as far as investment clubs are concerned. On the face of it trusts are doing exactly the same job as clubs – selecting a group of shares from those quoted on the Stock Exchange and trading them in order to make a profit. And the trusts charge a management fee for doing the job, which seems a bit superfluous for clubs. After all, why pay a dog if you can bark yourself?

Certainly when I first became involved with the investment club movement in the early 1990s I poo-pooed the idea of clubs investing in trusts. Apart from those obvious management costs there was another reason I was not enamoured: typically a trust will invest in anything between 50 and 100 shares, sometimes slightly less but often many more. The principle, presumably, is that they are spreading the risk, which is commendable but, in my opinion, they are taking things much too far. Let me explain, and keep in mind the comparison with your investment club.

Imagine you're the boss person of a unit trust or an investment trust (I'll explain the difference in a moment). You and your small team of maybe half a dozen analysts and helpers have to choose 100 shares which are going to produce overall profits that will make your investors so happy they will want to entrust more of their savings to your fund. However, there are some restrictions on which shares you can choose because your trust will undoubtedly specialize in a particular kind of share or part of the world – capital growth, or high-income yield, or smaller companies, or Europe or Latin America, whatever (don't worry, I'll come back to these restrictions later, for the time being just follow my thought process). You and your team are specialists in whatever your trust concentrates on and you know a handful of crackers in that sector that will show you wonderful returns. But 100? Or even 50? That's ridiculous. There is absolutely no way your 49th choice is going to be as well researched and have the same profit potential as your first

AT FIRST SIGHT INVESTMENT TRUSTS

AND UNIT TRUSTS WOULD SEEM TO

BE A WASTE OF TIME AS FAR AS

INVESTMENT CLUBS ARE CONCERNED.

ON THE FACE OF IT TRUSTS ARE DOING

EXACTLY THE SAME JOB AS CLUBS.

UNTIL A FEW MONTHS AGO,

I BELIEVED THAT TRUSTS WERE LITTLE MORE THAN THE IDLE PERSON'S VEHICLE FOR INVESTING ON THE STOCK MARKET.

handful of crackers. Nor are you going to be able to monitor them with the same diligence as your favourites.

By comparison, your investment club is fleet of foot. The club itself is a collection of experts and your specialist knowledge, although it may not be to the same depth as a trust's, is much more diverse. And, most importantly, you can restrict your choice to that handful of real crackers, club favourites in which you can confidently invest your savings. And you can monitor them. And you will take much more care than those trust people because you are shepherding your own money and there's nothing like having your own cash involved for concentrating the mind.

It's not difficult to understand why, until a few months ago, I believed that trusts were little more than the idle person's vehicle for investing on the stock market. Then fate stepped in and I began sharing the seminar platform with the lovely people from the AITC, the Association of Investment Trust Companies. Although I realize Daniel Godfrey (director general of the AITC), Geoff Procter (director) and Annabel Brodie-Smith (communications director) are paid to be slightly biased, what they said made sense and to a degree they

have changed my opinion. I now believe that for some clubs, but not all, it is worth considering trusts as a home for a minority percentage of their portfolio.

But before you decide whether yours is one of the clubs that would benefit let's look at how these collective funds – in America they're called mutual funds and over there they are very, very popular – are made up and how they operate. We'll look at three kinds, the unit trust, the investment trust and a relatively new kid on the block, the OEIC, nickname 'oik', which stands for Open-Ended Investment Company (more jargon, it puts you off before you start).

Unit trusts

A unit trust is a collection of shares or bonds chosen by a fund manager or managers. It gets its name from the fact that you buy a unit in the collection. Usually the shares are picked with a specific investment purpose in mind and this purpose often dictates the risks the managers are prepared to take. You choose the approach that suits you. Let's put it on a personal basis, because after all these funds are really designed to appeal to individuals rather than clubs.

For instance, you may be fast approaching the 'doddery old devil' stage of life and just want a regular income to supplement the meagre pittance that the government gives you. Buy a new motorized wheelchair, one of those Stannah stairlifts, go on a cruise, move into a luxury rest home, enjoy it while you can. You're not interested in capital growth – why leave it to the kids? They'll only squander it. Fine, you're on the lookout for a high-yielding unit trust which concentrates on providing good regular dividend payments.

But maybe, like me, you are a Young Turk still making your way in life, wanting to salt a large proportion of your substantial salary away so that your savings will bloom and grow. You are not particularly interested in dividends, you want your capital to increase in value. You are looking for a unit trust that invests in new, vibrant industries. They are out there just waiting to be found, but of course they haven't yet proved their worth, their potential is built on hope and promises, so they are riskier than the high yielders. Maybe you are prepared for even higher risk and potentially higher reward, so you look for trusts that invest in emerging markets around the globe. Yer pays yer money and yer takes yer choice.

A unit trust is called 'open-ended' because it grows or contracts according to the amount of money placed by the customers who buy the units. The unit price is established by comparing the number of units sold with the value of the share portfolio. There are all sorts of unit trust funds dealing in a variety of investments from shares to corporate bonds and gilts.

Investment trusts

The concept is the same – managers choosing a collection of investments for you – but the set-up is slightly different. Actually, these are not really trusts at all, they are companies with shares you can trade, that's why they appear on the same pages as the quoted companies in the *Financial Times*. They are companies that invest in the shares of other companies. They have a board of directors and managers for each of the specialist groups of investments.

Investment trusts are closed-ended, which means they have a fixed number of shares in issue and the people who run them reckon this puts them in a better position than their unit trust cousins because they can make long-term investment plans without having to worry about investors bailing out, thus causing shares to be sold for the wrong reasons. I can see the point they are making. Another factor in their favour is that investment trusts can borrow money if they see an exciting investment opportunity. Unit trusts can't borrow.

I confess to not having analyzed the costs associated with the two kinds of trust though I believe that on the whole

unit trust management services are slightly more expensive. But when it comes to pricing I think the unit trusts have the edge. The unit price exactly reflects the value of the shares or other 'financial instruments' the trust owns. But the quoted price of the investment trust takes into account a discount or a premium to net asset value, which is the total value of all the investments the trust owns divided by the number of issued shares. The discount or premium figure reflects the supply and demand situation and the popularity of the trust, so I believe it's an unwanted distraction. To me, that net asset value figure is vital and the only way to value the trust.

Split-capital investment trusts

Sounds complicated but it isn't because, like Ronseal, it does exactly what it says on the tin. 'Splits' have a limited life – they are wound up after a set period, usually five or 10 years – and the choices within the split are designed specifically to suit the requirements of the buyer.

You can go for the zero-dividend preference shares option which offers a predetermined capital return when the trust is liquidated (safe as houses, this one, but as you might expect you will need a magnifying glass to examine the rate of return). And remember, the zero dividend in the title of this option means you don't get your hands on a penny until the end payout.

If you want regular money coming in look at the income shares option. The income rate usually hovers around the bank or building society rate and you just might get some capital growth too, but don't bank on it. There are a couple of variations worth mentioning: the annuity income shares option offers a decent regular income but you are kissing goodbye to the vast majority of your capital; the income and residual capital option attempts to balance a reasonable income with a share of the surplus assets when the fund is wound up.

Finally, there is the capital shares option. If you choose this option be aware that you are last in the queue when payday comes and the split is wound up. Those who opted for income have been taking their regular payments from the fund and the preference people are before you. Then it is your turn. You took the biggest risk and you are potentially the biggest winner but it all depends on how the managers managed the fund.

Oiks

An oik is a hybrid, a sort of combination of the two kinds of trust, and it is becoming more popular by the minute. Indeed many of the big unit trust companies are favouring the system and promoting it.

I don't want to waste space explaining the intricacies of an oik save to say that the main difference you will notice is that there is no bid/offer spread. The price quoted is the price you can buy or sell the oik at. And that, to me, is sensible.

Why do I say these various trusts may be of interest to your investment club? After all, their main appeal is to the individual who has little or no interest in the stock market and just wants his or her savings to work in the most effective way. Trusts can be held in an ISA (Individual Savings Account) but that is of no interest as far as a club is concerned.

However, there is a number of potential areas of club appeal that I believe you should consider:

- The trusts enable you to access areas of equity investing where you do not have expertise. In particular I am thinking of overseas markets. For British private investors and clubs, with the possible exception of the American market, these are still difficult and expensive to access. They also present problems of assessment and monitoring but there is an argument for saying that a truly balanced large portfolio should include an element of overseas investment. The specialist trust is an easy and relatively inexpensive way to invest overseas.

- It could be that your club comprises a membership that has an extremely focused area of expertise. Remember the club of chemists I mentioned earlier? Whiz kids when it came to pharmaceuticals but useless at anything else. Trusts could be a way of achieving portfolio balance if you are determined to restrict your club to members who are clones of each other.

- If your club has an overall policy of blue-chip investment and doesn't feel comfortable with speculative smaller companies it may nevertheless see the wisdom of balancing its portfolio by having a minor exposure in this

TRUSTS COULD BE A WAY OF ACHIEVING PORTFOLIO BALANCE IF YOU ARE DETERMINED TO RESTRICT YOUR CLUB TO MEMBERS WHO ARE CLONES OF EACH OTHER.

area. There are a number of trusts which specialize in smaller companies and they have the knowledge to make well-considered selections.

1. If you are interested in finding out more about unit trusts and open-ended investment companies get a list of members and any other free information available from AUTIF (The Association of Unit Trusts and Investment Companies) by ringing 020 7831 0898, or look on their website: www.investmentfunds.co.uk.

2. Investment trusts: Contact the AITC on 0800 085 8520. Website: www.itsonline.co.uk.

3. If you are interested in split-capital investment trusts and would like a free daily detailed analysis of them all, log on to www.splitsonline.co.uk. Data is provided by Fundamental Data and the site is sponsored by Aberdeen Investment Trusts.

4. Decide exactly what kind of trust, in terms of risk and specialist subject, you are looking for.

5. Check the past-performance league tables showing how successful or otherwise the various trusts have been. They are published regularly in those monthly magazines you see on the newsagents' shelves. In the world of trusts what happened yesterday is an imperfect guide to what is going to happen tomorrow but at least it is an indication based on fact rather than picture painting.

6. Don't expect financial miracles from trusts. At best they will do OK. A £1,000 investment in the average investment trust 10 years ago would have grown today to £3,198 (Source: Fundamental Data, 31 March 2001). You should expect your club portfolio to perform considerably better than that.

So, dear, you want to follow in your father's footsteps. No problem with that, it's not a bad old life. But before you definitely decide this is the way you want to go you must be quite sure you know what you're letting yourself in for. Nothing is quite as it seems. Come to me and I'll tell you a few stories that might make you think twice.

Wise Parent

FAMILY FORTUNES

··

He that diggeth a pit shall fall into it.

Ecclesiastes 10:8

A TAXING
MATTER

So I said to Her Royal Highness, Princess Anne: 'Please excuse me, ma'am. I'm afraid I'm going to be sick.' She didn't bat an eyelid. 'I quite understand,' she smiled. 'When you've got to go, you've got to go.' And, as I tottered down the companion ladder to the main cabin and hence to what is euphemistically called the heads, she carried on her conversation with round-the-world sailor Chay Blyth as if nothing untoward had occurred.

It happened on board the yacht *Great Britain II*, a superb craft which Chay had built for the Whitbread Round-the-World Race in 1972. I was his business partner at the time and, together with the sponsor, Jack Hayward, and a crew of paratroopers, we were taking the yacht on her proving voyage through the choppy waters of the Solent.

Princess Anne, who had graciously agreed to launch the boat for us, had also accepted Chay's invitation to join us on a private sail. She arrived at our rendezvous driving her new Reliant Scimitar – they were all the rage in the early 1970s – accompanied by her fiancé, Mark Phillips. The princess and the army captain had announced their engagement the previous day so as we set sail there were congratulations all round. Following in father's footsteps, the princess is a keen sailor and soon she was clearly enjoying the exhilarating sense of speed as Chay and his crew tested the prowess of the new yacht.

If Princess Anne was having a good time, I certainly wasn't. Sailing and me are just not compatible. But as this was only my second time at sea I was not aware of just how opposed we were. My first voyage had been on Chay's previous yacht, *British Steel*, and on that occasion I had attributed my unhappy stomach to the fact that I had fallen down the companion ladder within two minutes of setting sail (two broken ribs and not an ounce of sympathy from Chay).

As I deposited my breakfast, plus the inevitable tomato skins that inexplicably appear on these occasions, down the bowl in the heads of *Great Britain II* while Princess Anne and Mark billed and cooed on deck, I realized I was a victim of the most violent seasickness. Since that embarrassing occasion I have discovered that, despite my best efforts – everything from little pills to witchdoctors' remedies – it is incurable. Every time I set foot on a boat, even one of those tiny ones on the lake in the park, those tomato skins prepare themselves for a grand entrance into daylight.

I mention this matter to illustrate yet again that we can't all be good at everything. Remember the saga of the chalk and the dartboard? I'm no good at sums. Or sailing. Or filling in tax forms.

When it comes to dealing with the Inland Revenue I get that tomato skin feeling again. It all looks so complicated and, because it involves sums, I have hitherto avoided it like the plague. So it was with mixed emotions and a certain amount of trepidation that a few months ago I agreed to ProShare's suggestion that I should be part of a team put together to discuss investment club tax returns with the Inland Revenue. I think

A FEW MONTHS AGO I AGREED TO
PROSHARE'S SUGGESTION THAT I SHOULD BE
PART OF A TEAM PUT TOGETHER
TO DISCUSS INVESTMENT CLUB TAX RETURNS
WITH THE INLAND REVENUE.
I THINK PROSHARE FELT THAT IF
I COULD UNDERSTAND
THE SITUATION AND PROCEDURE TO BE ADOPTED
THEN ANYONE COULD.

ProShare felt that if I could understand the situation and procedure to be adopted then anyone could.

Both ProShare and the IR were keen to examine the situation because, while in capital gains terms investment clubs have started off as small fry, the movement had expanded fast and in the light of experience it was sensible to see if it could be made more efficient. As I write our discussions are not completely finalized but we have agreed most of the principles and we are in the process of producing a revised reporting form which should hopefully be available for club returns in the not-too-distant future.

The history of investment clubs and capital gains tax is easy to explain. In the early 1990s, when the movement was in a fledgling state, clubs were not sure how the question of tax should be dealt with.

Discussion between the powers-that-be produced sensible guidance that satisfied the IR and the clubs. Briefly, the requirement was for the clubs to produce an annual return for their local tax office which would give details of (a) the club's capital gains and dividends from shares during the relevant year and (b) the names and addresses of the club members and the amount of the profits – or losses – attributed to each of them. The club's responsibility was to provide this information to the IR and each member of the club.

The Inland Revenue was quick off the mark and produced forms and guidance for clubs. At the heart of the policy was Form 185-1 which represented a Simplified Tax Scheme for small or newly formed investment clubs. At the moment this is still in use, a three-page form which requires a minimum amount of information about the club, its members and its investments. It can be used provided that:

1. the club does not have more than 20 members in total at any time during the relevant year

2. the annual subscription has a maximum rate of no more than £1,000 per member

3. the total net gain of the club does not exceed more than £5,000 in the relevant year

4. the average investment per member on the cost price does not exceed £5,000

5. all members have agreed the division of the capital gains.

From requirements 3 and 4 you will see that after a few years most clubs will have accumulated assets which will make them ineligible for the Simplified Scheme so they are then required to fill out the Standard Form of Agreement which requires slightly more detailed information about the club, its members and its activities. It is certainly not complicated, even for a layman like me, and in fact I find it easier to understand than the so-called Simplified Scheme.

There's just one other form, catchily titled 185-2, which is completed by the club secretary or treasurer, whoever is delegated to do the job, and provided to each member of the club. It details his or her share of the profits or losses made from share dealing and his or her share of dividends received. What the member does with Form 185-2 is up to the individual. If he or she is a private shareholder and trades on his or her own

account and the profits exceed the standard capital gains tax allowance, the proportion of the club's profit or loss can be added to or subtracted from the individual's personal tax returns. If the member has no other capital gains income and the share of the club's profits does not exceed the capital gains tax allowance there is no need to include it in the tax returns.

In the new arrangements we are discussing with the IR the basic requirements will not change. However, we are agreed that the present Simplified Scheme is really no longer necessary and we are working with the IR to replace it with a single form which all clubs, no matter what stage of development they have achieved, will fill in.

I can't give you the final format of the form yet but it will answer the following requirements which have been stipulated by the IR and made available by the Capital Gains Tax Division to their local offices. Inevitably they are written in official-speak so when I feel they need a Janet-and-John explanation I have put it in italics (if you think I'm being overly simplistic then be patient and feel smug because, believe it or not, there are people around who are not as bright as you).

Investment clubs

Arrangements For Assessment of Capital Gains

1. **In the following paragraphs 'holding' means the proportionate share of the assets of the Club owned by a member.**

2. For each year ended 5 April the Secretary (or the responsible officer) of the Club shall compute the net gains or net losses (by deducting allowable losses from gains) accruing from all disposals of investments ('capital gains'). *It's the secretary's or the treasurer's job to do the overall sums and fill in the main form.*

3. On or before 6 June in each year the Secretary (or other responsible officer) of the Club shall deliver to the Inspector of Taxes for the District in which the Club holds its meetings a return (on a form provided by the Board of the Inland Revenue) of the net gains or losses of each Member and other particulars necessary for the proper assessment of gains. *It's the secretary's or the treasurer's job to make sure the information is correct and the form is delivered to the local tax office.*

4. Any gain or loss so reported in respect of a Member shall be included in the computation of the gains of the Member for the appropriate year and shall be deemed to arise from an asset separate from any other asset owned by the Member in the year. *This clarifies the situation that arises when the club owns shares in a company and an individual member may him- or herself own shares in the same company, probably bought at a different time. For all purposes, including tapering (of which more later) they are treated separately.*

5. Gain or losses accruing on disposals of investments by the Club shall be allocated to Members by reference to their respective holdings and in accordance with the rules of the Club. *You can't allocate profits on the basis that certain members have not used up all their annual capital gains tax*

YOU CAN'T ALLOCATE PROFITS ON THE BASIS THAT CERTAIN MEMBERS HAVE NOT USED UP ALL THEIR ANNUAL CAPITAL GAINS TAX ALLOWANCE. THE DIVISION OF SPOILS HAS TO RELATE TO THE AMOUNT OF EACH MEMBER'S SUBSCRIPTION DURING THE YEAR.

allowance. The division of spoils has to relate to the amount of each member's subscription during the year.

6. The consideration for disposals made by the Club shall be allocated to Members on the same basis as 5 above. (Members need this information for Tax Return purposes. The Return requires taxpayers to know whether in any year they made gains in excess of the capital gains annual exempt amount for that year and whether they disposed of assets – excluding principal private residence – worth in total more than twice the annual exempt amount for the year.) *Interesting one, this. The club has to inform the member of his or her share of the profits or losses and the dates on which the assets were bought and sold so that the member can calculate whether any taper relief is due to him or her. It is also important for the member to know if any of the shares sold were worth more than twice the annual capital gains allowance – for example, if the allowance is £7,200 and the club or the individual sells a share with a value of more than £14,400 it has to be reported in the capital gains section of the person's tax return. Not many people know that.*

7. When a Member disposes of the whole of his holding, his chargeable gain or allowable loss shall be computed as follows:

a. From the amount receivable on disposal there shall be deducted as 'allowable expenditure' the total of –
 i. the total of his subscriptions in acquisition of or additions to his holding and
 ii. the total of
  A. the interest (net after the deduction of income tax) and dividends (before the addition of tax credit) allocated to him/her from time to time and
  B. the net capital gains allocated to him from time to time (net losses will be deducted from the total)
  to the extent that the amounts under A and B have not been distributed.

b. When a Member disposes of his/her holding there shall be a deduction of a corresponding proportion of the 'allowable expenditure'.

c. For disposals qualifying for taper relief (see below) the club shall make the appropriate calculation and inform the Member so he/she can make an individual claim.

This explains what happens when a member leaves. The suggested procedure for a resignation is explained thoroughly in the ProShare manual, as is what should happen on the death of a member.

Because some clubs alter these rules to suit their specific purposes I will not go over the procedure in detail so let us just assume that there is a time and date when a resignation is accepted.

At that time the club (probably the treasurer) calculates the amount owing to the member based on (i) his or her subscriptions since he or she joined; (ii) interest and dividends due; (iii) capital gains due to date; and (iv) any taper relief due.

8. **Where at any time a Club makes a distribution to Members in proportion to their holdings specifically out of accumulated income and gains, the distribution shall not be treated as part of the disposal but the 'total' referred to in paragraph 7a (ii) in respect of each Member shall be reduced by the amount of the distribution made to him.** *If, for any reason, you have made a withdrawal from the club at any time during your membership this must be taken into account when you leave the club.*

9. **Where the rules of the Club allow a Member to withdraw income and gains, any withdrawal so permitted may be treated as reduction of the 'total' referred to in paragraph 7a (ii) of the Member and not as a part disposal of his holding to the extend that it does not exceed the undrawn income or gains which have been** credited to the Member in the three years ended 5 April next before that date of withdrawal. *This relates to someone who withdraws part of his or her funds in the club. As long as the amount taken out is less than the accumulated income and gains made by the member in the previous three tax years it will not be regarded as a part-disposal of shares.*

Your local tax office will probably ask your club secretary or treasurer to sign an acceptance of these IR requirements (or, rather, ones that have been amended to incorporate taper relief) and may well ask to see a minute authorizing the acceptance signed by each of your members.

Taper relief

I'm not even going to try to explain the intricacies of taper relief. It has replaced indexation, but as I never fully understood how to work *that* out I don't feel competent to discuss this new concession in detail. But basically, taper relief encourages the investor to invest for the long term – an admirable aim – by reducing the amount of your capital gain that is taxable the longer you hold the share. In other words, the longer you own the share, the less you hand over to the taxman. There are different scales depending on whether the share is classed as a business asset or a non-business asset but in the case of an investment club it is virtually certain that all the shares in the portfolio will be regarded as non-business assets. Taper relief will kick in after you have owned the shares for three years and the amount of relief will gradually increase annually until you have owned the share for 10 years when only 60 per cent of your profit will be subject to CGT. Exact details of taper relief will be found in the new draft of the Inland Revenue publication CGT1 and it can also be found on the Inland Revenue website www.inlandrevenue.gov.uk.

To help explain in more detail the workings of this rather complicated subject I asked the IR to come up with some actual examples of taper relief at work. They kindly gave me four for-instances.

Investment club taper examples

Example 1

Mr A joined the investment club in January 1997. The club acquired shares in a listed plc in December 1997. On 7 July 2001 the club disposes of the shares in the listed plc. The club has made no other acquisitions or disposal of shares in this company. An indexed chargeable

gain of £10,000 is computed at the club level. Mr A's share of the gain is £1,000. Mr A has no losses to use against gains and he has gains in excess of the annual exempt amount for 2001/02.

For taper relief Mr A is treated as having held the shares from 6 April 1998 [the earliest date taper can start from] to 7 July 2001 [the date of disposal]. There are three complete years in Mr A qualifying holding period. If, in regard to Mr A, the shares are not business assets, then Mr A will qualify for the 'bonus year' for assets held before 17 March 1998 [when the club held the shares and Mr A was a member] and still held at 6 April 1998.

The amount of gain remaining chargeable after taper relief for a non-business asset with four years in the holding period is 90 per cent. So, Mr A has a chargeable gain of £1,000 × 90 per cent = £900.

If the shares were business assets in relation to Mr A throughout the period from 6 April 1998 to 7 July 2001 then there will be three complete years in this holding period. The bonus year is not available for the disposal of business assets on or after 6 April 2000. The amount of gain remaining chargeable after taper relief for a business asset with three years in the holding period is 50 per cent. So, Mr A has a chargeable gain of £1,000 × 50 per cent = £500.

Example 2

Mrs B joins an investment club on 1 May 1999. On 1 December 1997 the club purchased shares in a listed plc. The shares are disposed of on 1 September 2001. The club has made no other acquisitions or disposal of shares in this company. An indexed chargeable gain of £15,000 is computed at the club level. Mrs B's share of the gain is £2,000. Mrs B has no losses to use against gains and she has gains in excess of the annual exempt amount for 2001/02.

Mrs B's holding period for the shares begins on 1 May 1999, the date she joined the club, and ends on 1 September 2001, when the shares are sold. There are two whole years in the qualifying holding period. Mrs B is not entitled to the bonus year. No taper relief is due on a non-business asset where there are only two years in the qualifying holding period.

If the shares were business assets in relation to Mrs B throughout the period from 1 May 1999 to 1 September 2001 then the amount of gain remaining chargeable after taper relief for a business asset with two years in the holding period is 75 per cent. So, Mrs B has a chargeable gain of £1,000 × 75 per cent = £750.

Example 3

Mrs C joins an investment club on 1 June 1998. On 1 December 1998 the club purchased shares in a listed plc. The shares are disposed of on 1 January 2002. The club has made no other acquisitions or disposal of shares in this company. An indexed chargeable gain of £20,000 is computed at the club level. Mrs C's share of the gain is £3,000. Mrs C has no losses to use against gains and she has gains in excess of the annual exempt amount for 2001/02.

Mrs C's holding period for the shares begins on 1 December 1998, the date the club acquired the shares, and ends on 1 January 2002, when the shares are sold. There are three whole years in the qualifying holding period. Mrs C is not entitled to the bonus year.

The amount of gain remaining chargeable after taper relief for a non-business asset with three years in the holding period is 95 per cent. So, Mrs C has a chargeable gain of £3,000 × 95 per cent = £2,850.

If the shares were business assets in relation to Mrs C between 1 December 1998 and 1 January 2002 then the amount of gain remaining chargeable after taper relief for a business asset with three years in the holding period is 50 per cent. So, Mrs C has a chargeable gain of £3,000 × 50 per cent = £1,500.

Example 4

Mr D joined the investment club in August 1997. On 7 June 2001 the club disposes of 1000 shares in a listed plc. The club acquired 2000 shares in October 1997 and 2000 on 4 June 1998 and has made no other acquisitions or disposal of shares in this company. An indexed chargeable gain of £10,000 is computed at the club level using the share identification rules [last in first out – LIFO]. Mr D's share of the gain is £2,000. Mr D has no losses to use against gains and he has gains in excess of the annual exempt amount for 2001/02.

The LIFO rules mean that the shares disposed of on 7 June 2001 are identified with some of those acquired on 4 June 1998. This is Mr D's holding period and there are three complete years in that period. If the shares are not business assets in relation to Mr D then the amount of gain remaining chargeable after taper relief for a non-business asset with three years in the holding period is 95 per cent. So, Mr D has a chargeable gain of £2,000 × 95 per cent = £1,900.

If the shares were business assets in relation to Mr D then the amount of gain remaining chargeable after taper relief for a business asset with three years in the holding period is 50 per cent. So, Mr D has a chargeable gain of £2,000 × 50 per cent = £1,000.

I doubt whether there will ever be a perfect resolution to the relationship between investment clubs and capital gains tax. There will always be an anomaly that arises to prove that no set of rules is infallible, and there will always be a Mr and Mrs Wotif who will take delight in constructing a set of circumstances that are seemingly not covered by the guidelines produced by ProShare or the Inland Revenue.

To those who think they can wriggle around the rules to decrease the amount of tax they have to pay I have a word of warning. I have a letter from the Inland Revenue which clearly states: 'Membership of an investment club should not provide opportunities for tax avoidance. The Revenue reserves the right to refuse to allow a club to continue to operate the Standard Scheme if members are using it for avoidance.'

To nerds like Mr and Mrs Wotif I say – go get a life. Stop wasting valuable club time. Concentrate on the main reason for the club's *raison d'être* – choosing shares that are going to increase in value.

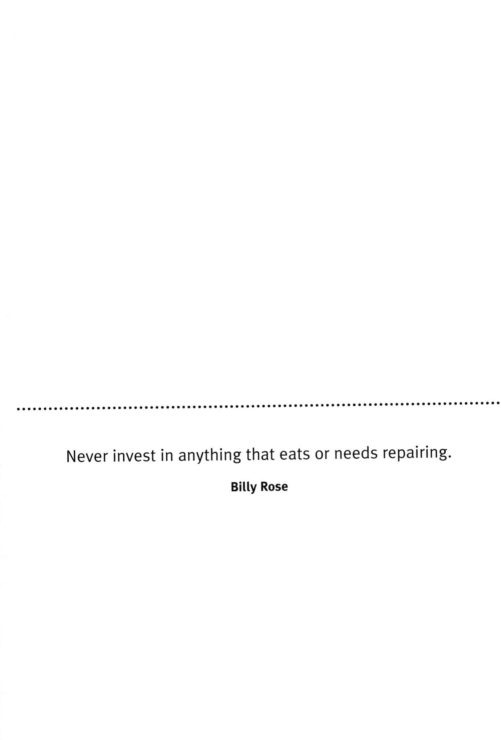

Never invest in anything that eats or needs repairing.

Billy Rose

CHAPTER 16

CLUBS?
WHAT CLUBS?

It's fair to say that until relatively recently only a handful of people in Britain had any idea what an investment club was. In the mid-1990s there were around 350 known clubs and I guess fewer than half of those were active. Then, for reasons I explained earlier, the whole thing took off. Clubs became a phenomenon, almost a cult, and like Topsie they just growed and growed.

As I write this particular chapter ProShare is celebrating the formation of its 11,000th club and you can be certain that by the time you read this book there will be many, many more. The froth that hit stock markets around the world at the beginning of this century has settled now – in one heady month we received registrations from 1,000 clubs – but despite uncertain times there are still hundreds of new clubs setting up, from Land's End to John O'Groats, the Isles of Scilly to the Hebrides.

Thousands of clubs, scores of thousands of members. But who exactly are they, these small groups of people who come together once a month to pool their precious savings and get pleasure from pitting their wits in the share marketplace? It is ProShare's job to encourage and guide the development of the investment club movement and to help them to do the job

- 8,500 investment clubs
- 300+ new clubs every month
- 1999 3,800 clubs
- 1996 300 clubs

Fig 16.1 The current position (September 2000)

properly they carry out regular research to find out about these men and women, what motivates them, and how they go about selecting shares.

....
The research

Carrying out such research is a mammoth task involving over 1,100 postal interviews. And because the results must be accurate the questions have to be carefully structured and posed in a consistent and reliable way. It's a job for specialists so ProShare uses a survey company called Objective Research.

- Postal survey
- Random sample
- July 2000
- Objective Research
- Sample 1070

Fig 16.2 The research

The results are valuable, not just for curiosity's sake, but because they enable ProShare to plan its future relationship with the clubs, to assess their needs and collate their experiences. The picture is also essential for the movement's supporters, organizations such as stockbrokers and information providers, who can adjust their services to suit the requirements of the clubs. Remember, we are talking about a big business here. It's estimated that in a couple of years investment clubs in Britain will collectively have around £500 million in the market and once that figure starts to roll there will be no stopping it. In five years it will almost certainly top £1 billion.

IT'S **ESTIMATED** THAT IN A COUPLE OF YEARS INVESTMENT CLUBS IN BRITAIN WILL **COLLECTIVELY** HAVE AROUND £500 MILLION IN THE MARKET AND ONCE THAT FIGURE **STARTS TO ROLL THERE** WILL BE NO STOPPING IT. IN FIVE YEARS IT WILL ALMOST CERTAINLY TOP £1 BILLION.

Let's take a look at the last set of results available as I write, from a survey carried out in the autumn of 2000. For your edification I have added my interpretation of what is revealed.

How long have clubs been in existence?

The majority have been formed for between one and three years. The interesting point here is that there are, on average, 14 members in a club. How does this reconcile with my statement that it is difficult for wannabe clubbers to join an existing club because the whole concept is so popular that they quickly become full? The rules say you can have 20 members so how come the average is 14? Good question, and it has two answers. The first is dictated by space: a significant percentage of clubs meet in members'

homes and this means space is restricted. I live in a cottage in the heart of the Oxfordshire countryside and more than a dozen people in the sitting room causes claustrophobia. Apart from that we don't have enough glasses (not strictly true, I haven't counted those cut crystal glasses we've collected over the years, but I certainly wouldn't be allowed to use those for actually drinking out of). The second reason is more nebulous: several clubs I've spoken to feel that a membership of 20 is too many. They are more comfortable with a lower number.

Relationship between members

Here's a prime example of why you have to use a professional market research outfit to carry out a meaningful survey. At first sight this question would seem misleading because of course most of the

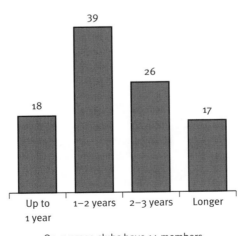

On average clubs have 14 members

Fig 16.3 How long have the clubs been in existence?

members would be friends, you would hardly decide to spend your leisure time with a group of folk you didn't like. But we wanted to know how people came together to form their club in the first place. It turns out that a big percentage were just friends and the link started when the motivator – there always has to be one person who sparks the idea off – decided to contact people he or she believed might be interested.

It's also significant to note that a lot of clubs are formed by work colleagues. You get to know people at work, you can assess their abilities and opinions and form a sixth sense about the contribution they can make to the club. My gut feel is that clubs formed by people who are together for much of the day are among the most successful. However, a word of warning: experience shows that it is better to hold the meetings away from the workplace. Rushed meetings at lunchtime or a session in someone's office at half-past five are not really satisfactory. Your club is a leisure activity and its home should be away from the daily toil.

Sector the club member works in

This is an interesting graph with confusing abbreviations at the bottom of the columns. For goodness sake, what is 'Trns'? And what do 'Man' and 'Primary' mean? Is it manual workers and people who teach toddlers? Fortunately, I can answer these questions for you. From the left the columns are:

1. Education, medical and public sector
2. Banking and financial services
3. Retail, travel and transport

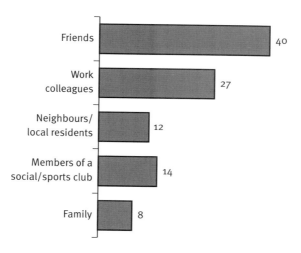

Fig 16.4 Relationship between members

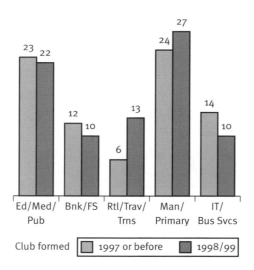

Fig 16.5 Sector the club member works in

4. Manufacturing and primary industry (that itself needs further explanation, apparently it refers to raw materials businesses, things like mining and forestry)

5. Information technology and business services.

Age of investment club member

Traditionally, private investors have come from what we politely call the more mature – it's nearly bus pass time – sector of society. Understandable really, because it's only when you reach the twilight years that you realize the government really means what it has been trying to tell you for ages, the state pension will hardly keep you in bread and water. The workhouse beckons unless you try to build up your own nest egg. Either these inescapable truths have dawned on investment club members earlier or they just want to have bigger eggs, because the average age of a club member is at least a decade less than the individual investor. It's gratifying to note

IT'S ONLY WHEN YOU REACH THE **TWILIGHT YEARS** THAT YOU REALIZE THE GOVERNMENT REALLY MEANS WHAT IT HAS BEEN TRYING TO TELL YOU FOR AGES, THE STATE PENSION WILL **HARDLY KEEP YOU IN BREAD AND WATER.**

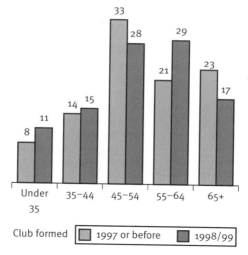

Fig 16.6 Age of investment club member

too that there is a goodly percentage of younger members.

Internet usage

Five years ago when I spoke at investor conferences and asked for a show of hands from those who used the Internet regularly for research, a smattering of arms were raised. When I ask the same question now it is a forest. The technology revolution has empowered the private investor and levelled the information playing field.

Club meetings – when and where

Pretty much what you would expect. Of those who don't meet every month there are some who meet every week (I think that's too often) and a few that meet

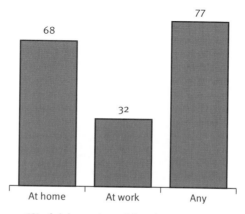

38% of club members visit websites every day

Fig 16.7 Internet usage

- 88% meet monthly
- 84% meet in the evening
- 42% meet in the pub
- Monday/Tuesday the most common day
- 48% of the clubs use e-mail to communicate
- 6% have their own website

Fig 16.8 Club meetings – when and where

- 78% of clubs hold shares in a nominee account
- Average value per trade is £1,180
- Buy an average of 9 times a year
- Sell an average of 6 times a year
- 17% trade using the internet
- 15% of clubs have switched brokers
- 30% of those established before 1998 have switched

Cost is the main reason cited for switching.

Fig 16.9 Club's trading activity

quarterly, usually because the members live far apart. I was in one of the latter clubs, we met four times a year in London and originally had members from as far away as Paris and Glasgow. After a couple of years we decided that three months was too long a gap between get-togethers so now we meet six times a year. The Paris chap is no longer a member but Jack Murdoch from Scotland never misses a meeting.

The number of clubs using e-mail has leapt up and now scores of clubs have their own websites.

Clubs' trading activity

A wealth of interesting information here for the companies who have a pecuniary interest in the success of investment clubs. By far the majority of clubs hold shares in a nominee account, that's partly because they can see the advantages of a paperless share-dealing society but the main reason is that the stockbrokers offer them no alternative. Low dealing prices mean automated processing and such items as share certificates and share registers cause hiccups and delays.

I believe that, the majority of brokers offering inexpensive execution-only services to investment clubs insist on the shares being held in the broker's nominee account and the shares are registered in that name with the appropriate company. In any case the shares could not be held directly in the name of the club because a club is a partnership and company registrars quite rightly would refuse to cope with multi-ownership. I have many an argument with clubs that insist on going down the route of appointing club trustees to hold share certificates on behalf of the club. What happens when a trustee leaves the club or, worse still, dies? It involves sorting out the situation with the executors of the dead person's will, special club resolutions, the cancellation and re-registration of shares with the company registrars – the whole thing is an administrative nightmare.

The perennial questions asked by the Mr Wotif of your club will be: 'What if the stockbroker goes bust? What evidence is there that our club owns the shares?' Don't panic. There's plenty of evidence. You receive written confirmation of your transaction from the broker, and all

CLUBS? WHAT CLUBS? **227**

qualified stockbrokers are properly insured, so you won't lose and the worst that can happen is that there will be a delay while things are sorted out. It's worth pointing out though that the delay can be a long one, as I know from experience. I had a share-dealing account with a stockbroker, Branston & Gothard, which did have to call in the receiver. It was at a time before nominee accounts were popular and I had share certificates; nevertheless, I did get that sinking feeling when the letter arrived telling me that the company liquidators had been appointed by the Securities and Futures Authority, which is the governing body overseeing all share trading in this country. My queries were easily sorted out on the telephone and I didn't experience any delays but obviously things were in a terrible mess because the SFA ordered the broker to cease trading in April 1998 and the latest report to creditors, with a covering letter asking for anyone who is still owed money to claim, arrived in May of 2001. That's over three years and the end is not yet in sight. Still, it provides jobs for the boys because the joint liquidators have been paid over £390,000 so far and there's more to come.

There was one fascinating snippet that caught my eye in the creditors' report. In the section dealing with the assets they had identified, the report says: 'B & G held a 'B' share in the London Stock Exchange, which was thought was of little value.' Fortunately, someone checked, and when the LSE decided to go public the 'B' share was converted to 100,000 new

ordinary 'A' shares which were then sold for £2.2 million.

Back to the graph. The other statistics here show that: (a) clubs are active traders, which is exactly what the brokers want; and (b) the investors are not afraid to change horses when it comes to dealing accounts. It used to be the case that, in the cloistered world of investing, your broker, like your doctor and your solicitor, was there for life. In the last couple of years there has been a price war going on as brokers compete for club business because they know that today's club member is tomorrow's individual private investor. My advice is to shop around and keep an eye on the special offers, after all when you cut through all the mystique, brokers are only order takers.

Subscriptions

Golden rule: Subscriptions must always be at a level everyone is comfortable with. The money you individually put in must be such that if you lost the lot it would be an aggravation but not a disaster. A complete wipe-out is very unlikely, but there's certainly a possibility that in the early days of a club's life you might experience a setback or two. I've never met a club of any substance that has picked winners every time. Equally, there will be a reticence among members to suggest potential investments if they think a significant amount of money is going to be risked on their recommendation. I can't repeat enough times that the money you have tied up in

I CAN'T REPEAT ENOUGH TIMES THAT THE MONEY YOU HAVE TIED UP IN AN INVESTMENT CLUB SHOULD BE RELATIVELY UNIMPORTANT. YOUR AIM IS TO TAKE THE CREAM OF THE INVESTMENT IDEAS THAT ARE DISCUSSED AT YOUR CLUB MEETINGS AND APPLY THEM TO YOUR PERSONAL PORTFOLIO. THAT'S THE WAY TO REALLY GET RICH.

- Average subscription per member £39.20
- 52% pay £20–£25 per month
- 21% pay over £50 per month – only 15% in 1999
- 76% paid a lump sum to join a club
- Average lump sum £250

Fig 16.10 Subscriptions

an investment club should be relatively unimportant. Your aim is to take the cream of the investment ideas that are discussed at your club meetings and apply them to your personal portfolio. That's the way to really get rich.

Most clubs chip a lump sum into the pot at the beginning to get the club started, and £250 seems about right. And the number of clubs paying over £50 a month is increasing, but that's inflation for you.

Clubs' investment approach

I find these statistics most gratifying. There is an opinion among the ill-informed that investment clubs do little more than chase the dragon, existing on hot tips and penny shares. The research shows that, on the contrary, by far the majority are intent on building a properly balanced portfolio, a diversity of shares that reflects the breadth of their specialist knowledge. The high riskers are a fairly insignificant single-figure percentage, which doesn't seem to alter with the years. Good to see too that quite a few clubs specialize in identifying growth stocks. To my mind that's where the real opportunities lie.

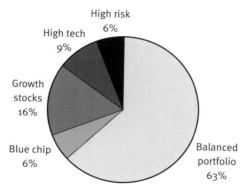

The number pursuing a high tech/high risk
approach is unchanged year on year

Fig 16.11 Clubs' investment approach

Information sources used by clubs

No real surprises here, though it is interesting to note how few clubs contact the company direct when they are researching a share. I usually do, even if it's only to get the latest press releases or a copy of the interim accounts. However, it may be that the increasing use of the Internet means clubs get this kind of information from the company's website, which I suppose counts as contacting the company direct. On a personal point, I'm

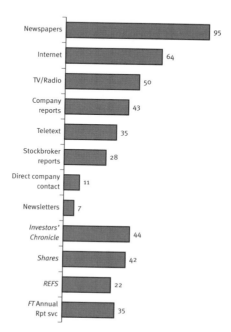

Fig 16.12 Information sources used by clubs

pleased to see *Shares* magazine is giving *Investors' Chronicle* a run for its money. Ever since I can remember the old *IC* held an autocratic and seemingly unassailable position as the only weekly around for private investors. Its design and layout was reminiscent of the dark ages and it talked loftily to its readers. Then along bounced a ginger-haired Aussie called Ross Greenwood, full of energy, enthusiasm and ideas. He launched *Shares* magazine with a flourish at exactly the right time, just as the bull market was getting into its stride. No holds barred, he went for the new investors and wooed them with a promise of riches, which was fortunately mixed with a dollop of common sense. Penny shares, information technology and telecom punts, they all had a place in *Shares* and the investors lapped it up. To its credit, the *IC* did not just roll over and let *Shares* tickle its tummy. With an attitude of 'If you can't beat 'em, join 'em' the old lady took the upstart on at its own game. Splash headlines replaced the staid messages on the *IC*'s front page. Colourful pictures instead of dreary drawings caught the eye of the bookstall browser. I'm looking at recent issues of the two magazines now. On one the cover headline says DIVE! DIVE! DIVE! – HOT PROSPECTS FOR THE BOTTOM FISHERS and the other EXPOSED – WHY YOU NEED TO KNOW WHO'S GUILTY OF CREATIVE ACCOUNTING. I defy you to guess with any certainty which one comes from the old lady and which from the upstart, but the winners in the war are undoubtedly the private investor and investment clubs.

It wouldn't be fair to ignore another weekly for the private investor that has appeared on the scene. *Investors' Week* is a tad more serious than *Shares* but to my mind it has still to decide where its niche in this marketplace is. If it were mine I would aim at the serious international investor and include information and tips for markets overseas, particularly in Europe and the United States. But what do I know? I'm not a publisher.

Investment club assets

Each year the portions of the cake that refer to club portfolios valued at over £20,000 get larger. That's because clubs are becoming more mature, they have a constant stream of new funds coming in every month, and they trade their holdings to increase their profits.

Here's an anecdote to illustrate what is possible when you begin to achieve success with your club. Every year ProShare organizes awards for various categories of investment club – Best Overall, Most Impressive New Club, Best Performance in Percentage Terms, the Club That's Done the Most for the Movement, and so on. In 1998 the winners of the best-performing club were a group of medical men from the Midlands. If memory serves me right their portfolio had shown something over 200 per cent profit in the year and we had much pleasure in presenting them with a handsome trophy and a cheque. The following year, 1999, the Midlands club was no match for its successors, The Golden Eagle Nest Club of North Yorkshire, that made an

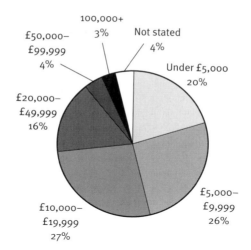

Fig 16.13 Investment club assets

incredible 2,400 per cent profit. At the awards ceremony in March 2000 I spoke to the secretary of the Midlands club. He told me their profits for 1999 had again been well over 200 per cent and their portfolio was valued at over £700,000. 'We are going to use options to protect our position,' he said. 'We can feel a downturn coming.' How right he was.

Average club assets

This figure rises substantially each year because there are more and more well-established clubs and, usually, as clubs get older so their performance improves. Remember what golfer Gary Player said: 'The more I practise, the luckier I get.'

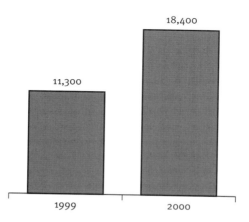

Fig 16.14 Average club assets

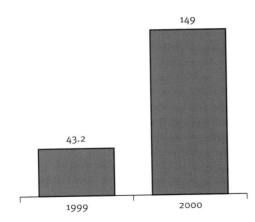

149

43.2

1999   2000

Fig 16.15 Total club assets (£m)

Total club assets

Dramatic increase. Clubs are big players in the game now.

Where do clubs invest their money?

Another one in the eye for those who thought investment clubs were populated by loonies who did nothing more than feed the minnows in the hope they would grow into whales. On the contrary, the bulk of the companies chosen by clubs are in the FTSE 100 and FTSE 250, substantial outfits with strong financial backing. Sensibly they see that a portfolio should be built on firm foundations. And very few clubs trust their funds to the hope stocks that come to the market via OFEX. The inference too is that they avoid new issues, which pleases me personally.

Not so long ago there was a big hoo-ha because private investors were not being given equal access to company flotations. The justifiable complaint was that new issues were often a carve-up

with priority being given to the institutions and a chosen few favoured ones. We ordinary investors didn't get a look-in. This cartel still operates today and when the really good new issues come to the stockmarket it is invariably as a placing, which means that all available shares are allocated beforehand. Private investors and clubs have to wait until the market opens before they can buy and more often than not they have to pay substantially more than the issue price stated in the prospectus. That is an annoyance and organizations like ProShare are continually lobbying the powers that be to level the playing field, but there is a subsidiary problem that is not just annoying, it is downright dangerous.

It is in the nature of man that he craves what he can't have, so when there is a chance of getting in on new issues the less wary among us leap in without too much thought. Enter the new issue that in reality is little more than a speculative idea looking for financial backing. Usually it is something easy to understand, like a company that is going to produce an all-British film, or an executive recruitment firm, or a website aimed at grandparents. No doubt some of these once-in-a-lifetime-opportunity-but-you've-got-to-get-in-quick deals are worth looking at, but the vast majority will haemorrhage your money. A recent survey in *Growth Company Investor* magazine proved that over the past year new issues that came to the market as placings had made money for the chosen few because the shares were on average

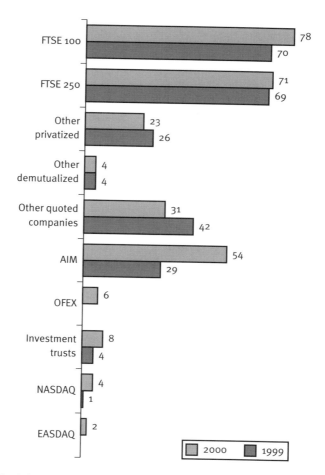

Fig 16.16 Where do clubs invest their money?

trading at a premium, whereas the majority of those that came as open offers were now trading at well below their issue price. In most cases you should avoid these tiddlers, let someone else take the risk.

Having said all that, I'm cautiously pleased to see that AIM, the Alternative Investment Market, is becoming increasingly attractive to clubs. The entry conditions for companies wanting a quote on AIM are not so stringent as those required for a position on the main

exchange; nevertheless, it is governed and policed by the London Stock Exchange. This means that there are opportunities for bright young companies to access private investor money and thus finance their business.

So am I talking with forked tongue? In one paragraph I say avoid the tiddlers and in the next I witter on about good opportunities presented by new young businesses. Both statements are correct. New issues are a prime example of where you must take time to sort the wheat from the chaff. Several publications list the details and contact numbers of companies that are planning a flotation in the near future. Most importantly, they usually include brief details of the business.

- Check whether any of the businesses fall within your club's circle of competence. If you have a member who has experience in the field it is a flying start for you. Remember: *Know what you own and own what you know.*

- Get hold of the prospectus and check it out thoroughly. With your member who knows, decide whether you think the ambitions will be realized. Is the business up and running yet or is it still one man, a dog and a dream?

- Is there a management team in place to cover all aspects of the business? Check out their pedigree, qualifications, and achievements to date.

- Is the competition identified? It should be. Why is the new company going to beat its competitors? Trying harder is not good enough, if there's a fresh face in the ring it should have unique features.

- Talk to potential customers for the new product or service. Do they know about it? If not, why not? What snags do they foresee? Would they be interested in investing themselves? This part of the research is essential because experience has taught me that management can be blinkered by enthusiasm for their business. They are deliberately trying to mislead when they say sliced bread will have a competitor, they are so consumed by their passion for the product that criticism is considered an affront from people who just don't understand. Management is understandably biased so it is vital that you take dispassionate but informed advice from those who can see the bigger picture.

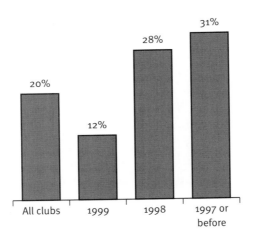

Fig 16.17 Over the year the average profit of all clubs was 20%. But the larger established clubs performed best

Investment clubs' performance

The graph in Figure 16.17 illustrates vividly that the more experienced a club becomes – the longer it has been formed – the better its investing performance. We've been through some rock 'n' roll years in recent times and these figures are most encouraging because they indicate considerable outperformance when measured against any other form of collective investment. However, I wouldn't want to mislead you; I regard them as an indicator rather than a strictly accurate measure because the figures are compiled only from the clubs that provided replies to this section of the questionnaire. It could be (although I'm only guessing) that some clubs left it blank because they were so ashamed ... Also, surveys like this are historical and you can be certain that the average client performance in the 2001 survey will be considerably down on its predecessors.

What is exciting is the performance of the all-female clubs. I made a jokey reference to this earlier, but I'm the first to admit it is a fact and proves beyond doubt that women are definitely not the weaker sex. Less prone to knee-jerk reaction, more inclined to do research, less tempted by penny share punts – whatever the reason they have graphically proved they are the champions.

It is also interesting to note that single-sex clubs perform better than the average of all clubs. I have always been an advocate of mixed clubs but that is based on nothing more than a personal opinion. I prefer to spend my leisure time in mixed company because I believe women are more interesting than men when it comes to conversations about people but men have the edge when matters such as sport are discussed. I'm sure it must be a proven fact that women are also much more accurate than men when it comes to first impressions. How many times have I had to admit she was right when she said: 'I told you that so-and-so was a bad lot,' or 'I told you at the start that was a stupid investment'?

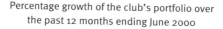

Percentage growth of the club's portfolio over the past 12 months ending June 2000

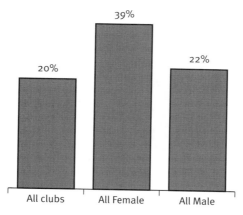

Fig 16.18 Investment clubs' performance according to sex of club members

Frequency of share purchase before joining an investment club

This is the reason why ProShare puts its weight and money into building the investment club movement in Britain. The mission has always been to widen and deepen sensible share ownership and clubs are the perfect way to do it. The vast majority of members had little or nothing to do with shares before they joined their club and those are the people ProShare wanted to reach and educate.

It is early days yet, but in Figure 16.25 below you will see that an increasing number of members start actively investing for themselves. I'm hoping that we will continue to mirror the American experience. The movement there is about five years ahead of us and at this stage of their developments they had around 60 per cent unsophisticated investors in their clubs. Recent research in the US has revealed that 60 per cent of that 60 per cent have now created individual portfolios and are active investors in their own right. Club

membership gives you the knowledge and the confidence to use shares as bricks to build your own future. (I should have been an advertising copywriter.)

Individual's perceptions of club membership

If ProShare's aim is to increase people's ability to invest, then it's working. Look at how many club members are learning and having fun at the same time. At least half of them agree that they are making more money from their personal investments since they became a club member, which gives credence to my argument that a private investor is not being fair to him- or herself if he or she doesn't join a club. It makes you a better investor.

Where do individual club members invest their money?

The idea that when you go to a club meeting you are more tempted to experiment is borne out by Figure 16.21.

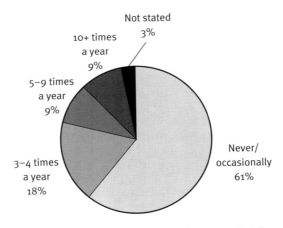

Fig 16.19 Frequency of share purchase before joining an investment club

1. I have learned more about investing since joining a club.
2. I get more enjoyment out of investing since joining a club.
3. I have increased the value of my own portfolio since joining a club.
4. Membership has made me more confident when taking investment decisions.

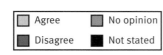

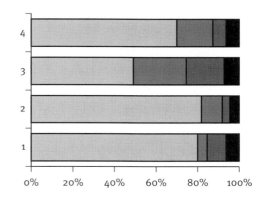

Fig 16.20 Individual's perception of club membership

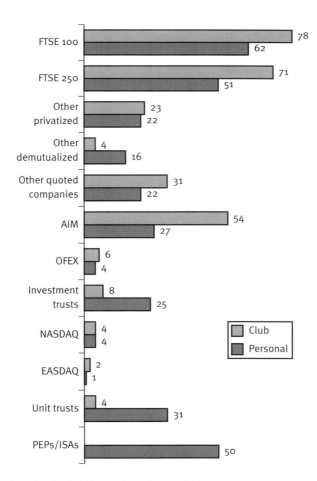

Fig 16.21 Where do individual club members invest their money?

In the case of AIM investments particularly it shows that you are twice as likely to be comfortable with this admittedly riskier area. The reason could be something to do with confidence – a collective assessment of risk is more reassuring than an individual opinion – but I believe it is more likely to be the comparatively small amount of personal money involved. If there are 20 members in a club and it decides to buy shares in an AIM company for £1,000 each member's involvement is just £50.

It's good to see that PEPs and ISAs play a big part in the portfolios of individual club members. They are a considerable tax concession for serious investors.

The amount of capital gains tax you will have to pay depends on your overall income and the ifs and buts are so many that I won't attempt to explain them here. The best move, if you have any doubts or need guidance, and you haven't got a professional financial adviser so plan to fill in your own tax return, is to ask your local Inland Revenue office or ring the IR Helpline (0845 9000 444). However, whatever your personal circumstances you must fill in the capital gains section of your return if the following two points apply to you:

1. When you tot up the gains and losses you made from share trading during the year, you made a total profit of more than £7,200 (that's the current tax-free allowance, watch out for chancellor-type changes). For the avoidance of doubt, we are talking about actual realized cash gains, not an increase in the value of your portfolio.

2. You disposed of chargeable assets in the year worth more than £14,400. This is a fuzzy area because a number of big items such as cars and houses are usually, but not always, exempt from this list of chargeable assets. Ask your taxman for details, but the point I am making is, if you sold shares to the total value of more than £14,400, never mind the profit – you have to tell the taxman on your tax return. Not many people know that.

I've spoken to my Deep Throat contact at the Inland Revenue about this last point and we are of the opinion that you should only take into account your share of the gross disposals of your club. So you divide the total club sales by the number of members and use that figure as the one for your personal tax return calculation.

Please don't take this advice as definitive guidance for filling in your tax return. If you have any queries relating to tax or indeed any other matter detailed on the form, use the Helpline. I've rung it several times and, contrary to popular opinion, there is not a Horrible Hector on the other end of the line out to get you. You will talk to a Helpful Hector or Harriet who invariably supplies not only the answer to your query but the reasoning behind it. But be prepared for that infuriating 'Sorry, all our operators are busy at the moment' twaddle before you eventually get through.

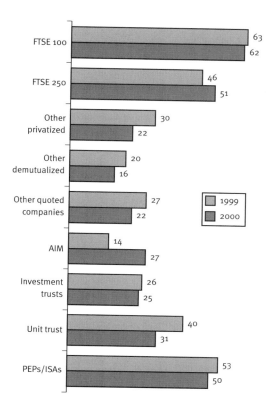

Fig 16.22 Changes in members' own portfolios in the last 12 months

Good to see too that unit trusts and investment trusts feature in private portfolios although I secretly hope not many choose those mindless tracker funds. I know, I know – they're a low-risk way of following market trends which is OK because over time the trend is always upwards, but how boring! As you will see from Chapter 14 I believe they should be used, by individuals and clubs, to buy into specialist sectors and overseas markets.

Changes in members' own portfolios in the last 12 months

Unsurprisingly, not much change here except that the AIM is beginning to feature more strongly.

Investment club members' personal investment patterns

- 15% have personally used an on-line broker
- Buy 6 times a year on their own behalf
- Sell 4 times a year on their behalf
- 68% aim to choose shares that will appreciate in the long term

Fig 16.23 Investment club members' personal investment patterns

Inevitably the percentage of investors logging on to the Internet and going into their brokers' secure site to buy and sell is increasing. It was bound to happen, even though the move from telephone and snail mail is a major sea-change for those who are past the full flush of youth. Look at the advantages:

- It's quick.
- It's easy.
- It's cheaper.
- It's secure.
- You can take your time.
- You can decide the price you want to buy or sell at.
- You can change your mind at the last minute.
- You make an offer – i.e. leave an order on the books for the rest of the day.
- Every deal is confirmed by post and there's no unnecessary paperwork.
- No share certificates to lose.
- You can view your updated portfolio.
- You can check on prices real time.

Of course there's a downside. I don't kid myself, brokers introduced Internet dealing and nominee accounts for their own benefit, not ours. You have to use a nominee account so your name doesn't appear on the company's share register. You don't automatically get annual reports and communications from the company. I use an execution-only broker for my Internet dealing. I have made sure he is adequately insured to cover my portfolio and a lot more besides. And I rattled his cage and threatened to take my business elsewhere until he agreed to send me the annual reports of all the companies in which I own shares. So far, touch wood, the system is working and I like it.

The comparative infrequency of trading and the finding that most people are looking to choose shares for the long term are statistics that reiterate the fact that the most sensible and profitable attitude to share selection – buy and hold – prevails.

Individual portfolios of club members

Look at the total value figure at the bottom of Figure 16.24. It's staggering. It also makes brokers almost whimper with glee because when they communicate with investment clubs this is the potential market they are talking to.

In addition the chart illustrates that a large proportion of high-net-worth

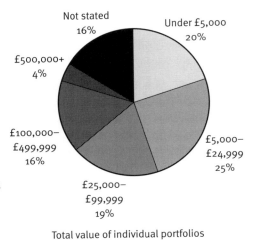

Total value of individual portfolios
= £13,080,000,000

Fig 16.24 Individual portfolios of club members

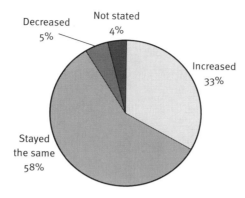

41% of those in clubs formed in 1998 or
before have increased their individual trading

Fig 16.25 Change in level of individual trading activity since joining an investment club

individuals (jargon for 'rich people')
understands that joining a club
protects their wealth and makes them
better investors.

Change in level of individual trading activity since joining an investment club

A significant proportion of investment
club members become more confident in
their own ability to make a profit from
buying and selling shares.

The investment club movement is a
living, growing thing. Its appearance
adapts to the changing state of the
economy and the stock market. Since
this survey was completed we have had
several months of uncertain markets and
we have tasted recession. Like all other
investors, clubs have been hit in their
pockets as the realization dawns that, as

- Growth in numbers highlights appeal
- Internet having a big impact:
  www.proshareclubs.co.uk
- Awareness of the needs to undertake research:
  Investors' Toolkit
- Encouraging a balanced approach
- Impressive returns
- More active individuals portfolios
- Funds for smaller companies
- £149m today £500m 2003

Fig 16.26 Assessing the impact

it says on the packet, the price of shares
can go down as well as up. However, this
year I have talked with hundreds of
investment club members and spoken at
several seminars organized by ProShare
for its members, and I know that the vast
majority of the people are not
discouraged. Far from walking away from
the stock market they see depressed
times as opportunities to buy.

Good clubs know that when they make an investment they are buying into a company, not an index or an economy. It is the mechanics of a single organization they have checked out and become familiar with, not a country or an amorphous thing like the FTSE 100 or the Dow or whatever. Of course, economic circumstances affect companies but if the management is aware and the product is right the company will be profitable and its shareholders happy.

GOOD CLUBS KNOW THAT WHEN THEY MAKE AN INVESTMENT THEY ARE BUYING INTO A COMPANY, NOT AN INDEX OR AN ECONOMY. IT IS THE MECHANICS OF A SINGLE ORGANIZATION THEY HAVE CHECKED OUT AND BECOME FAMILIAR WITH, NOT A COUNTRY OR AN AMORPHOUS THING LIKE THE FTSE 100 OR THE DOW OR WHATEVER.

For the private investor, the good news is there's never been so much free research information available. The bad news is there's never been so much free research information available.

Justin Urquhart-Stewart

NO TIME TO READ IT

Look at that pile of bumph in the corner. Books, newspapers, magazines, newsletters, annual reports, brochures, supplements. Some you bought, some came free, all of them are waiting to be read and if you are like me you feel guilty that they remain unopened. Log on to the Internet via your personal computer, type in some catch-all phrase like 'investment information', and you will be confronted with hundreds of thousands of sources. Move to one of the financial chat lines where investors exchange ideas and insider whispers and you can waste hours scrolling through them. If you have a digital receiver turn your television to one of the many business channels and watch and listen as the breaking news is churned out.

Information is a drug and it seems the more we have the more we want. The supply is unstoppable and while a first reaction is one of delight because our research is so easy to carry out there are two obvious dangers: the confusion that such a plethora of facts is bound to induce; and the problem of sorting the wheat from the chaff.

I guess I suffer more than most because I am targeted by the information providers as a private investor as well as a journalist and communicator. And I am a willing recipient, I eagerly await Danny who brings the newspaper and Mary, the postlady, I surf the Net interminably and can spend a whole afternoon in a bookshop. Seeking and soaking up facts and the thoughts of others can been a great, if pleasurable, timewaster.

Being aware of the dangers I have attempted to introduce some discipline into my absorption of information and I recommend you do the same. I also urge you to use your investment club to help.

My first attempts at cutting down on the information drug were fairly futile. As one of my New Year resolutions I decided Sundays were sacrosanct, a time for getting away from the world of shares and money, and that there would therefore be no Sunday newspapers delivered. Ostensibly the arrangement worked fine at first but I wasn't exactly achieving the objective because I used the barren Sundays for catching up with the paper mountain that arrives every Saturday. Then the *Telegraph* offered me half-price newspapers as long as I committed to four years of seven-days-a-week *Telegraphs*, and Mondays seemed to be dominated by fellow investors wanting to talk about articles I had surely seen in the *Sunday Times*, the *Observer*, or whatever. I have compromised and taken the *Telegraph* offer, principally because Neil Bennett seems to uncover good business stories and Luke Johnson is a thought-provoking columnist as well as being an interesting entrepreneur.

My other efforts on restricting the time I spend reading and watching have been more successful. Now I never, ever, turn to the information exchange pages – the chat lines – on the financial websites. I spent two hours a day for a week looking at this source of information before I came to my draconian decision because I wanted to be sure that I was

not cutting off my nose to spite my face. I moved from one chat line to another, checking the messages, backtracking the tips, using hindsight to decide the efficacy of the ideas. My conclusion: the information contained within the messages is, in the main, unadulterated drivel. Worse, it is dangerous unadulterated drivel.

Some of the crap is easy to spot. 'Hey, everyone! Rumpodumpo Mines have finally done it! Hit oil in the South China Seas and the gusher is a mile high! I filled my boots at 3p. Get in quick! Kev The Pixie.' Kevin, a vertically challenged anorak sitting in a terraced council house in Balsall Heath, Birmingham, has bought

£250-worth of Rumpodumpo stock today and is hoping to create a run on the market. A sad soul, he is working on the 'greater fool' theory.

No-hoper Kev is easy to spot but there are cleverer liars than him around. 'Help! I'm worried. Just heard from a very reliable personal friend who is a senior manager at Quacky-quack (a FTSE 350 company) that they're not far away from a profits warning. They've had poor sales in the last couple of months and are about to lose a big order. Anyone else got any info? I'm in for thousands but I'm thinking of getting out. Doctor John.' This is followed by several messages from other contributors (who are no doubt in cahoots with Doctor John) confirming the warning and adding some more depressing insider information about Quacky-quack plc. Search around and you will find similar messages on other chat sites.

Why do Doctor John and his mates do it? Two reasons. They may be short sellers and have made substantial spread bets on the price of Quacky-quack dropping. Or they may be starting a rumour so that they can buy when the price drops and subsequently benefit when the price bounces after the rumours are proved to be unfounded. It may seem unbelievable that individuals, or a gang of just a handful of investors, can manipulate the market in this way but, believe me, it happens. Addiction to the chat lines is not just a disease suffered by the small investor, those who control the portfolios of institutions read the drivel too and they are human, a worm will be implanted and confidence will be dented.

It used to be a mantra in the City that the private investor had little or no influence on share prices because his or her purchases were so small and fragmented as to be insignificant. That is probably still the case as far as bigger stocks are concerned but it certainly doesn't apply to shares in companies with a market capitalization of less than £200 million. A television programme taught me that lesson.

At the height of the tech stock boom I was invited to go for an audition to co-host a daily lunchtime show being produced by an independent company, Princess Productions. The programme was called *Show Me The Money* and was to be on Channel 4 for 13 weeks. For those of you who didn't watch or can't remember, the formula was simple: each day of the week a different 'investment club' team of four people (they were chosen from actual clubs) would manage their portfolio of shares and buy or sell on the evidence of their own researches and after hearing a one-minute sales pitch from the chief executive of a plc. Their choices would be commented on by a shares expert and that was the job they were testing me for. I didn't get it, Tom Winnifrith did, and quite right too. He is a knowledgeable lad when it comes to tiddler stocks. He's also younger and a tad more handsome than me. The programme got good audience ratings and was a particular hit with a large section of the new investor set, those good folk who had been attracted into the share-buying game by the promise of overnight riches as the new economy stocks shot skywards.

I happened to be in the dealing room at Barclays Stockbrokers one lunchtime when *Show Me The Money*, which went out live, was on. The phones were going mad. Here's the actual transcript of a typical call I listened in to:

'Name's Smith, number's 123353. I want to buy £500 worth of those shares that chap's just mentioned on the telly. Quick, before the price goes up.'

'Yes sir, what was the name of the stock?'

'I don't know! It was that one the man on that shares programme talked about.

He's the boss off it. Quick! You're wasting time, the price will be going up as we speak.'

Multiply that call by hundreds, maybe thousands, and you have a real picture of what was happening in execution-only dealing rooms everywhere in Britain. The company market makers were in seventh heaven, they knew which company boss was booked to make a sales pitch. Unless the boss was a real dummy – and there were those that deserved that description – the price of the featured share was marked up and the demand flowed in. At the end of each programme the presenter was able to say, 'Today, after hearing from Fred or Freda Bloggs, the chief executive of Notahopeinhell company, our share club chose to put a fantasy £2,000 into the stock. Great decision guys, because while we've been on air the share has gone from 14p to 21p so you're already showing a £1,000 profit.' This triggered a further frenzy in the dealing rooms as fledgling investors thought they had spotted a bandwagon and blindly jumped on board.

It was all good knockabout fun but it was bound to end in tears. Sure enough it did because those loony investors who let greed overcome their common sense – no one in their right mind makes an investment decision based on a one-minute pitch from a person who is paid to say only nice things about his or her company – bought at an artificially inflated price and suffered as the euphoria disappeared and the share price slumped. As Sir Jimmy Goldsmith so famously said, 'If you see a bandwagon, it's too late.'

My advice then is to ignore the amateur chat lines on the Internet and the quiz-show type of television programme. By all means use them for entertainment and amusement if you must but never let them influence your investment decisions.

Each investor will choose his or her investment sources based on personal choice and this depends on all sorts of factors. Age, sex, interests, available time, artistic or scientific bent, lifestyle all affect the newspapers and magazines we buy, the radio programmes we listen to and the television shows we watch. It is therefore invidious for me to tell you what to read, hear or see. If you are a young

NO ONE IN THEIR RIGHT MIND MAKES AN INVESTMENT DECISION BASED ON A ONE-MINUTE PITCH FROM A PERSON WHO IS PAID TO SAY ONLY NICE THINGS ABOUT HIS OR HER COMPANY.

mother who also fits in a full-time job you are not going to thank me for suggesting you buy the *Financial Times* instead of one of the quickly read tabloids and there would not be much point in me recommending *Working Lunch* as good viewing in the middle of the day. If you haven't succumbed to satellite and had an ugly Sky dish slapped on the side of your house I would be wasting my time wittering on about the CNN business news service.

However, I am keen to provide you with guidance on how to find out about information sources that will improve your knowledge and assist you to be a better private investor, so I have three areas for you to consider:

- the sources I use on a regular basis
- an inexpensive publication that gives an unbiased opinion on information sources
- books I suggest you read next.

My choice

Let me say immediately that what follows are not recommendations, they merely illustrate the methods I use to keep in touch with what is happening, to stimulate ideas and to provide opinions which I know from experience can be treated with respect.

Daily newspapers

The *Financial Times*. I can hear the groans, the murmurs of 'boring, boring'. You are so, so wrong. The pink paper is a unique treasure trove of information, an exciting daily miracle that can be yours for a pittance. But there's no gain without pain, like *REFS*, you have to learn how to read it and how to get the best out of it. Take my advice, plunder £16.99 from your piggy bank and buy *The Financial Times Guide to Using the Financial Pages*, it has recently been updated and the fourth edition has now been published. Buy today's *Financial Times* newspaper, set aside a couple of hours and start to learn. Read the paper and use the book as a reference when you come across anything you don't understand. It is a fascinating exercise, the time will flash by, and your knowledge will increase by the minute.

If you really haven't got the time to enjoy the *FT* every day make sure you buy the Saturday edition. It is worth every penny of whatever it costs, not just for the financial information but because it contains a host of informative and entertaining features. In my opinion the *Financial Times* is the best newspaper published anywhere in the world.

At home we have the *Telegraph* delivered, I suppose because we always have. It suits my wife and me, we know how to find our way about it, the business section is good, particularly now it is at the back of the main paper, and its politics are sufficiently radical for me to have violent disagreements with the editorials.

On London days I buy the *Independent* and occasionally *The Times*. Helen will opt for the *Daily Mail* and turn straight to Nigel Dempster's page. During the train journey home I read the *Evening Standard* because it is free in first class and I enjoy Anthony Hilton and Victor Lewis-Smith but not much else.

Sunday newspapers

As I have already mentioned, with the honourable exception of the *Sunday Telegraph*, I am trying to do without them. It's hard. I miss the *Sunday Times* because of the hard-hitting, go-for-the-throat features which cover topical business items in depth. *Sunday Business*, a newspaper I predicted would have a short lifespan because it attempts to appeal to people like me who are trying to have one day of the week free from finance, has proved me wrong. It's an excellent read. The beauty of these weekend newspapers is that they can give you a perspective view of what's happened during the week as well as flagging up the events

of the next seven days. When my self-imposed purdah is over poor old Danny will have to add them to his Sunday bag again.

Magazines

Difficult, because there are an increasing number and in the main they are useful. Let me emphasize again that these are the ones I subscribe to and they will not necessarily suit you.

Buying more than one or two can cost a small fortune and this is where your club comes in. Either allocate club funds for subscriptions or, perhaps more fairly, get a few members who are really interested to decide between themselves who will subscribe for what, then suggest they set up an exchange system so that everyone gets a bite of all the cherries. At least one club has taken this a step

EITHER ALLOCATE CLUB FUNDS FOR SUBSCRIPTIONS OR, PERHAPS MORE FAIRLY, GET A FEW MEMBERS WHO ARE REALLY INTERESTED TO DECIDE BETWEEN THEMSELVES WHO WILL SUBSCRIBE FOR WHAT, THEN SUGGEST THEY SET UP AN EXCHANGE SYSTEM SO THAT EVERYONE GETS A BITE OF ALL THE CHERRIES.

further by having an informal meeting of the three magazine subscribers every Saturday lunchtime in the local pub. Each person has read his publication and highlighted articles and news items he or she considers are worth looking at. They exchange magazines and also ideas and opinions, it is a small club within a club and they find their thoughts form the basis of the share discussions at the next club meetings.

Back to my choice. I take that grand old lady of the private investor business, the *Investors' Chronicle*. She's been going for over 140 years and there's no one out there that can quite touch her although there are plenty of new pretenders to her throne. Chief amongst them is that young upstart I told you about earlier, *Shares* magazine. It is not easy to describe the difference between the two but if I had to choose phrases I would say the *IC* is dignified and responsible while *Shares* is irreverent and chock full of ideas.

On a monthly basis I look at *Bloomberg Money* because I find most of the articles of interest and it has some wise contributors like Justin Urquhart-Stewart, Jeff Prestridge and, occasionally, me. I also like MoneyWise.

Reference publications

The bible. *Really Essential Financial Statistics. REFS*. I devoted a whole chapter to this publication so you already know the importance I place on it. I have the book version, the CD-ROM and *REFS Online*. Greedy, aren't I? I believe this is the best information source I have. I am also impressed by the *Estimates*

Directory, another monthly publication which contains brokers' forecasts for over 1,400 UK companies. The publishers are Barra (0131 473 7070) and they also have an excellent service relating to directors' dealings – if you are interested ring them and ask about it.

Incidentally, if you are a chartist – I'm not, I regard it as one step up from trying to read the stars, but there are a lot of investors who swear by charts so who am I to argue? – there is a monthly publication to which I don't actually subscribe but I see it because one of my friends is a disciple. The *Equity Chartbook* is produced by Investment Research of Cambridge and you can call them on 01223 356251.

Newsletters and tipsheets

Here's a hot potato. I realize I'm going to get calls from friends screaming 'What about us?' so let me apologize to them in advance.

Let us examine what exactly these publications are trying to do, what we expect from them and what they want from us. To deal with the latter requirement first, they want our money and invariably it has to be in the form of an annual subscription. You can't just wander in to Smith's or Menzies and buy these publications off the shelf. You must make an annual commitment which is a bit rich if you decide after a couple of months that the information doesn't live up to your expectations and you don't want to subscribe any longer. To get over this I suggest you ask for a sample copy of the latest issue because if the publishers have any faith in their offering they will be happy to oblige.

What do we expect from them? It has to be more than tips and news, otherwise we might as well stick to the *IC* or *Shares* magazine. There are those among us who subscribe because we hope that somehow we are going to open the door to a world of winners, a list of red hot opportunities that have only been spotted by this particular newsletter. There is an implication that the authors have the brains of Einstein and a network of influential contacts that would make the royal family look like loners. If you believe that you will believe anything.

Sensible investors who subscribe to newsletters do so because they expect the share recommendations to be well researched and carefully assessed. They want the background work to be done by competent people who know what they are doing and have years of experience in a specific method or approach to share selection.

Alternatively they will be experts in a particular sector of the market.

Top of my list is a publication that does not like to be described as a newsletter and certainly not a tipsheet. The owner of the *Analyst*, Jeremy Utton, will take issue with me over its inclusion under newsletters and tipsheets but it is available only by subscription and I am praising its content so he should not be churlish. To be fair, *Analyst* does stand out from the rest if only because of its standard of presentation. Most of these newsletters look as though they have been produced using a John Bull home printing kit, two-colour offerings on poor-quality paper with no sense of graphic design. At least *Analyst* looks and feels like a proper and professional magazine. The contents measure up to the appearance because the research is painstaking in its search for outstanding companies. It attempts to uncover value companies that have achieved substantial returns in the past and are able to reinvest retained earnings at

MOST OF THESE NEWSLETTERS LOOK AS THOUGH THEY HAVE BEEN PRODUCED USING A JOHN BULL HOME PRINTING KIT, TWO-COLOUR OFFERINGS ON POOR-QUALITY PAPER WITH NO SENSE OF GRAPHIC DESIGN.

above-average returns. Find out more about *Analyst* by calling 01454 642481.

One other publication that takes its graphics seriously is *Growth Company Investor*. It uses full colour and includes profiles of investor stars as well as properly reasoned recommendations, mostly from the AIM and OFEX areas. Get subscription details from 020 7430 9777.

Perhaps my most selective sieve when I consider the potential of a newsletter or tipsheet is that the compilers should, at the very least, have talked in depth to, and asked searching questions of, the chief executive of the company they are examining. Preferably they will have visited the company premises for a face-to-face interview. Such a requirement sorts the men from the boys. One monthly publication that measures up is *Small Company Sharewatch*, a newsletter run by a modest young fellow called Smit Berry. Smit is a substantial investor in his own right so I guess he puts his money where his mouth is. Certainly I find he does thorough research to produce recommendations on small dynamic growth companies and you know by reading the newsletter that he has asked the right people the right questions. One of his criteria is to spot information that might trigger a re-rating. I have made money from cherry picking Smit's recommendations in *Small Company Sharewatch*. You can find out about subscription rates (and hopefully get a sample copy) by ringing 020 8656 4648.

In an uncertain world – and there is nothing more uncertain than the technology section of the stock market –

one looks for sanity based on experience. That's why I like *Techinvest*, a newsletter produced not in the hothouse of the City of London but in the much quieter and more reasonable atmosphere of Dublin's fair city. Conor McCarthy is an Irishman with at least two decades of experience in the technology business and his publication has been a rock during the manic period of recent years when many of us made and lost paper fortunes as we followed the high-tech dragon. His experience and technical knowledge enabled him to factor in the downside as well as the upside potential of the myriad propositions that came our way. Of course he made mistakes (didn't we all?) but on balance he was the best of the guides through that turbulent time.

Techinvest tells it like it is and on the back page there is a 'Trader Portfolio' into which Conor puts what he considers are going to be his best selections. There's no hiding place for publications that do this because from month to month subscribers can see just how good the tips are. Trader Portfolio 1 started with a capital of £20,000 and ran from March 1985 for exactly eight years when it was terminated with a 2,214 per cent profit – the £20,000 had become £462,874. Trader Portfolio 2 started in March 1993 with £50,000 and when it closed just over three years later the portfolio was worth £276, 691. Portfolio 3 ran for four years and turned £50,000 into £570,402. Trader Portfolio 4 results to date are by no means as spectacular. Little wonder, because it was started with £100,000 at the dawn of the new millennium,

1 January 2000. You will recall that the tech-stock crash started around March when the fund was only three months old and since then (17 months on) the overall movement has been strictly downhill. Nevertheless in the June 2001 issue of *Techinvest* the portfolio was worth £110,371 which is a 10 per cent profit. Over the same period the FTSE 100 was down over 15 per cent and the more relevant FTSE techMARK Index was down over 44 per cent. Well done, Conor. To contact *Techinvest* from the UK ring 00353 1 670 1777.

My last suggestion in this area is *Investing for Growth* and I read it because the basic tenet is to identify undervalued growth shares. Ring 020 7837 8281.

I'm not going to recommend you look at any of the penny-share tipsheets, and this will not endear me to a number of my friends who specialize in this area. Frankly, I think these publications are dangerous because they imply that fortunes can be made by gambling on rank outsiders with no track record becoming the darlings of the City overnight. It just doesn't work like that. As one very successful investor sagely said to me: 'Why do you think they're penny shares? It's because everyone who knows – the owners, the stockbrokers, the market makers, the big investors – thinks that is what they are worth. Do you believe they're all wrong and the penny share tipster is right?'

STOP PRESS As we near the end of this book I can let you in on an embryo idea that is particularly relevant to the foregoing section on newsletters. For some time now Jim Slater and I have been thinking about producing a newsletter which we believe would provide what every investor wants – capital profits and income with safety.

Safety is established by investing in leading companies that have already proved themselves and are strong financially. They are better equipped to withstand the downturns that will inevitably occur. They also have the added advantage that it is usually possible to deal in their shares very easily without moving the price. Money is saved because the spread between the buying and selling price is much less than for other less marketable stocks.

Another vital route to establishing a margin of safety is to adopt strict investment criteria and these would govern the content of our proposed newsletter. Shares on very high price-to-earnings ratios would be avoided like the plague. We would seek out shares with low price-to-earnings ratios, strong cash flow and strong balance sheets.

The newsletter title we are contemplating, *Blue Chip*, makes it clear that we would be concentrating on the great companies that are to be found mainly in the élite FTSE 100 club. Each month we would produce one main recommendation that has been researched in depth and explain in simple language why we believe it would be a successful investment.

In these uncertain times many investors need a safe and growing income so we would have a section on stocks with a good dividend yield. We would also produce blue-chip selections each month based on the O'Higgins system.

Because Jim and I believe it is important for investors to learn as well as earn we have discussed the inclusion of a monthly educational article dealing with such topics as price-to-earnings growth factors (PEGs), return on capital, margins, price-to-sales ratios and the like.

Although most of the *Blue Chip* recommendations would come from the FTSE 100 we would not restrict our researches and, provided they met our strict criteria, we would also include a page of small cap selections.

If we go ahead with our *Blue Chip* newsletter it would not be for gamblers. It would be for patient investors and investment clubs who want to invest for the long term with a substantial margin of safety and allow the power of compounding to do its wonderful work.

As I write our plans are not yet finalised but I can promise you that, as a reader of *The Company of Successful Investors*, if Jim Slater and I do decide produce *Blue Chip*, you would qualify for the most advantageous subscription rates available. To find out more send me an e-mail: terry.bond@hemscott.net.

Radio

I love the wireless. Having said that, there's not much on for investors but if you search around there are a handful of programmes for us. Let me take you around the clock. If you are an early bird tune in at 5.45 a.m. on weekdays to *Wake Up To Money* on *Radio Five Live*. This is the first business news bulletin of the day and, like the rest of *Five Live*, it is a breath of fresh air. There seem to be different presenters on different days and you can look forward to a bit of informative fun if Mickey Clark or Adrian Chiles are in the chair. There's another financial new

bulletin called *Money Check* on the same wavelength at 1.45 p.m. on weekdays.

At the end of every weekday, just before you snuggle down, turn the bedside radio on at 11.15 p.m. to the *Financial World Tonight*. It's a brief resume of the financial day. And on Saturdays (noon) or Mondays (3 p.m.) listen to *Money Box*, it is not strictly for investors but I find it most informative on personal finance generally.

Television

Television and investment are slowly waking up to each other, and with mixed emotions. Those who subscribe to Sky do reasonably well because CNBC and Bloomberg are both excellent. Let's hope they survive because two of the smaller independent stations devoted to the world of finance and shares, *The Money Channel* and *Simply Money*, died the death in 2001 after short and financially disastrous lives. I have not yet succumbed to the digital world so my two mainstays now are the business section of *BBC Breakfast News* – Tanya and Sarah are without doubt the most glamorous people on television and Declan Curry is a breathe of fresh air – and *Working Lunch* which is screened on weekdays for half-an-hour at 12.30 p.m. The latter is a remarkable programme. Produced by Tracey Hobbs and with Adrian Chiles and Adam Shaw as its main presenters, it has developed a personality of its own and for me it is unique in proving that money and business can be interesting and entertaining.

Software and Data Services

I have to be careful here because I am no expert so I can only write with authority about what I use personally. This is not really fair because, for instance, I know from having seen it demonstrated that the Updata service, developed by David Linton, seems superior to anything I have got. I will certainly be looking at having it installed in the near future and I suggest you find out about it by ringing 020 8874 4747.

So let me tell you what I use now but do not accept it as an objective assessment of what is available or indeed a description of all the bells and whistles that my software can be used for. It does what I want it to do and probably much more. I will never know.

I have described elsewhere how much I rely on the CD-ROM and On-line versions of REFS so I will not dwell on the again, save to say they are my lifeline.

For managing my various portfolios I use *Finsight* and have done for years (it used to be called Infotrade). First thing I do when I go into my office in the morning is switch it on and press the Update button. This downloads all the LSE price information from the previous day as well as company results and the latest data changes. I suppose it takes less than a minute but I have never timed it.

I then press the button that takes me to my portfolio details which have been simultaneously updated. This is a real delight because they are all separately identified and with a click of the mouse I can enter each portfolio and examine the individual shares to see how they have moved from the previous day. If dividends have been paid, share splits have taken place, anything unusual that has occurred to a company's financial standing, it is all automatically recorded and available for my inspection.

Throughout the day I can log on direct to *Finsight* and all the portfolios will show me near real-time prices (I believe they are about 20 minutes delayed).

Perhaps because I am used to it, maybe because it is so clear and simple to operate, I am truly satisfied with this level day-to-day management. I have been tempted by more sophisticated services, flashing screens constantly changing and an in-depth analysis of the balance of my portfolios, but all I can say is that they are not for me. It all becomes too confusing, I am a simple soul and a devotee of the easy life. *Finsight* details available on 01675 430102.

I also update my Sharescope programme on a daily basis. I find this service is invaluable for share analysis because it enables me to sort and select shares using all sorts of criteria. There are over 40 technical analysis tools built in and they work at an amazing speed. To get the best out of the software – and I'm sure I don't at the moment but I keep promising myself I will – Sharescope run workshops. For details, and a copy of their demonstration CD, ring 020 7561 6000.

Investment Club Software

The software thousands of UK clubs use is COW, the awful acronym of Computer Office Workshops. It was designed and developed by one of the stalwarts of the investment club movement, Derek Richards, who is a grand fellow living in the depths of Cornwall. Very much a traditionalist, Derek nevertheless listens and talks with most of the users of COW and over the years has changed it and added improvements.

I am no club treasurer (I suffer from number dyslexia, if there is such a complaint) but those I know who have attained that exalted position seem quite happy with the current COW product. Others prefer to work their own spreadsheets out and there is a minority that eschew such technical wizardry as the personal computer and opt for pushing an old fashioned pen.

If you want to know more about COW software I suggest you make contact through ProShare because I believe ProShare clubs get preferential rates. Ring them on 020 7220 1730.

Websites

I use websites every day for information and frankly I could not operate without them. I have kept a diary for a month to make a list of those I use at least once a day and others that I log on to regularly. Again I must point out that it is a personal list and represents only a fraction of what is available. Also the Internet scene is changing daily and the gestation period of a book is such that by the time you read this some of the sites may no longer be running.

DAILY

www.hemscott.co.uk This is my server site so when I log on I reach Hemscott automatically. Rather like your daily paper of choice it is like a friend you feel comfortably with. I use it to check financial news, real time prices, archive news and so on. I also read the recommendations and subscribe to their excellent new Hemscott Analyst service because (a) I respect the research and analytical ability of the editor, Tom Stevenson and (b) as I write their tips are showing good progress.

www.ft.com Best in the business. General and business news throughout the day, well-informed articles and the finest news archive I have come across.

www.proshare.org Investment clubs and ProShare are synonymous. IT manager John Ring and his colleagues have developed a good interactive site and more and more clubs are using it to hold their portfolios which are secure and can only be accessed by the individual club's members.

REGULARLY

www.investorschronicle.co.uk I find this an extremely useful site and it was considerably improved for subscribers to the magazine in mid-2001. There's a good daily news update plus analysis of British, European and US stocks. The article archive goes back to 1997.

www.itruffle.com News, company announcements, detailed company information, stock screening. Good email alert service.

www.iii.co.uk Excellent all-round investor site. Two of the clubs I belong to have there portfolios based here.

www.fool.co.uk Good educational site with a sound philosophy.

www.carol.co.uk A forerunner of what will be commonplace in the future. Up-to-date extracts of the main facts from company annual reports and accounts. Very useful and saves you searching for individual company sites.

Annual Reports

I rank the *FT Free Annual Reports Club* alongside *REFS* as the most helpful developments I have come across since I have been an investor. To obtain the latest annual report for any of the companies marked with a club sign in the *Financial Times* ring 020 8770 0770. It is a free service.

THE INFORMATION SOURCE FOR INFORMATION SOURCES

It's called *The Investor's Guide to Information Sources* and it is a reasonably comprehensive list of the contact numbers and cost for most of the information providers.

They have been marked by experts for 1. Simplicity of English. 2. Ease of use. 3 Value for money. 4 How up-to-date the information is.

The guide will cost you just £5.95 post-free. Get it from ProShare 020 7220 1730.

BOOKS

I reckon that, whatever you pay, a book is cheap. For just a few pounds you can gain access the author's wisdom and experience, often a near-lifetime of knowledge and imagination that has been assembled and edited then passed on to you in an understandable way. In the investor's world this is particularly apposite because writers who have usually already proved their abilities by making themselves rich still have the urge explain their techniques in the pages of a book. I have no hesitation in suggesting that your investment club quickly creates its own library of investment publications, volumes that can be passed around between members, read and re-read to increase the competence of the club as a whole.

The trouble is, most of the best investment books are written by Americans. I'm not sure why this is, but as I look along my bookshelves a rough estimate tells me that 80 per cent of the volumes have American authors. I believe this adds unacceptable complications for the UK investor because inevitably all examples are based in $$$s and cite US company examples. Anecdotes are based on Wall Street and not London's Square Mile. I am not prepared to compound this imbalance by recommending US books for your library so my list is confined to British books which deal with UK investments.

Here are my Top Ten:

1. ***The Investor's Guide to Selecting Shares That Perform. 10 Ways that Work*** Written by Richard Koch and published by Prentice Hall. Koch is a City entrepreneur who masterminded the turnaround of Filofax and provided start-up finance for Belgo. His strength is that he recognises all investors have different personalities and can cope with different levels or risk. Do his test for yourself and find out what kind of an investor you are.

2. ***The Financial Times Guide to Reading the Financial Pages*** Written by Romesh Vaitiningham and published by Prentice Hall. Buy it and

read it in conjunction with today's *Financial Times* newspaper. It will make you a better investor.

3. ***Investment Made Easy*** Written by Jim Slater and published by Orion. Jim is a no-frills author who has the ability to explain finance in a way everyone can understand. He also has a unique grasp of his subject.

4. ***The Astute Private Investor*** Written by Kevin Goldstein-Jackson and published by Right Way. Kevin must be one of Britain's most successful private investors but he is a modest man and the nearest he gets to a public face is an occasional column in the Financial Times where, among other things, he forecast the 1987 stockmarket crash. I'm not sure whether this grand little book is still in print (probably not, because I notice the cover price on my edition is £3.99) but if you can find a copy buy it.

5. ***The Intelligent Guide to Stockmarket Investment*** Take Control of Your Financial Future. Written by Kevin Keasey, Robert Hudson and Kevin Littler, published by Wiley. This is a good book of reference which I believe was sponsored by the Halifax Group. It covers a host of subjects from a history of the stockmarket to investment gurus.

6. ***The Zulu Principle. Making Extraordinary Profits from Ordinary Shares*** Written by Jim Slater and published by Orion. No apologies for

putting another of Jim's book on the list. He has an uncanny ability to identify undervalued shares and can forecast the market better than anyone I know. Reading this book will make you a better investor.

7. ***The First-Time Investor*** The complete Guide to Buying, Owning and Selling Shares. Written by Debbie Harrison and published by Prentice Hall. A book of reference by a woman journalist who knows her subject. It is free from jargon and covers subjects from ethical investment to tax management.

8. ***Traded Options*** A Private Investors Guide. Written by Peter Temple and first published by Batsford Business Books. I'm delighted to see it has been updated and reprinted by Prentice Hall recently because options can be a useful tool in the investor's armoury provided always that they are fully understood. Peter Temple explains his subject in an understandable and useful way.

9. ***The Money Makers*** The Stock Market Secrets of Britain's Top Professional Investors. Written by Jonathan Davis and published by Orion. You won't recognise many of the names – Anthony Bolton, Ian Rushbrook, Nils Taube, Colin McLean and so on – but these are the men who make millions from the market. Davis explains succinctly how they do it.

10. ***How to Make Your Million from The Internet*** And what to do if you don't. Written by Jonathan Maitland and published by Hodder and Stoughton. Give yourself a laugh. We've all dreamed of doing it. Selling the house and speculating the lot on shares. Television presenter Maitland did it at the height of the tech boom. Oops!

I have enjoyed writing this book for you. If you have any queries or would like to comment on anything, please e-mail me at terry.bond@hemscott.net

INDEX